creative
crafts
you can do in a day

NORTH LIGHT BOOKS

Cincinnati, Ohio

www.artistsnetwork.com

table of contents

Simple Glass Seed Beading
page 382

Making Greeting Cards with
Creative Materials
page 268

introduction

Creative Crafts You Can Do in a Day is designed to both inspire and instruct. All the projects in this book have step-by-step instructions, and many have ideas for variations so you can try your hand at something original. You'll be introduced to ribboncraft (ribbon is one of life's little luxuries that turns the everyday into the exception); glass beading, where you'll learn to create and embellish stunning jewelry, accessories and other great gifts; papercraft, where you'll finally be able to use all of those gorgeous decorative papers you have left over from other projects; and making greeting cards with creative materials such as fabrics, tags, fibers and trinkets you don't want to part with, but can't seem to find a use for.

You probably have most of the necessary materials for these projects at home already; all you need is a little inspiration to get started. Consider *Creative Crafts You Can Do in a Day* that inspiration and get started now!

bright ideas in papercrafts

susan niner janes

NORTH LIGHT BOOKS
CINCINNATI, OHIO
www.artistsnetwork.com

bright ideas in papercrafts

TABLE OF CONTENTS

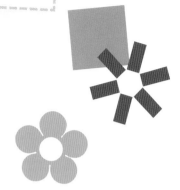

I t's great to be a twenty-first century papercrafter, because the Golden Age of Papercrafting is here and now! Never before has such a fantastic selection of specialized papercraft products—both gadgets and materials—been available, offering exciting and limitless creative possibilities.

Thanks to the archival-quality, acid-free papers and adhesives devised for the making of memory albums, it is now possible to make keepsake projects which will last for many, many years. It's a papercraft revolution—one giant leap!

Scrapbookers are a dedicated bunch of crafters, always on the lookout for new ways to present their memory album pages. Because of them, many innovative papercraft products have been introduced: paper-cutting equipment, paper punches in all shapes and sizes, paper edgers and corner rounders, and tools and templates for cutting out paper shapes. Other developments include machines for bonding and laminating papers and acid-free papers in an inspirational array of patterns, colors and textures.

If you are a devoted scrapbooker, then you are almost certainly accumulating an ever-growing collection of gadgets. You probably have a stash of decorative papers in search of a project. You may have been searching for any other craft applications for these marvelous tools and materials—not to mention your considerable papercraft skills—besides the making of memory albums. Look no further. This book is packed with useful ideas that reach beyond the confines of the two-dimensional album page.

You don't have to be a scrapbooker to create these projects. This book will update and fine-tune your skills, introducing you to the current crop of papercraft innovations.

Learning how to use the new generation of papercraft products will bring a new dimension—literally and figuratively—to how you approach papercrafting. You'll bubble over with creative ideas of your own, eagerly anticipating future papercraft innovations and trends.

Getting Started

Whenever I go to a scrapbooking or hobby store, I am faced with the dazzling array of paper in rainbow colors and the amazing selection of papercraft tools on display. If you are new to papercrafting, you might just be a bit overwhelmed or a little confused by the sheer volume of what's available to buy. The bottom line is this: papercraft is mostly about cutting paper—and most papercraft tools are mechanical devices for doing exactly that. Simple, really.

Some papercraft tools, like a craft knife—which is really just a razor blade on a stick—are pretty basic. Others, like a ShapeCutter, are sophisticated, state-of-the-art feats of engineering smarts. What it boils down to is this—they are different methods of cutting paper. The trick is knowing which gadget is right for the job at hand.

The old adage "a good craftsman knows his tools" holds true for paper-crafting. The good news is that getting acquainted with your papercraft tools is fun! You can learn the basics in minutes. As always, practice makes perfect. As you get to know your tools and their capabilities, you'll expand your cre-ative repertoire. For instance, once you master paper edgers, you'll progress from using them exclusively for trimming paper edges to fashioning paper chains and more.

Familiarity with what your papercraft gadgets can do will leave you burst-ing with ideas and the delightful knowledge that if you have a papercraft tool kit and a stash of paper, a finished project is just minutes away.

The following pages give you some basic information and tips about paper-craft materials, techniques and equipment—what you need to get started and how to get the most out of them.

MATERIALS

Paper Primer Variety of choice makes papercrafting a joy. Some papers don't even look like paper. For instance, they can be fabric-like or have metallic finishes. Whatever the paper, it is usually easy to cut and glue—in my opinion, it's the perfect handicraft material.

Here's a brief rundown of some of the papers you are likely to use in your crafting:

SCRAPBOOKING PAPER AND CARDSTOCK: Acid-free, archival-quality paper, created for use in memory albums. Cardstock is a heavier paper. Since scrapbooking paper is specially manufactured to minimize deterioration over time, it is ideal for keepsake projects. Scrapbooking papers come in a fantastic array of printed patterns and solids. Some of the designs are themed for special occasions. Double-sided patterns are often available. Scrapbooking vellums—that is, translucent papers—are also available. Standard sizes are 8½" × 11" (22cm × 28cm) or 12" × 12" (30cm × 30cm). The latter size is the standard measurement of a scrapbook page.

CORRUGATED CARDBOARD: Has a textured finish. Most familiar is fluted, which has tube-like ridges. You can buy corrugated paper in fine flute or coarse flute to suit your project. Other textured patterns include waves and basket weave.

EMBOSSED PAPER: Has raised surface designs.

GIFT WRAP: Ideal for papercraft projects with a limited life span. It is inexpensive; you can find it everywhere; there's an incredible choice of patterns, colors and finishes; and its wider width often comes in handy.

HANDMADE PAPER: Often softer and more fabric-like than machine-made paper. It may include plant matter for a natural-look decorative effect.

MIRROR CARDSTOCK: Has a high-gloss metallic finish. It comes in silver, gold and jewel-bright colors. Ideal for festive occasions.

ORIGAMI PAPER: Not just for folding! It comes in plain, reversible and printed varieties. Washi paper is a bit thicker and comes in larger sheets.

PEARLESCENT PAPER: Has a luxurious, shimmery, iridescent finish.

TIP

Clip sheets of paper onto a clothes hanger for convenient storage. This method is especially good for oversize sheets of paper that would be difficult to store flat.

Adhesives and Supplies

When choosing adhesives, you must consider the end use of your project. For short-use projects, use ordinary, everyday adhesives. For keepsake projects, use archival-quality adhesives (from a scrapbooking supplier). Always read the label to know how to best use your adhesive.

Keep all the following items in your craft box. These are the supplies you will find yourself turning to again and again while papercrafting.

CRAFTER'S GLUE: The familiar white general-purpose craft glue. It dries clear.

DRY GLUE STICK: Rub-on stick glue for bonding paper to paper. Particularly good when large, smooth expanses are needed.

MASKING TAPE: For joining two surfaces temporarily during crafting. Drafting tape is a special low-tack tape that won't tear delicate papers.

TOOTHPICKS: The ideal papercraft glue applicator. A toothpick helps get into tight corners and aids in applying glue sparingly.

KNEADED ERASER: Removes pencil marks from projects without leaving a crumbly residue.

3-D DÉCOUPAGE SELF-ADHESIVE FOAM PADS: For sticking paper together quickly when you want to give dimensional "lift" to a project.

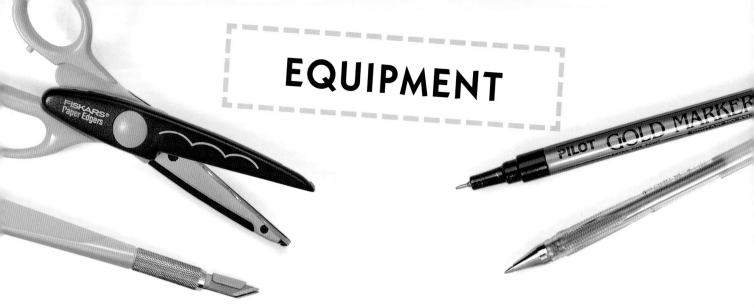

EQUIPMENT

Papercraft Gadgets and Equipment There are many tools for cutting, shaping and texturizing paper, including some absolutely genius gadgets and gizmos. Some papercrafting tools are essential, others less so—but all are fun and easy to use.

In this book, when a project calls for a specific papercraft tool, an effort has been made to suggest an alternative product whenever possible—because there's nearly always more than one way to get the job done.

The starred items on the following list are craft-kit essentials:

CIRCLE CUTTER: An adjustable, compass-like tool with a knife blade for cutting paper circles.

*CRAFT KNIFE: The most essential papercraft tool. A razor-sharp blade mounted in a handle, a craft knife gives a cleaner, more precise cut than scissors. It should be used with a self-healing cutting mat.

CORNER EDGERS: Special scissors for cutting decorative corners on paper and cardstock.

GEL PENS: Can be used for writing on light or dark colors. The inks flow on easily and come in a good range of colors.

MARKERS: Metallic markers can add a festive touch to special projects (be safe and make sure you choose non-toxic inks).

METAL RULER: For measuring and cutting out your paper crafts. When using a craft knife, you lean it against a metal straightedge in order to cut perfect straight lines. It is useful to have metal rulers in several sizes: 6" (15cm), 12" (30cm) and either 18" (46cm) or 24" (61cm) are recommended.

PAPER CRIMPER: A tool that texturizes plain paper by pressing it between two embossed rollers. The most common patterns are ridges or waves.

PAPER EDGERS: Papercraft scissors with patterned blades. Paper edgers can be used for cutting fancy edges and making paper chains. An amazing variety of blade patterns are available. Basic shapes are pinking (zigzag) and scallops.

PAPER PUNCHES: Gadgets for die-cutting shapes out of paper. They come in two varieties: press-action punches for larger shapes—usually $1/2$" (13mm) and larger—and hand punches, handheld squeeze-action punches for punching smaller shapes.

*RIGHT TRIANGLE: A 45° right triangle is handy for checking whether your measured corners are truly perpendicular. Get into the habit of using one.

*SCISSORS: Every papercrafter should have several different pairs of scissors kept expressly for papercrafting. Using scissors for other purposes would dull the blades. Small scissors are indispensable for delicate cutting. Use embroidery scissors or nail scissors. Curved nail scissors are good on curves. Handicraft scissors are blunt ended and smallish—about 5" (13cm) long. They are great for general craft use, such as trimming and coarse cutting.

*SELF-HEALING CUTTING MAT: Use as your cutting surface in conjunction with a craft knife. The mat protects the tabletop and has a resilience that makes cutting easier.

TIP

Papercraft tools are easy to use, but it's always a good idea to familiarize yourself with them before starting a project.

SHAPE CUTTER: The Fiskars ShapeCutter is a tool in which a swivel blade is suspended in a carriage. It can be used with stencil templates to cut out decorative paper shapes. Another method of cutting shapes out uniformly is to use a system of nested templates, such as the Coluzzle Cutting System. This comes with a special handheld swivel knife and cutting mat.

STENCIL KNIFE: A variety of craft knife that has two parallel blades. The blades produce a line of uniform width.

TRACING PAPER: Keep a roll handy for making pattern tracings. Thumbnail sketch paper is a less expensive alternative.

TWEEZERS: Can be useful for picking up and positioning small punched paper shapes. Choose straight-tip or angled-tip—not pointy ones.

XYRON MACHINE: This mechanically laminates, applies adhesive to bond paper together, and makes magnets and stickers. The device has different cartridges for each purpose.

Where to Find Papercraft Supplies
Try hobby superstores, scrapbooking stores and your local art supply store first when looking for papercraft materials and equipment.

Toy stores can be unexpected treasure troves. They can be sources of paper edgers and fun papers, such as metallics and origami paper. Consumer craft shows are often showcases for new products and hard-to-find items. The Internet can also be a fabulous resource for the papercrafter. You can find whatever you need and order it by e-mail. Check out the resource directory at the back of this book for some useful Web sites.

Finally, a browse through the classified section of your favorite craft magazine is likely to yield useful mail-order shopping leads.

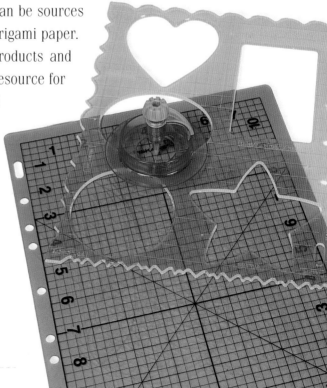

TECHNIQUES

Impressing a Pattern Impressing a pattern outline using a stylus is a convenient way to transfer pattern markings onto paper. Impressing takes a lot less time than tracing because you don't have to go over the pattern outlines in pencil on the back of the design before transferring the design onto the project paper. Unlike tracing, there are no pencil lines to erase when the project is completed.

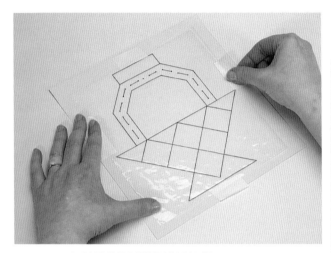

1. TAPE THE PATTERN IN PLACE

Enlarge or reduce the pattern on a photocopier until it is the correct size. Pencil-trace the pattern onto a piece of tracing paper. Tape the tracing onto the piece of decorative paper you have selected for the project.

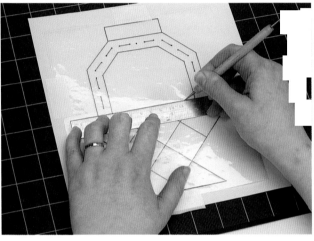

2. IMPRESS THE PATTERN

Place the taped pattern on a mat or a piece of scrap cardstock—not a hard surface. Use a stylus to impress the pattern into the paper. A metal ruler can help you keep the lines straight. A dry fine-point pen makes an excellent stylus. You can also use an embossing tool.

TIP

If you are going to use the pattern tracing several times, it is a good idea to reinforce it by applying a layer of clear, self-adhesive vinyl, such as book-covering material. This will make it durable for repeated use.

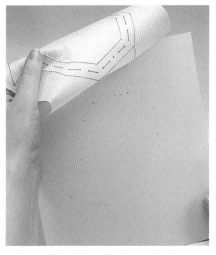

3. UNCOVER THE IMPRESSED PATTERN

Untape the pattern tracing to reveal the impressed lines. If the lines are hard to see, trace over them lightly with a pencil. On a dark surface, you may wish to outline the design in white gel pen—but only if the outlines will not be visible in the finished project, because the ink is permanent.

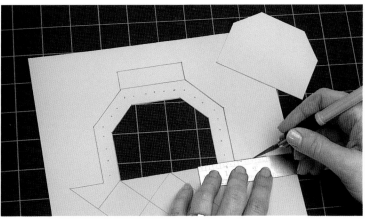

4. CUT OUT THE SHAPE

Use a craft knife and cut out the shape. Use a ruler to keep the lines straight. Always cut over a self-healing cutting mat. Use a fresh, sharp blade in the craft knife. It is time to change blades when the knife starts to drag on the paper. For cutting curves, you may find it easier to use small scissors, such as embroidery or nail scissors. Keep these expressly for paper use to prevent the blades from dulling.

TIP

Practice scoring on a test piece of the project paper. See if it is better to score on the inside or the outside of the paper. You'll know which side is right by how easily the paper folds. If you mistakenly cut too deeply, position a piece of cellophane tape behind the cut to mend the paper and salvage the project.

Scoring
In order to fold thicker papers and cardstock smoothly, you must first score the paper; that is, partially cut through it.

1. SCORING

Swipe the craft knife lightly across the paper, taking extra care not to cut too deeply. Lean the knife against a metal straightedge to score a perfect straight line.

2. FOLDING

Fold along the scored line. Use your thumbnail to crease a nice, crisp fold.

Using Paper Punches
An enthusiastic papercrafter (that's the only kind!) will soon build up a sizeable collection of paper punches.

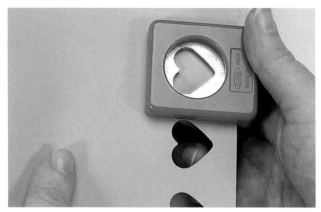

UPSIDE-DOWN PLACEMENT

If you hold your punch upside down, you can view through the "window," so you can position your punch precisely where you want it on the paper. Some punches have alignment notches on the casing to assist in placement. Mark a pencil dot at each notch, then match up the dot with the notch to place the adjacent cutout.

PUNCH MAINTENANCE

You can sharpen the punch by punching through a piece of aluminum foil several times. If your paper punch starts to stick, lubricate it by punching through a piece of waxed paper a few times.

Using Hand Punches
Another type of paper punch is the handheld squeeze-action punch. Hand punches are used for punching smaller shapes in quick succession.

Tweezers are great for picking up and positioning tiny punched shapes.

When making a border of hand-punched shapes, measure and mark punch positions on the back of the paper. For perfect alignment, draw a straight guideline, then make pencil dots along it at positions where the center of each punched shape should be located.

Some hand punches have a built-in "confetti catcher"—a compartment that collects the punched shapes. Remember to empty it periodically by swinging open the "trap door." Save the confetti, it might come in handy for future paper-craft projects.

The "confetti catcher" is an excellent source of confetti and extra punched shapes.

Cutting Shapes

The Fiskars ShapeCutter is a system for making paper cutouts. It consists of the ShapeCutter tool—a cutting blade suspended in a circular carriage, so it can swivel freely; a plastic template with stencils for making the cutout shapes; and a self-healing cutting mat. A large selection of ShapeTemplates is available for making shapes in various sizes. Themed templates are also available. The ShapeCutter can also be used for freehand cutting, but the projects in this book use it only for template cutting.

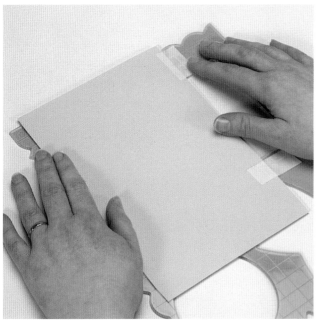

1. TAPE THE PAPER

Tape the paper onto the back of the template, so it doesn't shift during cutting. The smooth side of the template is the front, and the raised grid lines are on the back.

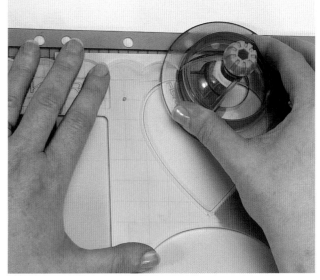

2. USE THE SHAPECUTTER

Hold the ShapeCutter by the textured outside ring, then slide it along the edge of the template. Start cutting at a straight side of the shape and align the blade parallel to the edge of the template. Slow down as you go around corners or extreme curves. If the cutter is not producing smooth edges, then it's time to replace the blade.

TIP

You may have to adjust the blade depth to suit the thickness of the cardstock. For cutting with a template, twist the orange knob clockwise to lower the blade and counterclockwise to raise it. Do a test run on a scrap of the paper you intend to use before you cut out your project "for real."

Using Paper Edgers

Paper edgers are a craft innovation that has caught on like wildfire. It's easy to see why: they're so much fun! Paper edgers are scissors with specially shaped blades that can cut paper edges in decorative patterns. They come in an amazing variety of blade patterns.

✿ In order to make the edged pattern continuous, you must realign the blades with every cut. After making your cut, advance the blade, at the same time matching it with the shapes on the cut paper edge.

✿ Each paper edger blade pattern has its own "feel." Get used to handling each design. Practice on scrap paper, especially the tricky bits, like negotiating curves and corners. More intricate designs require greater pressure while cutting.

✿ To cut a straight paper-edged line, rule a pencil line on the back of the paper, then cut against it.

✿ Save time by using straight scissors to cut the project out and then remove excess paper. Use paper edgers for the fancy trimming, after the basic shape has been cut out.

✿ When cutting a double-edged strip of paper, you must reverse the direction of the strip to cut the second side. (Or, you can fold the paper in half lengthwise and cut both edges simultaneously—but this method will leave a center crease.)

✿ Use specially designed corner edgers for a one-snip corner treatment.

Advance your blade each time you make a cut to keep the pattern continuous.

Use a pencil line to keep your cuts straight, and trim away excess paper before you begin.

Crimping Paper

Paper crimping allows you to incorporate an element of texture to a project. Texture can be an exciting and beautiful addition to any papercrafted project. Normally you would have to find the right textured paper to fit your project, but with a paper crimper it is easy to texturize plain paper. Corrugated ridges are the most common roller pattern. Insert the paper between the two ridged rollers. Squeeze the handles together tightly with one hand; this secures the paper. With your other hand, turn the key to advance the paper through the rollers. Once you master the basic techniques, experiment to find new ways to bring texture to your project using a paper crimper.

Check to make sure the paper goes through the rollers evenly.

To create a waffle effect, put the paper through a second time, perpendicular to the first.

To keep your paper correctly aligned, tape a piece of masking tape onto the center of the paper support bar (in front of the rollers). This mark will help you keep the center of the paper lined up. As you feed the paper through the rollers, check the tape to see if any adjustment is required. Straighten the paper gradually, if necessary.

To create a waffle effect, run the paper through the crimpers twice. Make a second pass perpendicular to the first one.

Make sure your paper is narrower than the crimper width. This sounds obvious, but mistakes can happen, especially if you pass the paper through the crimper a second time in another direction.

Papercrafting Projects

Back in the "Swinging '60s," paper dresses were made up as novelty items. A wacky idea, yes, but it does illustrate just what a versatile material paper is. In fact, you can make surprisingly more out of paper than the usual stuff that comes to mind because there are all sorts of innovative developments in both paper and papercrafting tools to take advantage of. It is my hope that the projects in this book offer some refreshingly different papercrafted creations in a range of categories including greeting cards, giftwrap ideas, ornaments, and home decorating accents. The projects are pretty, practical and fun.

This book is filled with exciting papercraft projects, such as handmade greeting cards. It's always a pleasant surprise to receive a handmade greeting card instead of a mass-produced one. With the help of the latest papercraft gadgets, such as paper punches and paper edgers, your cards can have a professional appearance. Not only will your handiwork earn keepsake status—it's likely to be put on permanent display.

But you'll find so much more on these pages. When you think of home decorating accessories, paper items may not immediately spring to mind. Think just a little harder, and—yes, paper homewares have always been there, doing what they do best—brightening things up colorfully and inexpensively. They are time-tested favorites re-invented to look fresh and new.

Every project in this book has a charm and personality, and I hope you have as much fun making them as I did presenting them to you.

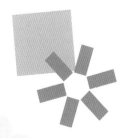

terrarium card

This card is a papercraft gadget interpretation of a fun 1970s pastime, sand-painting. Part of sand-painting's ongoing appeal is the "how'd you do that?" mystery factor. Well, the very same can be said of this papercrafted greeting card! It looks tricky to do—but appearances are deceiving!

Instead of sprinkling, poking and prodding grains of colored sand to build up patterns, paper "sand-painting" is crafted using glued cutouts—squiggly paper strips cut using decorative edgers—plus paper-punched shapes. "Elephant hide" paper, which has a grainy appearance, is ideal for creating a sand-like effect. The card has a top fold, so you can easily prop it up to display your handiwork!

1. TRACE AND CUT OUT THE CARD

Enlarge the pattern, given on page 29. Trace it onto a piece of beige cardstock for a top fold card. Lightly score the fold. Cut out the terrarium bottle shape from the card front.

2. TRACE TERRARIUM SHAPE ONTO THE BACKING PAPER

Cut a piece of blue cardstock exactly the size of the card front. Cut a piece of tan elephant hide (for the "soil") 2¾" (7cm) high by the width of the blue cardstock. Glue the tan paper onto the bottom of the cardstock using a dry glue stick, and lay the terrarium cutout directly over the two-tone backing card. Pencil the terrarium outline onto the backing card.

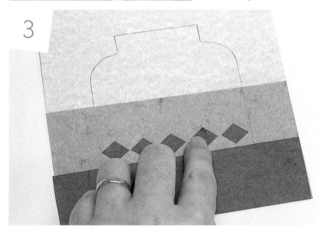

3. ADD THE DARK BLUE CUTOUTS

Cut a 1¾" (45mm) strip of dark blue paper and glue it onto the bottom of the backing card, overlapping the tan elephant hide. Also from dark blue, punch five diamond shapes. Glue a row of horizontal diamonds just above the dark blue strip.

4. CUT THE SCALLOP BANDS

Using the cloud paper edgers, cut the scallop bands from light green, dark green, and terra cotta paper. To start, draw a baseline across the paper. Cut along the line, aligning scallop points with the line. Discard the paper below the baseline. Next, using the previous cut as your new baseline, cut across the paper, aligning scallop points. Cut the scallop band about ¼" (6mm) wide. Make all the bands in this way.

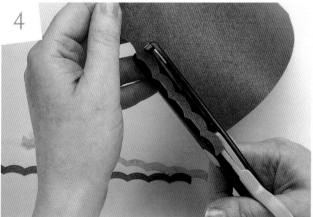

5. ADD FLOWER STEMS AND LEAVES

Glue the scalloped bands in place on the terrarium card using a dry glue stick. Use small scissors to cut the curved flower stems freehand. Glue the stems in place using crafter's glue applied with a toothpick. Punch out the leaves using a leaf-shaped paper punch. Glue the leaves onto the stems with crafter's glue.

6. ADD THE FLOWERS

Punch out three flowers and glue them in place using crafter's glue. Punch the flower centers with the ⅛" (3mm) circle punch and glue them in place. Next, remove the pencil outline using a kneaded eraser.

7. GLUE CELLOPHANE BEHIND THE WINDOW

Clear cellophane is used to create the appearance of a glass terrarium jar. Cut a piece of cellophane slightly larger than the terrarium cutout. On the back of the card front, apply a thin line of crafter's glue all around the cutout. Carefully smooth on the cellophane. Turn the card over. If any glue has crept onto the cellophane, clear it away with the tip of a toothpick or a moist tissue.

8. COMPLETE THE CARD

Glue the terrarium behind the cellophane window. Apply a line of crafter's glue across the top and bottom edges of the terrarium design and at the middle of each side. Position the terrarium behind the card front and smooth it in place. Finally, cut the terrarium "lid" out from corrugated cardboard and glue it onto the card front.

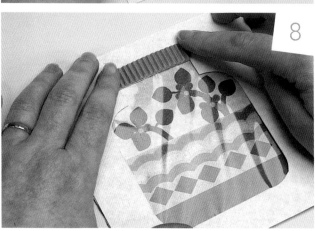

Get the Edge

Vary your sand-painted designs! Besides scallops, other paper edger blade styles are appropriate for mock sand-painted effects. Notch, wavy, heartbeat, and corkscrew patterns work well. Also try other punch shapes; geometrics, such as triangles, are best.

✿ VARIATION IDEAS

Using this same basic format,
you can create many more
"sand-painted" pieces of art
to give to friends and family!
The use of different colored
scalloped bands gives you a
vastly different card. A variety
of bottle shapes are available
to you. Make up several bottles of different shapes and
arrange them together for a
striking presentation.

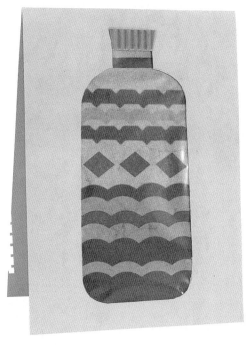

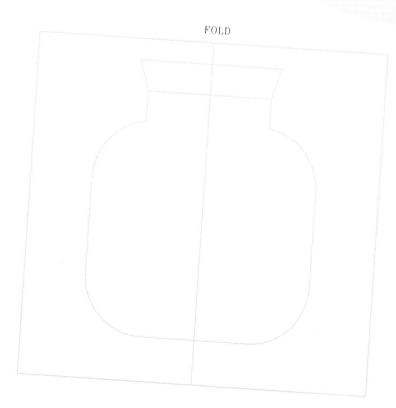

FOLD

Enlarge the
pattern 143%
for the front
of the folded
card.

crystal ball card

The whimsical crystal ball card works real magic. It brings a smile to the face of whoever you send it to. Plus, it is as much fun to make as it is to receive. The card is suitable for a variety of occasions—as a good luck card, a Halloween card or a greeting for a fantasy buff.

The inspiration for this card is snow globe toys—those childhood favorites, most often acquired as stocking stuffers or souvenirs. Instead of swirling snowflakes, this card produces a cosmic shower of shooting stars!

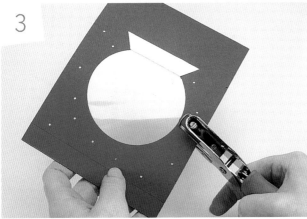

1. CUT OUT THE CARD

Enlarge the card pattern, given on page 35. Using the card template, trace and cut out the greeting card front and back pieces from navy blue cardstock. Trace the globe pattern onto the card front (card front has the top fold). Lightly score the top fold using a craft knife and ruler. Next, cut the circle out using the shape cutter.

2. GLUE ON THE CELLOPHANE

Cut a piece of pearlescent white vellum the size of the card front. This will be the back of the snow globe. Trace the globe pattern in pencil in the center of the vellum. Cut a piece of clear cellophane to fit behind the circle cutout. On the back of the card, apply crafter's glue around the circle edges sparingly and carefully. Smooth the cellophane in place.

3. PREPARE THE CARD FRONT

Trace and cut out the globe base from mirror cardstock. Attach it to the bottom of the globe with crafter's glue. Next, use the $^1/_{16}$" (2mm) circle hand punch to add a few random holes around the globe. When held up to the light, these holes will be "distant twinkling stars." Add as many or as few holes as you like.

4. BEGIN THE CRESCENT MOON

Use the $^1/_2$" (13mm) circle punch to make a crescent moon. This is done in two steps. First, punch a semi-circle from the mirror cardstock. To do this, the punch must overlap the card edge, as shown.

5. COMPLETE THE CRESCENT MOON

Use the back of the punch so you can look through the cutout for easy placement. Position the circle over the previously punched arc. Punch out the shape to produce the crescent moon.

6. DECORATE THE CARD FRONT

Punch out several stars from mirror cardstock. Affix them to the card front with crafter's glue. Also glue on the crescent moon.

7. CUT OUT THE WAND

Cut out a 2½" (6cm) long by ¼" (6mm) wide strip of mirror card. Add a tip of pearlescent paper to the wand with crafter's glue. Glue the wand onto the bottom of the card.

Recycled Artistry

If you've saved punch-outs from your other projects, you can use them in the cellophane globe! Keep your leftover punch-outs in a plastic bag, and use them for projects such as this that require extra punches.

Holiday Greetings!

Papercraft a snow scene—ideal for holiday greetings. Make a few triangle-shaped trees and add a distant cabin out of simple shapes. For the snow, use ⅛" (3mm) punched circles. Add a few bigger snowflake shapes, punched out of shimmery white pearlescent paper. You can find a snowflake punch at your local craft store. A perfect greeting card for the holidays!

8. PUNCH OUT THE SNOW GLOBE CONFETTI

Use your paper punches to cut a variety of shapes for inside the globe. For this card, we used twenty-five blue vellum ½" (13mm) stars. From the mirror cardstock cut four ½" (13mm) spirals, four ½" (13mm) stars, one crescent moon (see steps 4–5, above) and seven ⅛" (3mm) punched circles.

9. GLUE MIRROR SHAPES INSIDE THE GLOBE

The penciled circle on the pearlescent vellum (see step 2) is your guide for gluing on the mirror cardstock embellishments. Inside the circle, glue on the mirror shapes with crafter's glue, arranging them as you wish them to appear on your completed card.

10. ASSEMBLE THE CARD FRONT

Flex the card front a few times. This eases the paper so the shapes can move around freely within the globe. Next, place the card front face down on your work surface. Place the blue vellum stars in the center of the cellophane. Apply glue around the edges of the circle. Smooth the pearlescent vellum onto the back of the card front, with the mirror shapes face down. Add a bit of glue to the corners of the pearlescent paper to affix it to the blue card front.

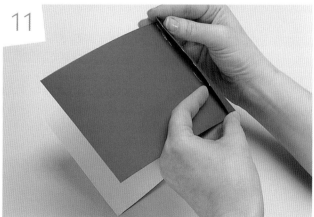

11. GLUE THE CARD TOGETHER

Crease the fold on the card front. Apply glue to the underside of the flap. Glue the flap onto the card back piece, as shown.

✿ VARIATION IDEA: STAR AND FLOWERS

Here's another quick-make idea. Use the shape cutter to cut out a star in the front of the card, then make a shimmery star to hang in the hole you've made. Front the star with a smaller, translucent card and stitch it in place with yarn. Fill the star with flower and circle confetti and glue more flowers and circles around the star for decoration. This card is sure to put a smile on someone's face!

✿ VARIATION IDEA: FISH POND

If you've made the crystal ball card, then crafting a fish pond is a cinch. Start with a shape cutter cutout, back it with colored translucent paper—and you've got the makings of a delightful papercrafted lily pond. Cut an oval pond shape, back with green vellum for the water, glue on punched paper water lilies and goldfish. Mount the hanging on your window using poster putty, or punch a hole at the top and add a ribbon hanging loop.

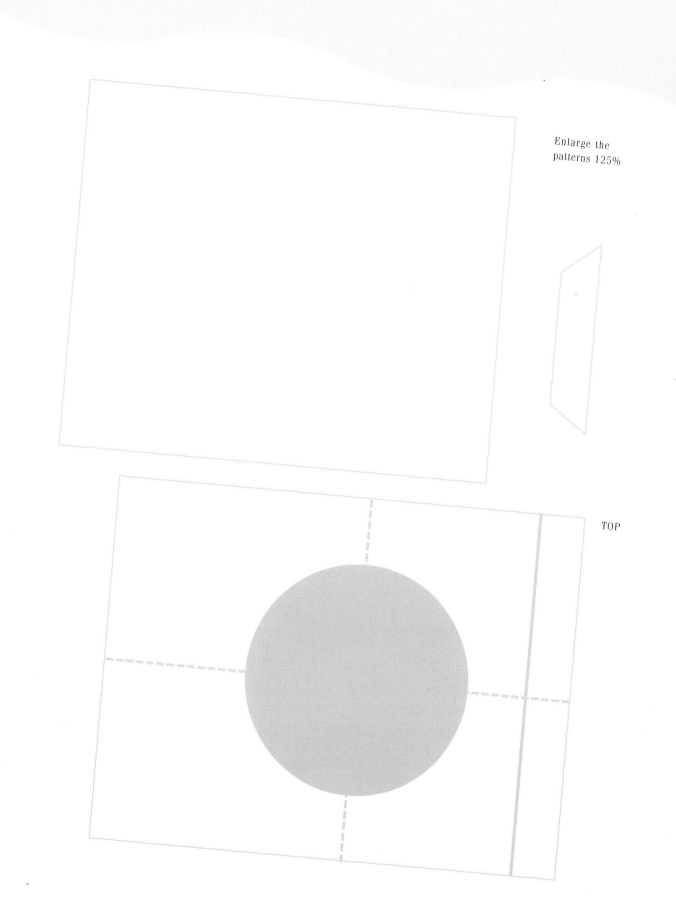

Enlarge the
patterns 125%

TOP

mola card

Mola embroidery is a style of reverse appliqué unique to the Cuna Indians who live on the San Blas Islands off the coast of Panama. A typical Mola design depicts the spectacular wildlife and lush vegetation of the rain forest using bold shapes and a burst of vibrant tropical hues.

Creating Mola embroidery is a time-consuming process. In fact, a Mola panel takes hours and hours of labor-intensive needlework to create. The good news is that this card can be produced in well under an hour! Papercraft gadgets make easy work of the Mola design. A stencil cutter is used for the swirly slitted background pattern, while hand punches and decorative paper edgers also contribute to the finished effect—a papercrafted tropical paradise!

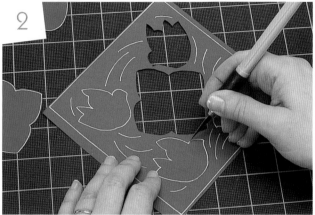

1. TRANSFER THE PATTERN

Enlarge the pattern given on page 41. Cut a piece of blue cardstock measuring 5½" (14cm) square. Tape the blue paper behind the pattern with masking tape. Use a stylus to impress the pattern outline onto the blue card. To see the outline more clearly, go over it with a white gel pen.

2. CUT OUT TWO DOVES AND THE FLOWER

Using the craft knife, cut out the upper right and lower left doves and the center flower. Make sure to cut just outside the white lines.

3. CUT THE DECORATIVE LINES

Using the stencil cutter, cut all the curved decorative lines that will be yellow in the finished design. Straddle the white lines as you cut, creating a line that is ⅛" (3mm) wide. A craft knife can be used as an alternative to a stencil cutter.

Paper Chase

Careful paper choice is crucial to the success of your Mola design. The distinctive feature of the Mola design is surface texture created by the cut away areas, so you want the depth of these to be noticeable. Choose cardstock thick enough to create a three-dimensional appearance, but thin enough to cut easily in double layers.

4. REMOVE THE CARD STRIPS

Cut across the short ends of each stencil cut strip with a craft knife, then remove and discard the card strips. The flattened tail of the stencil cutter handle can be used to pick out the cut card strips.

5. PINK THE EDGES

With pinking pattern decorative edgers, trim the blue card. Keep scissors inside the marked white lines.

6. PREPARE THE YELLOW LAYER

Cut a piece of yellow card 6" (15cm) square. Mark a border ¼" (6mm) inside the card edges. Glue the blue cut out centered on top of the yellow square. To do this, apply crafter's glue onto the back of the blue card, gluing around the doves and the flower cut out. Apply glue sparingly with a toothpick. Also glue all four corners and the middle of each side. Next, with a stylus, transfer the outlines for the design elements that appear red. Go over the outlines in pencil.

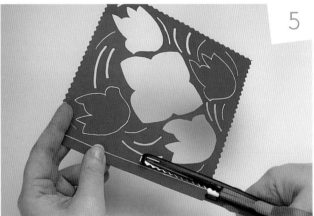

Speed Mola

If you are in a hurry, then you can approximate the look of Mola embroidery using glued-on cardstock cutouts. You can still use the patterns provided—only build up layers of cut outs rather than removing them. Still use the stencil cutter to create the background pattern, but glue on the curved strips instead of cutting them away. The finished design will lack the three-dimensional interest of the cutaway version, but it will still get across the unique quality of Mola designs in terms of shape, color and subject matter.

TIP

Tweezers can be helpful for positioning small glued elements. Straight-tipped tweezers are preferable to pointy ones— much easier to pick up the cutouts!

7. CUT OUT THE YELLOW LAYER

With the craft knife, cut out the design elements that will be red and the two remaining doves. Remember you are cutting through two layers of cardstock. Cut out the flower center, then cut out the cross and set it aside to glue on later. Cut out the decorative triangles on the yellow doves. With the stencil cutter, cut out the remaining curved decorative lines and the wings on the doves. Pink the edges of the card, as for Step 5. Place the yellow layer on the red card to check that you have cut out all the elements.

8. MARK THE RED LAYER

Cut a piece of red cardstock $6\frac{1}{2}$" (17cm) square. Mark a $\frac{1}{4}$" (6mm) border. Glue the yellow card onto the red, taking care to glue around the cutouts and at the corners. Tape the pattern over the design and use the stylus to trace the parts that will be green. Remove the pattern.

9. CUT OUT THE RED LAYER

Use a craft knife to cut out the elements that will be green: the center flower and the triangles on the red doves. Use the stencil cutter to cut out the wings on the red doves. Pink the edges of the red card. Cut a piece of green cardstock measuring $6\frac{1}{2}$" × 13" (17cm × 33cm). Score the middle of the card, then fold in half. Glue the red card onto the green card, centered, with the fold of the green card at the top.

10. COMPLETE THE CARD

Punch two green eyes and two red eyes with the $\frac{1}{8}$" (3mm) circle punch. Also punch out seven small green flowers. Glue these punched shapes and the yellow cross onto the card as shown.

❧ VARIATION IDEA: DIFFERENT COLORS, DIFFERENT CARD!

You can use different colors of paper to make strikingly different cards using the same patterns and techniques presented here. And with so many paper styles to choose from, you will never run out of possibilities. The card below was made by adding punched paper pieces, rather than cutting them away, as a quick-make technique. The gift tag was a quick-make as well, and would be a fabulous addition to any gift presentation. Speed Mola! Enjoy!

❧ VARIATION IDEA: MOLA BOOKMARK

This is a simplified version of the card design, so if you know how to make the card, the bookmark's a breeze.

Design Your Own Paper Mola

Think tropical rain forest for your subject matter and colors. (Wildlife: parrots, turtles, lizards. Color palette, rainbow: red, yellow, green, turquoise, magenta, orange.) Plan your design on paper (graph paper may help) using felt-tips to map out color areas. Keep it bold and simple. Start with a three-color design. (In authentic Molas, the top layer is often red.) Remember that you can "cheat" by including glued-on elements in addition to cutouts. In fact, authentic Molas often do include embroidered details and lettering. You can add "embroidery" to your design with gel pens. Simple lettering can be achieved using a scrapbooker's alphabet stencil.

Enlarge the pattern 125%. Dots (other than bird's eyes) show placement of punched flowers.

Enlarge the pattern 125%.

new baby keepsake card

Welcome the new arrival with a sweet and simple baby-bib motif greeting card. Tucked inside the bib pocket is a papercraft replica of a soft toy. Handmade with TLC from archival-quality scrapbooking materials, this easy-make card is both a heartfelt greeting and a long-lasting commemorative gift. The top-fold design of the card makes it easy to stand up for display.

Fun-to-use papercraft gadgets make crafting this card a cinch. The waffle-like texture of the paper bib, crinkled with a paper crimper, is a dead ringer for piqué fabric. Paper punches and corner rounders speed up card construction. Happy birthday, little one!

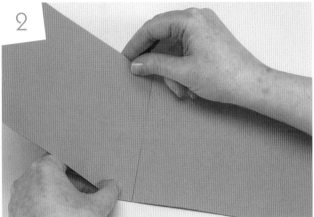

1. CUT OUT THE CARD

The greeting card is made in two pieces, so that you can fit it onto standard-size scrapbooking cardstock, either $8\frac{1}{2}$" × 11" (22cm × 28cm) or 12" × 12" (30cm × 30cm). Cut out the card pieces using a craft knife held against a metal ruler. Measure and cut out one 5" × 7" (13cm × 18cm) piece of card with a $\frac{5}{8}$" (1.5cm) fold added across the top. Cut the card back piece exactly 5" × 7" (13cm × 18cm). On the card front piece, score the fold line to make creasing easier.

2. GLUE THE CARD TOGETHER

With the scored line face down, fold down the flap. Crease the fold with your fingernail for a nice, crisp edge. Apply crafter's glue to the inside of the flap. Glue the smaller piece of card on top of this, aligning the top of the card with the creased fold on the flap. The flap belongs on the back of the card. The writing surface is inside the greeting card, on the smaller piece of card.

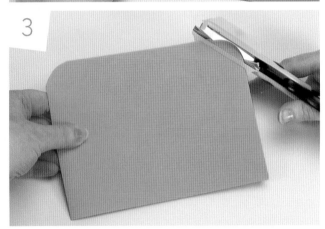

3. CUT THE ROUNDED CORNERS

Using the corner rounders, trim all four corners of the card. Open the rounders and slide the corner of the card underneath the guide slot until the paper is flush with the edges of the guide. Cut the corner, then repeat for the remaining three corners.

4. CRIMP THE BIB PAPER

Cut out a piece of blue paper about $4\frac{1}{2}$" × $6\frac{1}{2}$" (11cm × 17cm). Insert it between the rollers of the crimper, making sure the top edge of the paper is parallel to the lines on the roller. Squeeze the crimper handle tightly to clamp the rollers together, then crank the key toward you to advance the paper and create the corrugated ridges.

5. CRIMP THE PAPER AGAIN

Turn the crimped paper 90° and insert the paper, held lengthwise, between the rollers. Pass the paper through the crimper a second time. This creates a waffle-like texture. Enlarge the bib pattern (see page 47) and cut it out in cardstock. Punch holes where marked on the pattern using a $\frac{1}{16}$" (2mm) circle hand punch. Position the bib pattern over the waffle paper and trace around it with a pencil. Mark the holes for the ribbon, as well as the pocket fold.

6. CUT OUT THE BIB

Using the $\frac{1}{16}$" (2mm) circle hand punch, punch out the holes as marked at the bib top and along the bottom edge. Cut out the curved neckline using scissors, and use a craft knife held against a metal ruler to cut out the remaining straight edges.

7. CUT THE ROUNDED CORNERS

Using a ruler to keep the edge straight, fold down the bib pocket. Using the corner rounders (see step 3), trim all four corners of the bib, including the pocket corners.

8. THREAD RIBBON THROUGH THE HOLES

Cut a 10" (25cm) piece of $\frac{1}{8}$" (3mm) satin ribbon. Using a tapestry needle, thread the ribbon through the punched holes along the bib pocket edge. Sew an under-over running stitch. Make sure the ribbon doesn't twist. Cut the ends of the ribbon flush with the bib. Secure the ribbon ends with glue on the back of the pocket.

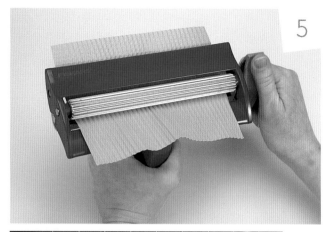

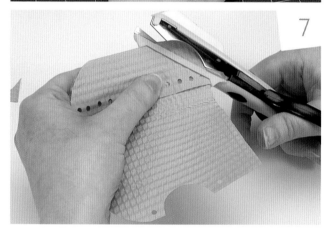

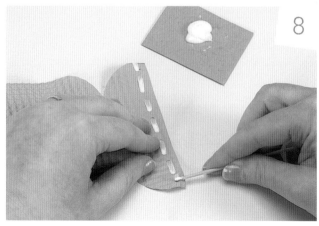

TIP

The craft knife tends to catch on the crinkled paper. The best way to cut through it is to swipe the knife lightly several times across the paper until it makes a cut.

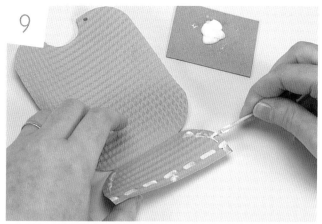

9. GLUE THE BIB POCKET

On the inside of the bib pocket, apply glue to the side edges. Also place a small dab of glue at the middle of the top edge. Fold the pocket up and gently tap the glued areas down.

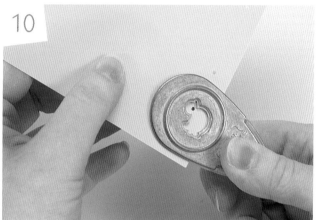

10. PUNCH OUT THE DUCKS

Using the 1/16" (2mm) hand punch, punch five holes in the paper for the duck's eyes. Space the holes a bit more than a duck width apart. Turn the paper punch upside down so you can see exactly where to position the eye. Punch out five ducks.

11. GLUE THE DUCKS ONTO THE BIB POCKET

Glue the center duck first, then space the remaining ducks evenly across the pocket. All the ducks should face the same way.

12. ATTACH THE BIB TIES AND BOW

Cut two 8" (20cm) pieces of 1/8" (3mm) satin ribbon for the ties. Slip the end of one ribbon through the punched hole. On the back side of the bib, glue down the ribbon tail at a 45° angle. Repeat for the other ribbon. Tie the ribbons into a bow. Use scissors to trim the ribbon tails, then seal the ribbon ends with crafter's glue.

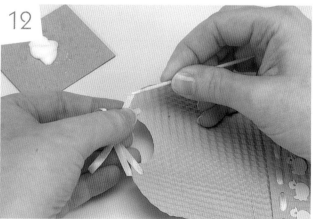

Same Card, Different Looks

✳ To add background interest, make the greeting card out of patterned scrapbooking cardstock. Many adorable new baby motifs are available.

✳ Tuck a paper teddy into the bib pocket instead of a bunny.

✳ No paper crimper? Make the baby bib out of handmade paper. It has a fabric-like feel and appearance.

✳ For a refreshing change from the usual pink/blue baby color scheme, try alternative pastel colors such as peach, lilac or mint green. Very appealing!

13. GLUE THE BIB ONTO THE CARD

Apply glue sparingly to the back of the bib. Glue the bottom edge of the bib, behind the pocket. Also apply dabs of glue at the midpoint of each bib side and on the backs of the ribbon ties (at the bib top). Glue the bib onto the card front. Tap the bib in place gently to avoid smoothing out the crinkles. Finally, attach the bow knot with a dab of glue.

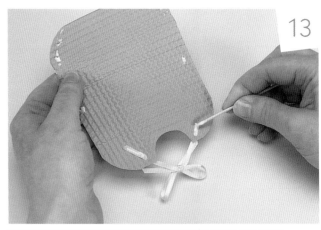

14. TRACE THE BUNNY

Trace the bunny pattern (see page 47) onto a small piece of pink cardstock (leftover from the card). Just make an impression of the bunny outline using a stylus, such as a dry fine-point pen. Go over the outline in pencil, if necessary. Use a gel pen to draw in the face of the bunny.

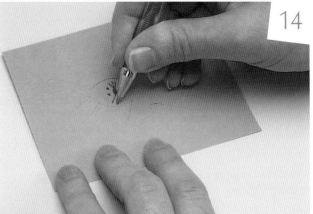

15. CUT OUT THE BUNNY

Use small scissors, such as embroidery or nail scissors. Cut on the inside of the pencil mark or the impressed outline, so the lines won't show on the completed cutout. Erase any lines left on the paper.

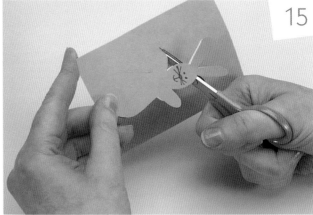

16. GLUE BOW ON BUNNY

Cut 3" (8cm) of ⅛" (3mm) ribbon for the bow. Tie a knot in the middle of the ribbon, trim the ends at an angle, then seal the ends as you did in step 12. Glue the bow onto the bunny and fold over one ear.

Forever Yours

For a truly lasting keepsake, make sure all your card materials are of archival quality: paper, glue and ink—no halfway measures! You can find these supplies in a scrapbooking store or in the scrapbooking department of a hobby superstore. Sales staff will be happy to advise you.

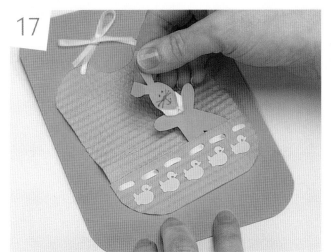

To finish the card, tuck the bunny into the bib pocket—there's no need to glue it down.

Overcast Pocket Edges

For a different look, overcast the edge of the bib pocket. You will need a 12" (30cm) piece of ribbon for this. Just sew the ribbon around and around over the pocket edge. For easier threading, use a ⅛" (3mm) hole punch for the stitching holes.

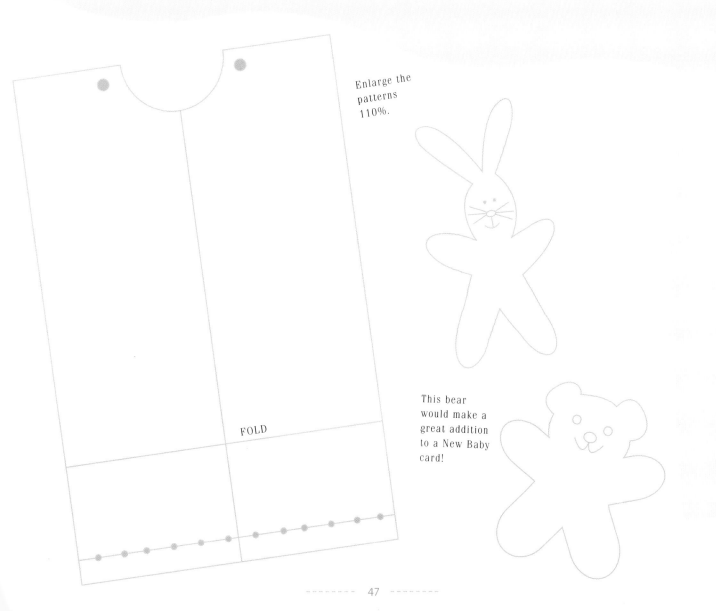

Enlarge the patterns 110%.

FOLD

This bear would make a great addition to a New Baby card!

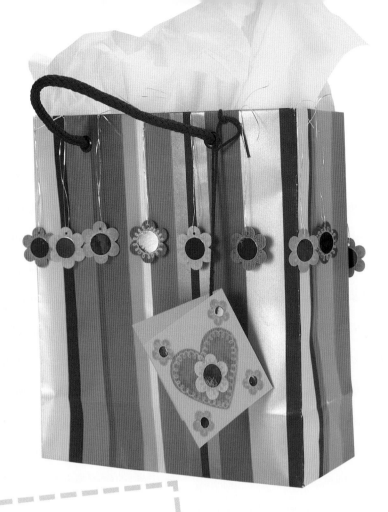

shisha spangles gift bag & tag

Splashes of color and flashes of sparkle transform this gift bag and tag into a gorgeous "hippie chic" sensation. The spangles take their inspiration from the traditional shisha embroidery of India and Pakistan. A shisha is a mini mirror, usually a round one, which is appliquéd onto a background fabric using decorative buttonhole stitches.

We dressed up a purchased gift bag, but shisha spangles can also be used to make over other store bought articles, especially stationery items. Glue spangles onto school notebooks in decorative patterns, or use them to jazz up a pencil holder or other desktop articles. For another shisha-inspired project, turn to the shisha CD gift box.

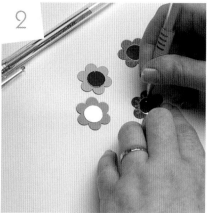

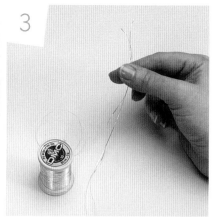

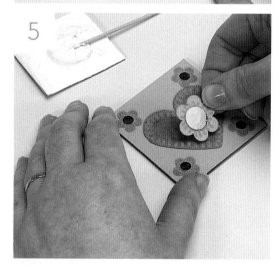

1. ASSEMBLE THE SPANGLE

Using the 1" (25mm) flower paper punch, make flowers out of brightly colored cardstock. Punch two $\frac{1}{2}$" (13mm) circles from mirrored cardstock for each flower that you punch. Using crafter's glue, affix a mirror circle to the center of each side of the flower.

2. DRAW A DESIGN

Use a gel pen to draw an embroidery-style design around the mirror circle. For example, a curlicue design is quick and easy to do. Use a gel pen color to contrast with the flower. Wait until the ink has dried, then decorate the flip side of the flower.

3. ADD THE SILVER THREAD

Punch a $\frac{1}{16}$" (2mm) hole in a petal of the spangle. Cut 12" (30cm) of silver thread and pass it through the hole in the spangle. Next, punch holes in the top of the gift bag for the spangles using the $\frac{1}{16}$" (2mm) punch; space the holes about $2\frac{1}{2}$" (6cm) apart. Thread each spangle through a hole in the bag and knot it in place.

4. CUT OUT THE GIFT TAG

Cut out a rectangle of green cardstock measuring $2\frac{1}{2}$" × 5" (6cm × 13cm). Score the cardstock and fold it in half. Next, cut out a pink 2" (5cm) heart, a 1" (25mm) flower and four $\frac{1}{2}$" (13mm) flowers. Then, cut out mirrored cardstock circles and glue them in place. You need a $\frac{1}{2}$" (13mm) circle for the larger flower and four $\frac{1}{4}$" (6mm) circles for the small flowers.

5. DECORATE AND ASSEMBLE THE TAG

Draw the embroidery designs around the mirrors and the heart, using a contrasting gel pen. Then glue the spangles and the heart onto the gift tag as shown. Punch a hole in the inside top left corner of the card. Cut about 12" (30cm) of burgundy embroidery thread and draw it through the hole. Tie the tag onto the gift bag handle.

star gift box

This five-sided gift box looks all starry, cosmic and other-worldly—really snazzy packaging for that special birthday surprise!

Hard to believe, but the gift box starts out as just two circles of cardstock! This is good news because it means you'll never be without a gift box as long as you have a couple of pieces of cardstock, a shape cutter tool and a few minutes to spare!

To get from flat circles to three-dimensional box, you just fold in the curved side flaps, join the top and bottom box layers, and the box takes shape. This sort of box is called a pillow box, because it plumps up like a fluffy pillow.

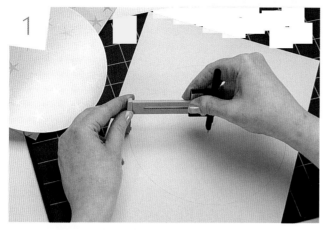

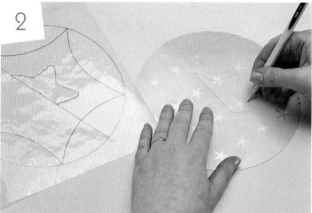

1. CUT OUT THE PAPER

Glue a piece of gift wrap onto a sheet of heavy cardstock with a dry glue stick. (Alternatively, a Xyron machine can be used to bond the gift wrap to the cardstock.) Using the compass cutter, cut out a 3½" (9cm) radius circle from the gift-wrap-covered cardstock. Cut out another 3½" (9cm) radius circle from plain green cardstock.

2. TRANSFER THE PATTERN MARKINGS

Make a tracing of the gift box pattern on page 55. Tape the tracing over the plain side of the gift wrap circle. Transfer the pattern outlines by pressing firmly with a stylus. Mark half a star in the middle of the circle, and the five curved side folds. On the plain cardstock circle, mark only the curved folds.

3. SHAPE-CUT THE STAR

Use the 3" (8cm) star on the shape template. Since you will be using only half of the star, begin cutting at the top point of the star, continue downward to the bottom point, then stop cutting! (For more detailed shape cutter how-tos, see page 21.)

Pick a Patterned Paper

To save time, make your gift box out of printed cardstock instead of gift wrap glued onto cardstock. Many fabulous scrapbooking papers can be found, some with double-sided designs. Reversible paper will work fabulously for the fold-back window cutout!

4. SCORE THE STAR FOLD

On the back of the circle, lightly score the fold line of the star. Turn the circle gift wrap side up, then fold the star back.

5. SCORE THE CURVED FOLDS

On the back of the circle, score the curved folds. Do the same thing on the second cardstock circle.

6. GLUE THE TRANSLUCENT PAPER

Cut a small piece of pearlescent vellum to fit behind the star opening. Use a toothpick to apply crafter's glue sparingly around the opening. Smooth the paper in place, making sure there are no folds.

7. MAKE THE GIFT TAG

Use the shape cutter to make two 3" (8cm) stars. Cut one star from green cardstock and the other from lightweight purple paper. Fold the purple star in half and use a dry glue stick to affix half the purple star to the green star, with star points matching.

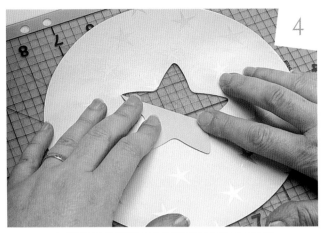

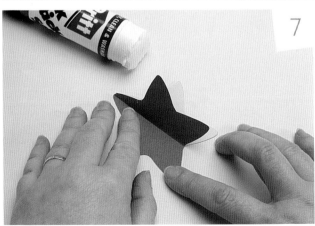

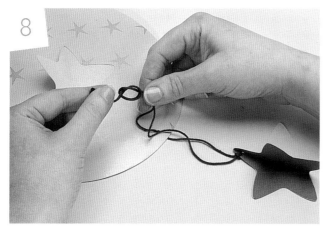

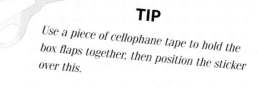

TIP

Use a piece of cellophane tape to hold the box flaps together, then position the sticker over this.

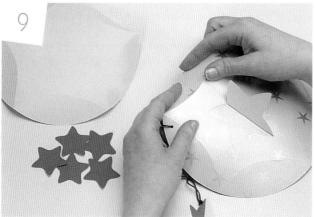

8. ATTACH THE GIFT TAG

Cut 18" (46cm) of purple matte embroidery cotton. Use the $1/8$" (3mm) hole punch to make a hole near the edge of the gift tag and another hole near the corner of a side flap. Tie the thread through the holes and knot to secure.

9. PREPARE THE BOX FOR ASSEMBLY

Use the shape cutter to make five $1^1/2$" (38mm) star-shaped stickers. To make the sticker material, use a dry glue stick to bond a piece of purple paper onto a self-adhesive mailing label. Next, crease the scored, curved edges on both the gift wrap and plain circles.

10. ASSEMBLE THE BOX

Hold the folded circles with insides facing, edges even, and curved flaps matching. Fold the top flaps over the bottom flaps one at a time, and seal the bottom edge of each flap with a star sticker.

11. FINISH THE BOX

Do not seal all the flaps; leave two sides open. Place the present inside the box, then fold down and seal the two remaining flaps.

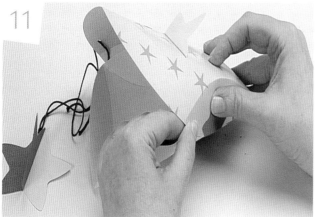

By simply changing the folds and the shape of the template, you can have an endless variety of gift boxes!

What You See Is What You Get

For our gift box, frosted vellum was used behind the star-shaped window opening. This is because we wanted the box contents to remain a mystery. However, if you are packaging food treats— such as candy or cookies—then back the window with clear cellophane to show off the yummy box contents!

Instead of a fold-back window, cut out the entire star shape, to give a better view of the goodies.

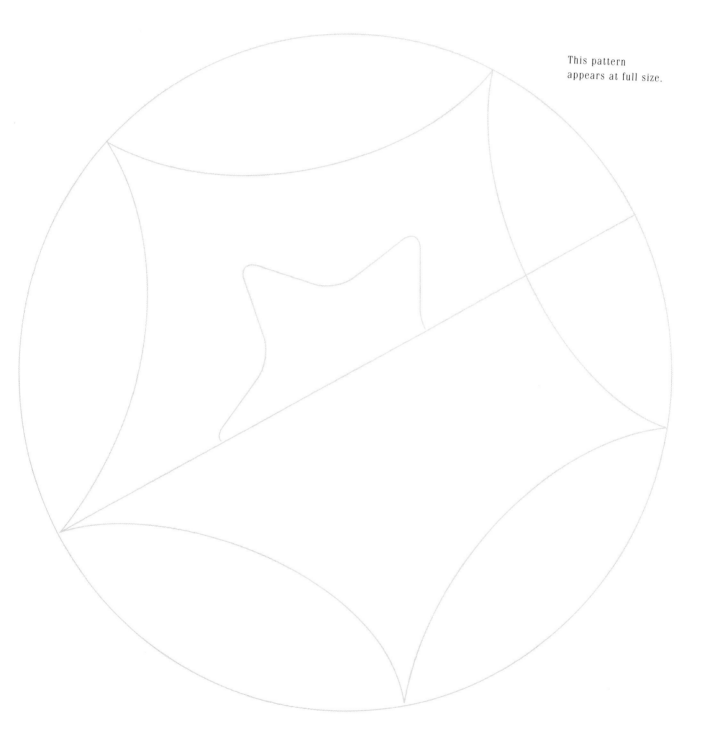

This pattern
appears at full size.

japanese-style gift bag & tag

This attractive gift bag is quickly and easily made from just a single piece of paper, plus a few trimmings. Once you know how to make the bag, you can make it in different sizes, so you'll never, ever be without a gift wrap solution.

The bag design is inspired by Japanese paper-folding traditions—and the hexagonal seal and tag resemble Japanese heraldic crests. The use of authentic Japanese washi paper for the patterned triangle carries through the theme. If you don't have any washi paper handy, then substitute patterned origami paper or a suitable piece of gift wrap.

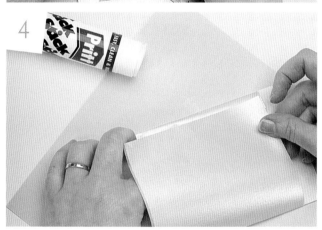

1. TRACE AND CUT OUT THE PATTERN

Enlarge the bag pattern (see page 59) on a photocopier, then trace it onto the back side of a piece of pearlescent paper. At the same time, enlarge the pattern for the gift tag and seal. Cut out the bag. Mark fold lines in pencil. Also, cut out a triangle from the patterned paper.

2. CREASE THE FOLDS; GLUE THE TRIANGLE

Using a ruler, crease all the fold lines. Next, glue the decorative triangle onto the bag front, the side with the flaps using a dry glue stick.

3. DRAW THE GOLD LINES

With the gold marker, outline the diagonal edge of the triangle and the top edge of the bag. Use a ruler to ensure straight lines, wiping it clean with a towel after each marker line. Work over a piece of scrap paper.

4. ASSEMBLE THE BAG

Turn the paper face down (white side up). Next, fold the long flap down and apply glue stick along its length (on the pearly side). Glue the flap in place, folding it inside the bag.

TIP

Use a cork-backed ruler to prevent the marker ink from running under the ruler and smudging. Or, stick several stacked pieces of masking tape onto the back of your ruler.

5. GLUE THE BOTTOM OF THE BAG

Glue the white side of the bottom bag flap (the shorter, wider flap). Fold it onto the bag back.

6. MAKE THE TAG AND BAG SEAL

Start with two plain white self-adhesive mailing labels. Use a dry glue stick to glue red pearlescent paper onto one label and matte gold paper onto the other. From each label, cut out a hexagon (use the pattern provided) and punch out a flower. Punch flower centers using the 1/4" (6 mm) hand punch. To assemble each medallion, peel off the backing from the flower, then stick the flower onto a contrasting-colored hexagon. For the tag, cut out a slightly larger hexagon from yellow card stock. To complete the tag, peel off the backing from the flower medallion and center it on the tag. The remaining flower hexagon sticker is the bag seal; set it aside.

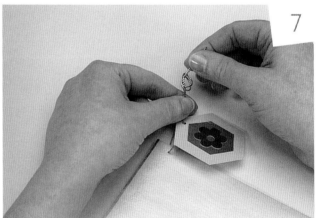

7. ATTACH THE TAG TO THE BAG

Using the 1/16" (2mm) punch, make a hole at the upper right-hand corner of the bag, and another one at a tag corner. Cut 10" (25cm) of thin gold cord. Thread the cord through the tag hole, then tie the tag onto the bag. Trim the cord ends even. Seal the cord ends with a bit of crafter's glue if necessary.

8. FILL AND SEAL THE BAG

Insert the gift in the bag. (A flattish present is recommended!) Fold the bag top down on an angle as shown. Seal the bag with the hexagon flower sticker.

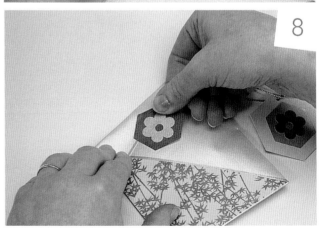

Hex Marks the Spot

The hexagons for our bag seal and tag were cut using a craft knife and ruler following the pattern provided. However, if you are a scrapbooker, then you may already own the Coluzzle Cutting System and have a template for making hexagons in graduated sizes. If you prefer, use this method to cut geometrically perfect hexagons for the tag and seal.

Enlarge the pattern 180%

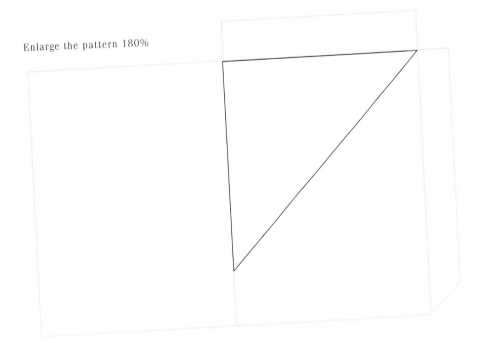

This pattern
appears at full
size.

🌸 VARIATION IDEAS

Choose different paper patterns
for a completely different look.
Increase the size of the pattern
for larger gifts.

★ MATERIALS LIST

PAPER

Pearlescent paper in pink and blue

Vellum in light and medium green, pink and magenta

Cardstock (for template)

ADDITIONAL SUPPLIES

Clear cellophane (sold by the roll as gift wrap)

Matte embroidery cotton in blue

Self-adhesive mailing labels

Crafter's glue

Dry glue stick

Toothpicks

Shape cutter

Shape template: hearts

Craft knife

Self-healing cutting mat

Hand punches: $1/16$" (2mm) and $1/8$" (3mm) circle; $1/4$" (6mm) flower

Paper punches: assorted flowers and leaf shapes

Metal ruler

Tapestry needle

wedding confetti pouches

Distribute these dainty purse-style confetti pouches to wedding guests—and add an extra sprinkling of romance and fantasy to the special occasion! Made of shimmery pearlescent paper in delectable sugared-almond colors, each envelope-style pouch is decorated with a garland of punched paper posies surrounding a heart-shaped "picture window." Inside are delicate floral confetti shapes made of vellum.

Each confetti pouch starts off as a square of paper. Add a heart-shaped cutout, glue on the decorations, then make a few basic origami folds to produce the finished project.

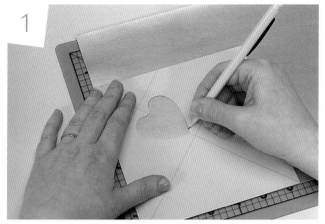

1. TRACE THE POUCH PATTERN ONTO PAPER

Enlarge the confetti pouch pattern, given on page 65. Cut the heart-shaped cutout in the template using the shape cutter tool. Next, trace the pattern outline—including the heart shape—onto the pearly side of the pink paper.

2. CUT OUT THE HEART

Cut the pouch square out of the pearly paper with your craft knife. Then cut out the heart using the 2" (5cm) heart-shaped template. For detailed shape cutter how-tos, see page 21.

3. GLUE CELLOPHANE BEHIND THE WINDOW

Cut a small piece of cellophane to fit behind the heart window. On the back side of the paper, apply crafter's glue around the edges of the heart-shaped window. Center the cellophane over the window; smooth it in place carefully. Turn the paper over to check if any glue has crept onto the cellophane. Remove glue quickly with the tip of a toothpick or a moist piece of tissue.

TIP

If you do not own a ShapeCutter tool, you can use an ordinary craft knife to cut out the heart shape.

4. FOLD THE PAPER IN HALF

With the white side of the paper inside, fold the paper in half diagonally, forming a triangle. Crease the fold with your fingernail for a nice, crisp edge.

5. PUNCH OUT THE DECORATIVE FLOWERS

Begin by punching the flower centers, using the 1/16" (2mm) circle punch. Next, punch out the flower itself, centering the flower punch over the previously punched hole. Punch out seventeen flowers with the hand punch.

6. PUNCH THE SHAPES FOR THE CENTER FLOWER

Using the 1/8" (3mm) circle punch, punch one flower center in pink. Also punch out a five-petal flower from blue paper, and two leaf shapes from green vellum.

7. GLUE THE FLOWERS ONTO THE POUCH

Assemble the larger flower at the heart top in layers. Start with the larger flower at the heart top. Using crafter's glue, glue on two vellum leaves, followed by the five-petal flower. Next, glue on the pink flower center. Glue a small blue flower just below the bottom point of the heart window.

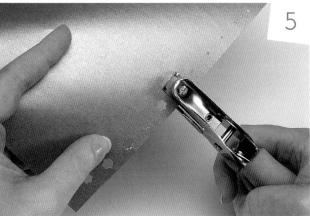

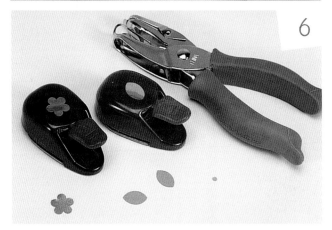

TIP
Turn the hand punch upside down and open the confetti catcher. You can now see if the hole is in the flower center.

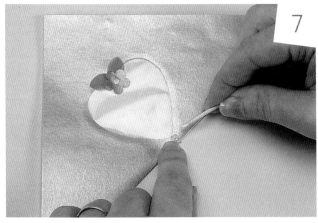

8. GLUE FLOWER GARLAND AROUND THE HEART

After you have glued on the bottom flower, glue the remaining small flowers around the heart-shaped window, spacing them evenly apart.

9. FOLD THE POUCH

With the window side face down, fold the right-hand triangle point across to meet the opposite side so the top and bottom edges of the paper are parallel. Crease the fold. Fold the left-hand triangle point over in a similar way, then crease the fold. Use a toothpick to glue beneath each triangle point and smooth the points down.

10. FOLD THE TOP FLAP

On the back side of the pouch, fold the top corner down to form the envelope flap. Crease the fold.

Posh Gift Packaging

With just one small change, the pouch design can be adapted to make elegant gift packaging for a small item of jewelry—such as a ring, earrings or a delicate chain. Simply eliminate the window cutout to add the gift-giving "surprise factor." Replace the window with a glued-on heart-shaped cutout of the same size. Use pearlescent paper in a contrasting color.

11. MARK HOLES FOR THE THREAD HANDLE

At each corner of the pouch front, mark two holes spaced vertically, $1/4$" (6mm) apart. Open out the pouch top flap and punch the holes using the $1/16$" (2mm) circle punch.

12. THREAD THE HANDLE

Cut 18" (46cm) of matte embroidery cotton. Using a tapestry needle, thread each end of the handle through the holes. Knot the thread ends below the holes.

13. FILL THE POUCH WITH CONFETTI

Using a variety of flower and leaf shapes, punch out the confetti from the vellum. Alternatively, if you are really pushed for time, you can use purchased confetti. Fill the pouch with confetti. Make sure the confetti shows nicely through the window.

14. MAKE A FLOWER-SHAPED SEAL

Glue a piece of blue pearly paper onto an adhesive label using a dry glue stick. Punch out a five-petal flower shape from the label. To complete the flower-shaped sticker, glue on a pink flower center using a $1/8$" (3mm) circle. Seal down the back flap with the sticker.

TIP

You can use six-strand embroidery floss as an alternative to matte embroidery cotton. Use all six strands.

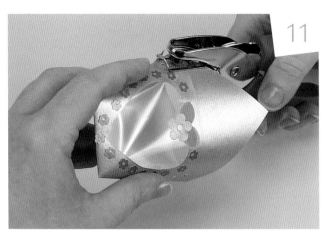

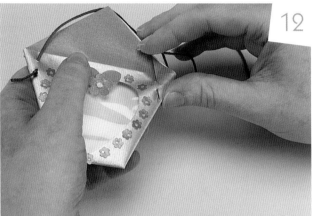

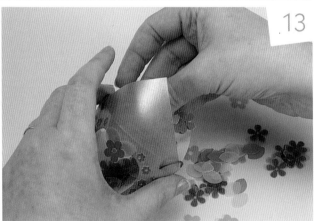

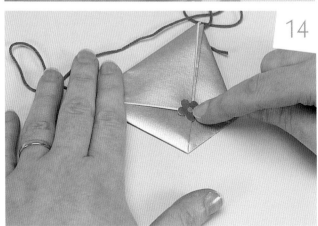

1. BEGIN THE FOLD

Once you've cut out the pattern and the heart shape, fold the pattern in half so it resembles a triangle. Mark the bottom edge of the triangle with dots, dividing it into thirds.

2. MAKE THE SQUARE

Fold the right-hand point to meet the dot at left, aligning the bottom edges of the paper; crease the fold. Similarly, fold the left-hand point to meet the dot at right and crease the fold.

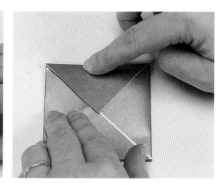

3. CLOSE THE FLAP

Fold down the top flap. Reverse the color scheme of the square pouch so it complements the colors of the cup-shaped pouch.

✿ VARIATION: SQUARE CONFETTI POUCH

You can make a square pouch from the same pattern as the cup shape, simply by folding the triangle in a different way. Magic!

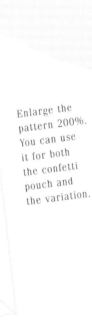

Enlarge the pattern 200%. You can use it for both the confetti pouch and the variation.

PAPER

One 12" × 12" (30cm × 30cm)
sheet of navy scrapbooking
cardstock, or two 8½" × 11"
(22cm × 28cm) sheets

One square of red origami
paper

One small piece of white paper

One square of blue origami
paper

One 6" × 6" (15cm × 15cm)
sheet of patterned origami paper
(red and white print)
or washi paper

ADDITIONAL SUPPLIES

Soft embroidery cotton in white

3-D découpage self-adhesive
foam pad

Crafter's glue

Dry glue stick

Masking tape

Stylus

White gel pen

Toothpicks

Craft knife

Self-healing cutting mat

Metal ruler

Paper punch: ½" (12mm)
heart

Paper edgers: scallop pattern

Hand punches: ¹/₁₆" (2mm),
⅛" (3mm) and ¼" (6mm) circles

Small scissors

Tapestry needle

sashiko cd gift box

Everybody enjoys receiving a CD, but a CD gift is a bit like getting a wrapped bottle of wine—no surprise—because of its easily recognizable shape and size. This attractive, reusable gift container brings back the surprise. It holds both a CD and its plastic case. It will show the recipient that you have spent as much thought and effort on packaging the gift as you did on selecting it.

This distinctive CD gift box is inspired by the boldly beautiful needle art of Japanese Sashiko quilting, in which designs are stitched onto contrasting-colored background fabric using large running stitches. For our box, we have chosen the traditional combination of white "stitching" on indigo. The hexagonal decorative medallions on the box are styled after Japanese heraldic crests.

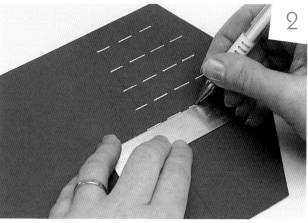

1. TRACE AND CUT OUT THE TEMPLATES

Enlarge the pattern templates on page 71 and make separate tracings for the two box pieces and the decorative hexagons. Trace and cut out the two box pieces from navy cardstock. Lightly score the fold lines as marked. Lay the tracings over the box pieces. Tape them in place with masking tape and with a stylus impress the "stitching lines". Use vertical dashes on the top flap, and horizontal dashes on the box bottom piece.

2. DRAW THE "STITCHING LINES"

Use a white gel pen and a straightedge to draw the lines on the CD box pieces using the pattern you impressed in the previous step.

3. CREATE THE DECORATIVE CRESTS

Trace and cut out the two larger hexagons from red paper and two smaller hexagons from white paper. Use the heart punch to make eight navy blue hearts. Punch out two ¼" (6mm) circles in red for the crest centers. With a dry glue stick, glue a white hexagon onto each red hexagon. Next, glue four blue hearts onto each white base. Glue a red dot in the center of each crest.

4. EMBELLISH THE BOX

Use the pattern tracing to cut out the V-shaped box trim from the printed origami paper. Glue the origami trim onto the cover flap of the box using a dry glue stick. Trim the ends of the origami paper with scissors if necessary. Use crafter's glue to attach one decorative crest onto each box piece.

TIP

I used a craft knife and straightedge to cut out our hexagons, but you may wish to use nested templates, such as the Coluzzle Cutting System, to cut geometrically perfect hexagons.

5. PUNCH A HOLE FOR THE TASSEL

Use the ⅛" (3mm) punch to make a hole at the center of the box flap.

6. ASSEMBLE THE BOX

Fold the box pieces along the scored lines, creasing firmly. Next, join the two box pieces. Apply crafter's glue to the underside of the bottom flap of the piece with horizontal dashes. Glue this onto the top flap of the piece that ends in the V-flap. Let the glue dry.

7. GLUE THE BOX SIDES

One side at a time, apply glue to the outside of each flap, with the angled edge at the bottom. Fold up the box front and press each glued side flap onto the inside of the box back. Reach inside the box to smooth down the glued flaps. Use a rubber band to hold the box together until the glue sets.

Prints Charming

If you can't track down patterned origami paper for the box trim, substitute a scrapbooking print. You should be able to find a good selection of Asian-style motifs. (For example, check out Paper Adventures Quadrants Papercrafting Packs.) Or, use a suitable gift wrap pattern.

5

6

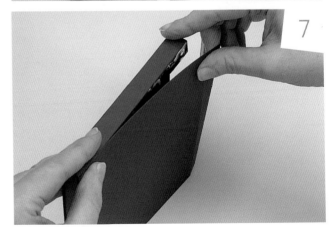

7

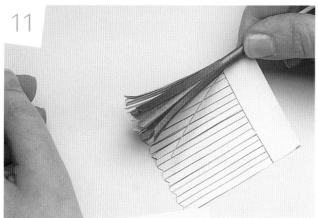

8. CUT OUT THE TASSELS

On the back of a piece of red origami paper, measure a rectangle 2½" (6cm) wide by 4½" (11cm) long. Draw a ⅝" (16mm) border along the top of the rectangle. Cut along the bottom edge of the rectangle with scalloped paper edgers. Cut out the rest of the rectangle with a craft knife.

9. MARK THE TASSEL FRINGE

Draw a vertical line from each scallop indentation to the border, then draw another line from the lowest point of each scallop to the border.

10. CUT THE TASSEL FRINGE

Use small scissors to cut the fringe along the lines marked in the previous step.

11. ROLL THE TASSEL

Tightly roll the uncut top border of the tassel rectangle around a toothpick. When finished, secure the end with a dab of crafter's glue.

Making Tassels

Tassels are easy to make and are a fantastic accent piece or embellishment for many paper-craft projects. Steps 8–13 can be used to make tassels for many of the projects in this book.

12. SECURE THE TASSEL

Cut a band of blue origami paper 1/8" (3mm) wide by 1 1/2" (4cm) long. Wrap the band around the tassel top, just above the fringe. Glue the beginning and end of the band.

13. PUNCH A HOLE IN THE TASSEL

Flatten the tassel top, then punch a hole in the end of the tassel with a 1/16" (2mm) punch. Make another tassel following steps 8–13.

14. TIE THE TASSELS ONTO THE BOX

Cut a 12" (30cm) piece of white embroidery cotton for each tassel. Fold the thread in half and thread the loop through a tapestry needle. Sew the loop through the tassel hole, then remove the needle and pull the thread ends through the loop. Repeat for the other tassel. Thread each tassel through the hole in the box flap. Knot the tassel threads on the back of the box and seal the knot with crafter's glue. To make a reclosable box seal, add a 3-D découpage self-adhesive foam pad under the point of the box flap.

No-Hassle Tassels

The paper tassels on the box are fun and easy to make—but, if you prefer, inexpensive ready-made tassels made of silky thread are available at notions counters or in the home furnishings department. Or, make your own tassel substitute: Tie on a bit of rattail cord, and thread the ends with beads. Knot the rattail below the beads. Looks great!

12

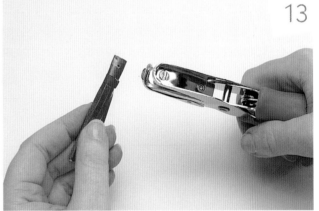

13

14

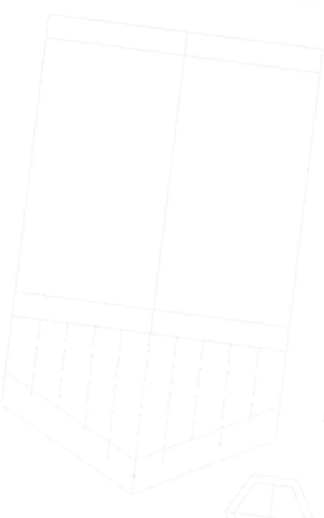

Enlarge the patterns 200%.

✿ VARIATION IDEA: BOX PAIR

To make a coordinating pair of CD gift boxes, use the templates for the red Sashiko CD box. Its stitching lines go in opposite direction to those on the blue box.

shisha cd gift box

Here is another take on the CD gift box, this time finding its inspiration in the colorful mirror embroidery of India and Pakistan (see Shisha spangles, page 48). The tassel-trimmed gift box resembles a typical shisha-work purse (shisha means mirror).

The origin of mirror embroidery can be traced back to the folk belief that the mirrors were good-luck charms that warded off evil spirits. It was thought that the evil spirits were frightened off by seeing their own reflections!

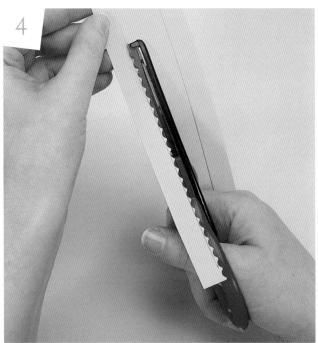

1. TRACE AND CUT OUT THE TEMPLATES

Enlarge the pattern templates on page 75 and make separate tracings for each of the two box pieces. Do not copy the dashes. They are for the Red Sashiko CD box variation. Trace and cut out the two box pieces from red cardstock. Lightly score the fold lines, then cut out the V-shaped flap using small-scallop paper edgers.

2. MAKE THE MOCK RICKRACK

Mark a straight line about 8" (20cm) long on a piece of green paper. Cut along the line with the clouds pattern (large scallops) paper edgers.

3. COMPLETE THE GREEN RICKRACK

To finish the rickrack band, cut another row of large scallops ¼" (6mm) below the first row. Position the paper edger blades so the scallop peaks are aligned with those in the first row. Make two more rickrack bands in this way.

4. CUT THE YELLOW BAND

On yellow paper, mark a band 1" (25mm) wide by about 8" (20cm) long. Cut the band out using the smaller scallop paper edgers. Make a second band in this way.

What's Inside?

Just because this box is CD-size doesn't mean you have to use it for its intended purpose. This box is the perfect size for small items of jewelry, such as bracelets or earrings. Or, it can be used as a container for small candy party favors.

5. EMBELLISH THE BOX

Use a dry glue stick to glue the embellishments onto the box pieces. You will have to cut the flap bands to follow the edges of the box. Begin with the green decorative trim.

6. CONTINUE THE EMBELLISHMENT

Next, glue on the yellow decorative trim. For the perfect-fit miter join, cut one band to fit from V-point to edge with a diagonal cut.

7. FINISH THE DECORATIVE TRIM

Turn the cut side of the yellow strip over and join it at the V-point. Also glue a yellow band with rickrack to either side of the bottom of the box front.

8. ADD THE MIRRORED CIRCLES

Using the 1/2" (13mm) circle paper punch, punch out ten circles from mirrored cardstock. Use crafter's glue to attach the "mirrors" to the yellow bands. When gluing on a row of circles, glue the center circle first, then work your way outward to keep the spacing even.

Perfect Cut!

Steps 6–7 offer a simple way to make perfect miter-joined paper borders. You can use this to embellish anything from cards to scrapbook pages.

9

9. DRAW THE GREEN DIAMONDS

Use a green gel pen to draw double diamonds in between the mirror circles. First, draw an X in pencil, then complete the ends to make two adjacent diamonds. Color the diamonds in. Use a red gel pen to outline the mirror circles and draw "blanket stitch" spokes. To complete the CD box, follow steps 5–14 of the Sashiko CD Gift Box. Make the tassels in colors to match the box.

Enlarge the pattern 200%.

starburst ornament

With the help of a shape cutter tool, you can quickly craft a tree full of these cheery three-dimensional "starburst" ornaments. Or if you prefer, hang them in doorways or in the window where the breeze will set the loop-top jingle bell tinkling.

Fans of 3-D découpage will find this project to be a special treat. Each ornament is comprised of a triple-decker arrangement of star cut outs in coordinating festive papers.

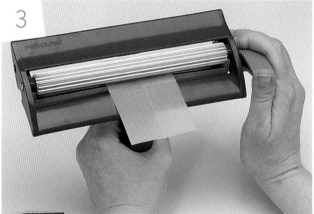

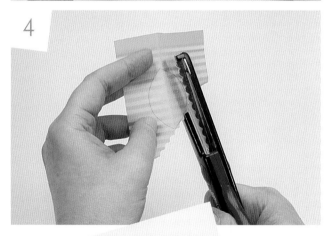

Sticky Pad Alternative

An economical alternative to using foam sticky pads is to make your own spacers by cutting little snippets of cardboard from a cardboard box. Attach these with crafter's glue.

1. CUT OUT THE STARS

Using the shape cutter, cut out three stars: one 3" (8cm), one 4" (10cm) and one 4½" (11cm). Use the gold embossed cardstock for the largest star and red cardstock for the medium star. For the smallest star, bond printed scrapbooking paper onto the red cardstock using a dry glue stick.

2. ATTACH THE STARS

Using the fine-point metallic gold marker, outline the two smaller stars. Then use the 3-D découpage self-adhesive foam pads to connect the stars. The largest (gold embossed) star is the bottom. Place a pad on the underside of each arm of the medium-size red star, but set it back a bit so the pad is not visible. Stick the red star onto the gold star, turning it slightly off center. Stick the smallest star on top, twisting it the same way.

3. CRINKLE PAPER FOR THE LEAVES

Cut out small rectangles of green vellum and dark green elephant hide (or, use flocked paper as an alternative). Crease the paper rectangles in half vertically. Feed each rectangle through the paper crimper with the crease in the vertical position. (For further instructions on how to use a paper crimper, see page 23.)

4. CUT OUT THE LEAVES

Cut out a leaf template (see page 79) from cardstock. Trace a leaf outline onto each piece of crinkled paper. Make sure you align the paper fold with the points of the leaf shape. Use scalloped paper edgers to cut out each leaf. Since these are holly leaves, you need to make concave scallops to create the pointy edges. To do this, hold the paper edger upside down to cut. Once done, use a kneaded eraser to gently remove the pencil marks.

5. GLUE THE LEAVES TOGETHER

Glue the dark green holly leaf on top of the vellum leaf, matching leaf points at one end as shown.

6. MAKE HOLES IN THE LEAF

Using a $1/16$" (2mm) hand punch, make two holes in the center of the darker leaf, $3/4$" (19mm) apart. Position the holes on the paper fold. Take 12" (30cm) of green velvet cord and lace it through the holes with the cord ends on top of the leaves. If you wish, thread the cord through a tapestry needle for easier lacing. Green yarn can be substituted for the velvet cord as an easy-to-find alternative.

7. ADD THE BEADS

Thread three red beads onto the cord nearest the overlapping leaf points. Slide the beads down the cord to the point where the cord emerges from the leaf. Knot the cord just below the beads.

8. ADD BEADS TO THE CORD ENDS

Thread a bead onto each of the cord ends. Knot each cord below the bead. Trim off any extra cord, then glue the leaves onto the center of the top star using crafter's glue.

Star Alternative

If you don't own a shape cutter tool, another way to cut stars in stepped sizes is to use a graduated-size template and knife set, such as the Coluzzle Cutting System. Using this method, you hand-cut the stars using a craft knife.

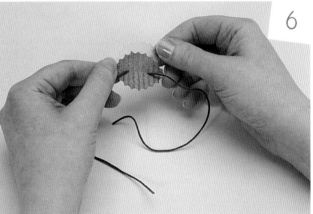

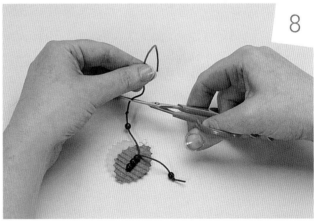

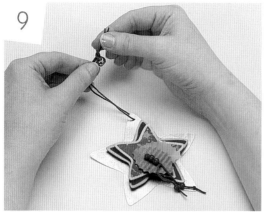

9

9. ADD THE HANGING LOOP

Punch a 1/16" (2mm) hole for the hanging cord at the top of the bottom (gold embossed) star. Thread 10" (25cm) of green cord through the hole. Next, add the jingle bell. Thread both cord ends through the loop on the jingle bell. Knot the cord so the jingle bell is contained by the knot.

10. ADD A BOW

Make a bow with 8" (20cm) of 1/8" (3mm) wide gold taffeta ribbon. Sew this through the cord knot just below the jingle bell.

10

Starry Garland

For a party decoration, make a garland by stringing a group of star-shaped ornaments side by side. Simply punch holes in opposite star points and tie the stars together. If you prefer, string the stars vertically and hang the cascade from the ceiling. A cascade is particularly effective with stars in graduated sizes.

❀ VARIATION IDEA: STARRY CELEBRATIONS

Make the star ornament in non-Christmas colors to suit other occasions such as birthdays, anniversaries, job promotions or graduations. Instead of going for gold, try a silver color scheme. Track down scrapbooking paper in an event-specific print. In place of holly leaves, glue a charm onto the center of the top star (add a mini bow to conceal the loop at the top of the charm). You can also use the star ornament to dress up a gift box, or as a detachable ornament on the cover of a homemade greeting card.

This pattern appears at full size.

stars foldout ornament

Here's another easy Christmas ornament craft-ed from ShapeCutter stars. Since this orna-ment can be viewed from all sides, it is ideal for hanging in a doorway, like mistletoe.

This ornament also looks great in holographic card-stock backed with velvety flocked paper. The latest velvety papers are very realistic-looking—they have a classy suede finish—and come in a good range of col-ors. Check some out next time you are in a scrapbook-ing store.

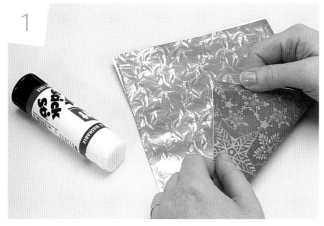

1. PREPARE THE PAPER

Glue a piece of gold embossed gift wrap and a piece of Christmas-print scrapbook paper together back-to-back, so it becomes double-sided. If you wish, you can use gold cardstock instead of gift wrap.

2. CUT OUT THE STARS

Use the shape cutter to cut out four 4" (10cm) stars and two 1½" (38mm) stars using the double-sided paper you created in step 1. Use the metallic gold marker to outline the Christmas-print side of the stars.

3. FOLD THE STARS

Fold the four larger stars in half. Since the double-sided paper is fairly lightweight there is no need to score the folds. (If, however, you use gold cardstock, you will need to score the folds.) Use a straightedge to keep the folds neat and crisp.

4. STAPLE THE STARS TOGETHER

Lay the four large stars on top of each other with points and folds aligned. Lay the first two stars with the gold side face up, and the last two stars with the print side face up. Once done, staple the stars together along the center fold; place one staple near the top and the other near the bottom.

5. ADD THE CORD

Punch two holes with the ⅛" (3mm) hole punch through all the stars, one near the top, and another at the bottom. Cut 12" (30cm) of green velvet cord. Fold the cord in half and pass the loop end through the hole. Next, pass the cord ends through the loop and pull them tight to secure them. Pull the cords gently so you don't damage the star.

6. ATTACH THE SMALL STARS

Using the ¹⁄₁₆" (2mm) hole punch, punch two holes in each of the two small stars. Punch one hole in a star point and the second hole about ¼" (6mm) below the first. Pass a cord through the holes in a star, thread on a bead, then knot the cord just below the bead. Attach a second star to the remaining cord end in the same way, but tie it on at a different length for variety. Trim the cord ends.

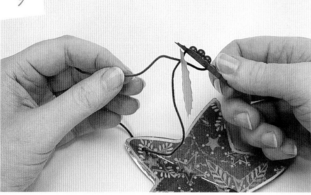

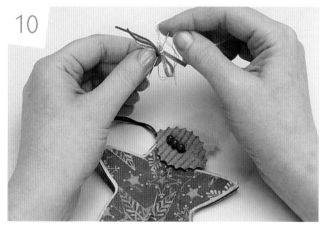

7. MAKE THE LEAVES

Create two holly leaves as for the Starburst Ornament on page 77, steps 3 and 4. Use the ¹⁄₁₆" (2mm) hand punch to make one hole near the bottom of the vellum leaf and two holes, spaced equally apart, on the center fold of the darker leaf.

8. THREAD THE LEAVES

Cut 18" (46cm) of green velvet cord, then thread the cord through the hole in the star point. Make sure the cord ends are level, then thread the cord through the bottom hole of both leaves, placing the darker leaf on top of the vellum leaf. Thread three beads onto the cord and slide them down to where the cord emerges from the hole in the darker leaf.

9. PULL THE CORD THROUGH

Draw the cord with the beads through the remaining hole on the dark leaf and then back through the single hole on the vellum leaf. Pull the cord so the beads are held snugly against the leaf.

10. ADD THE BOW

Knot both cords together, just above the leaves and tie another knot near the ends of the cord. This forms a hanging loop. Create a bow from 8" (20cm) of ¹⁄₈" (3mm) wide gold taffeta ribbon. Sew it onto the knot at the top of the hanging loop. Open out the folds of the star before hanging the ornament, for maximum three-dimensional effect.

Great Shapes

Foldout ornaments can be made in different shapes for use on holidays and special occasions. Simply choose a different shape template. For example, use hearts for Valentine's Day, or make gift-box-shaped ornaments out of rectangles for use as birthday decorations.

You can use this technique to make so much more than just ornaments. These two cards were made using a diamond shape template to make the hole in the card. The diamond template was also used to make the three-dimensional ornaments in the middle using the same techniques as the Star Foldout Ornament. As embellishments, I added a bow and bead at the top of the diamond. If you use archival quality paper, these cards are sure to become keepsakes!

❧ VARIATION IDEA: TREE ORNAMENT

The two-tone effect of this Christmas tree ornament is really eye-catching. Plus, the visual pun of hanging a mini tree on a real Christmas tree is smile-worthy. The tree template can be found on the Fiskars Christmas shape template. You will need green cardstock and red velvet cord for this project.

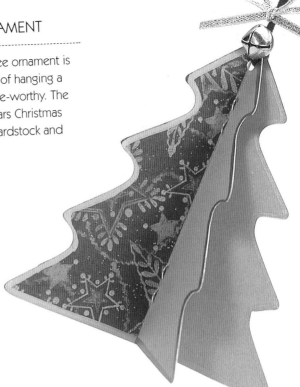

1. CUT OUT THE TREE

First, prepare the two-toned paper. Glue a piece of red scrapbooking print onto a piece of green scrapbooking cardstock so there is a straight line between them. Align the straight line with the center of the tree template. Cut out two trees this way. Outline the tree with metallic gold marker on both sides.

2. SCORE, FOLD AND STAPLE THE TREES

Score the tree shapes down the center where the papers join, then fold them in half. Next, place the trees back-to-back and staple them together. Place one staple near the top and another near the bottom, but not too close to the edge, so they will be less visible.

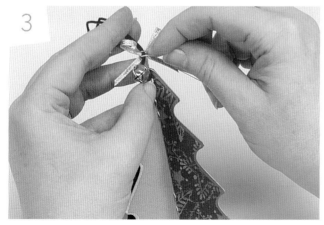

3. ADD THE HANGING LOOP

Punch a ⅛" (3mm) hole at the top of the tree. Cut 14" (36cm) of red velvet cord and pass it through the hole. Thread both ends through the loop on the jingle bell. Knot the cord so the jingle bell is contained by the knot. Make a mini bow from 8" (20cm) of ⅛" (3mm) wide gold taffeta ribbon and sew it onto the knot in the cord.

cathedral window ornament

This cube-shaped holiday ornament has the look of cathedral window patchwork, a needlecraft technique prized for its intricate-looking, beautiful and dimensional appearance.

The wonderful selection of printed scrapbooking papers available makes paper patchwork projects like this one a pleasure to create. Here a mix of green-and-white checks and florals has been used, but you could just as easily opt for a seasonal selection of Christmas-motif papers. Have a browse around your local scrapbooking supplier—and explore the paper patchwork possibilities!

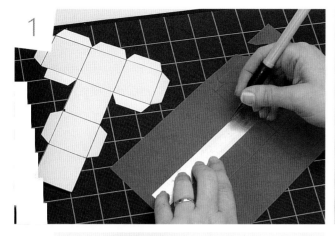

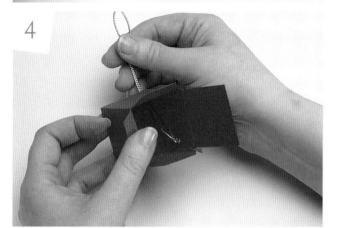

1. TRACE AND CUT OUT THE PATTERN

Enlarge and trace the cube pattern (given on page 91). Transfer the pattern outline and markings onto the red cardstock. Use a craft knife and ruler to cut out the pattern. Lightly score the fold lines.

2. PUNCH A HOLE

Use the 1/8" (3mm) hand punch to make a hole in the pattern (indicated by a dot). Next, use a kneaded eraser to remove any pencil lines from the cube pattern.

3. ASSEMBLE THE CUBE

Crease the scored folds of the box pattern, then assemble the cube. First, glue under the flap on the long strip to make a four-sided ring. Next, glue down one side of the cube, but leave the opposite side unglued. Use crafter's glue applied with a toothpick. Use a rubber band to hold the cube in place as the glue dries.

4. ADD THE HANGING LOOP

You must attach the hanging loop to the ornament before you close the cube. To do this, cut a 12" (30cm) piece of gold cord. Make a loop and knot the end three times, making a bulky knot. Starting from inside the cube, feed the loop carefully through the hole, making sure the knot remains inside. Once the loop is attached, fold down and glue the last side of the cube.

TIP

If you are going to make more than one ornament, it is advisable to make a trace-around template for the cube out of cardstock.

5. CUT OUT THE CIRCLES

Using the circle cutter, carefully cut out six circles from red cardstock, each measuring 2⅛" (52mm) diameter, a radius of 1¹⁄₁₆" (26mm).

6. CUT OUT THE PRINTED SQUARES

Cut out six squares, 1½" (38mm) on each side, from the decorative paper. You need five different printed patterns. Cut four squares from different prints and two squares from the same print. The squares fit perfectly in the circles. Glue a square onto each circle using a dry glue stick. Trim the squares, if necessary, to make sure they look neat.

7. SCORE AND FOLD THE CIRCLE EDGES

Lightly score the red cardstock along all four sides of each square. Next, crease along the scored lines, folding the edges of the circle in toward the center of the square. This completes the Cathedral Window patch.

TIP

Five different prints may seem like a lot, but you can buy reversible scrapbooking paper with double-sided coordinating prints—so you can get two different prints from a single sheet of paper.

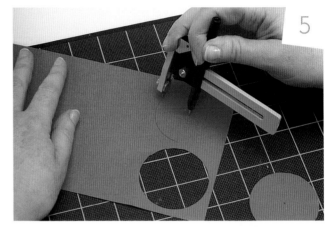

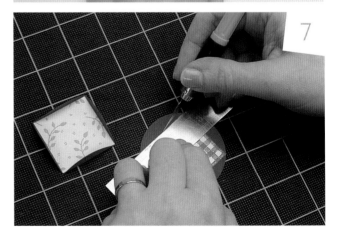

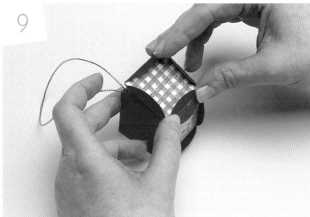

8. CUT A HOLE FOR THE TASSEL

At the cube corner directly opposite the hanging loop, use scissors to cut a small hole. This is for the tassel cord.

9. GLUE ON THE DECORATIVE SIDES

Using crafter's glue applied with a toothpick, glue a Cathedral Window patch onto each side of the cube. Glue the two identical prints onto opposite sides of the cube.

10. MAKE A TASSEL

On the back of a piece of matte gold paper, measure a rectangle 2½" (6cm) wide by 4½" (11cm) long. Draw a ⅝" (16mm) border along the top of the rectangle. Cut the bottom edge of the rectangle with scalloped paper edgers. Cut out the rest of the rectangle with a craft knife.

11. MARK THE TASSEL

Draw a vertical line from each scallop inden-tation to the border, then draw another line from the lowest point of each scallop to the border.

12. CUT THE TASSEL FRINGE

Use small scissors to cut the fringe along the lines marked in the previous step.

13. ROLL THE TASSEL

Tightly roll the uncut top border of the tassel around a toothpick. When finished, secure the end with a dab of crafter's glue.

14. COMPLETE THE TASSEL

Cut a band of decorative print paper ⅛" (3mm) wide by 1½" (38mm) long. Wrap the band around the tassel top, just above the fringe. Glue the beginning and end of the band. Next, flatten the tassel top and punch a hole through it with the ¹⁄₁₆" (2mm) hand punch.

15. ATTACH THE TASSEL

Cut a 10" (25cm) piece of gold cord and thread it through the tassel hole. Tie a few knots in the cord, just above the tassel. Once done, push the knot through the small hole you made at the corner of the cube and secure it with a bit of crafter's glue. For the finishing touch, cut a 12" (30cm) piece of ½" (13mm) ribbon and tie a bow. Sew the bow onto the hanging loop at the top of the ornament.

TIP

The eye of a tapestry needle or the tip of small scissors can be used to push the knot through the hole.

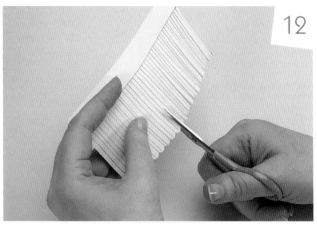

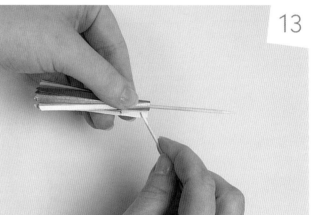

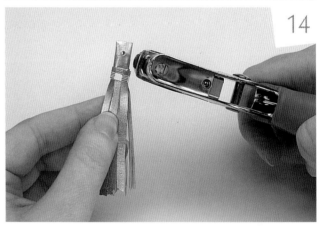

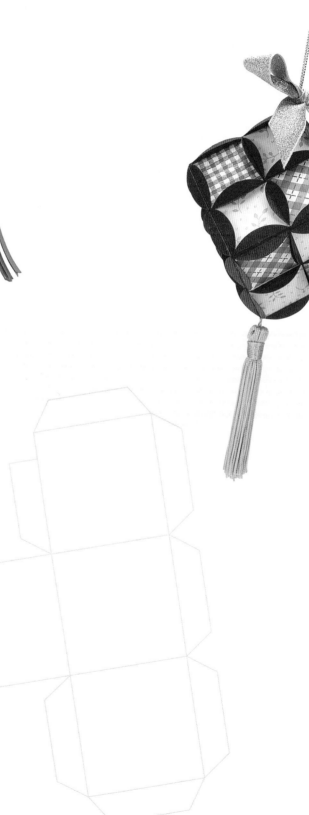

✿ VARIATION IDEA: JUMBO ORNAMENT

Display this large-size ornament in a window or doorway. To make it, size up the cube pattern so that each face measures 3" (75mm). Glue on Cathedral Window patches four to a side (you will need a total of 24 patches). For the finishing touch, add a silky purchased tassel.

✿ VARIATION IDEA: QUICK-MAKE ORNAMENT

Glue a Cathedral Window patch onto a cardstock circle with a $1\frac{1}{16}$" (26mm) radius, same size as for the patch backing. Punch holes at the top and bottom, then add a hanging loop and tassel. This ornament is compact, so it can easily fit inside an envelope. Send it as a greeting card enclosure.

Enlarge the pattern 118%.

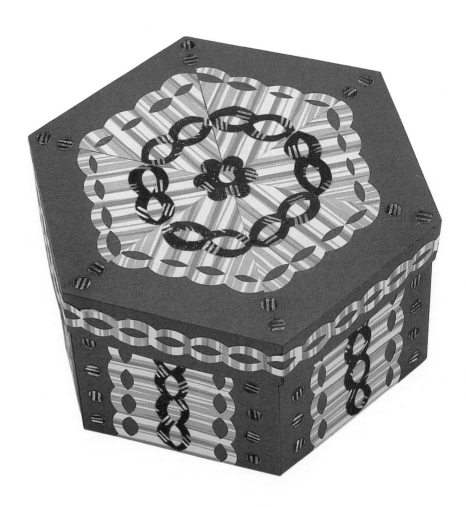

paper chain gift box

I t's time to play the chain game. This elegant fili-gree-effect gift box is embellished with paper chains fashioned with paper edgers. They are sim-ilar to the paper snowflakes and the chorus lines of linked paper dolls you made as a child.

The pleasing hexagonal shape of this gift box gives the medallion on the lid a snowflake appearance. The designs on the side panels and the box lid are coordi-nated using two scrapbook prints.

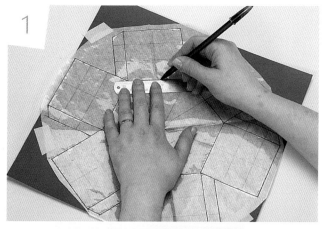

1. TRACE AND CUT OUT THE BOX AND LID

Enlarge the patterns on page 99 onto tracing paper. Tape each pattern piece onto a piece of forest green scrapbooking cardstock. Impress the pattern outlines and markings into the cardstock, using a stylus. Use a craft knife and ruler to cut out the box and lid. Then score the fold lines as marked.

2. CUT OUT THE DECORATIVE SIDE PANELS

On the back (the plain side) of the striped scrapbooking paper, measure out and mark in pencil six 2" × 3" (5cm × 8cm) rectangles. Make sure the stripes run perpendicular to the long dimension of the rectangle (see photo). On the long sides of the rectangle, make a pencil line margin ¼" (6mm) in from either edge. Cut out the rectangles using a craft knife and ruler.

3. CUT THE SIDE PANEL BORDER

Fold the side of the rectangle at the margin. Use the clouds (large scallop) paper edgers to cut along the fold. Do not cut to the full depth of the blade; cut with the tip of each scallop only. You must position the blade on the fold so the paper is cut just part of the way through. You must cut curved chunks out of the paper with little "bridges" in between. After each cut, reposition the blade for the next cut. Aim to cut to a consistent depth, so the cutouts are of uniform size. Cut both sides of the rectangle this way.

TIP

Making paper chains is more difficult to explain than to do! Do a few scrap-paper test runs and you'll soon master the technique.

4. COMPLETE THE SIDE PANEL BORDERS

Unfold the sides of the paper and use the paper edgers to cut a scalloped edge. Make sure to align the paper edger blade to echo the shape of the previous cutouts. Repeat for the other side of the panel. Make five more side panels, following steps 2–4.

5. CUT THE PAPER CHAIN TRIM

From the green striped paper, cut two strips, each measuring 1" (25mm) wide by 12" (30cm) long (the full width of the scrapbooking paper). The stripes should run crosswise across each strip. Fold each strip in half lengthwise and cut along the fold using the clouds paper edgers. Use the partial-cutting technique described in step 3. Remember, if you cut to the full depth of the scallops, the two sides of the strip will fall apart! Cut two 12" (30cm) strips of the rust-colored paper in the same way.

6. EDGE THE STRIP

Open out the fold. To complete the paper chain, cut a scalloped edge to either side of the leaf-shaped cutouts. Align the scallops to echo the curves of the leaf shapes. Turn the strip around to edge the second side of the chain. You need to make two green chains and two rust-colored chains in order to complete the box decoration.

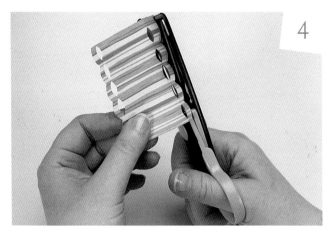

4

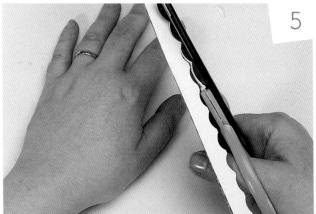

5

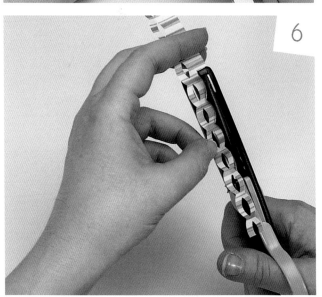

6

Faking It

The following method of cutting a paper chain is a bit of a cheat—but it looks great! First, cut out a narrow strip of paper and crease it in half lengthwise. Next, cut paper-edged borders on either side. Finally, fake a chain effect by using a hand punch to cut out regularly spaced decorative shapes down the center of the paper strip; use the crease as a positioning guide. You can use hearts, squares, stars—whatever motif suits the blade pattern!

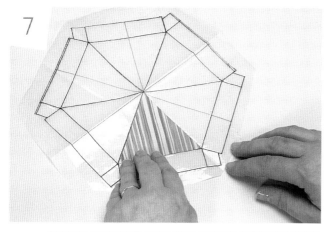

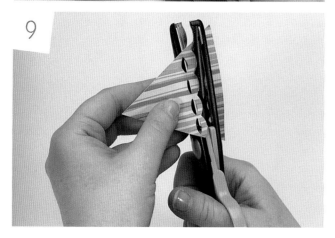

7. CUT OUT THE TRIANGLES

You need six paper triangles for the lid medallion. Cut them out from the striped green paper using the lid pattern. Position the stripes so they run vertically from the tip to the base of the triangle.

8. FOLD AND CUT THE TRIANGLES

On the back of a triangle, mark a ¾" (19mm) margin along the base. Fold the margin to the right side and cut it as for step 3.

9. EDGE THE TRIANGLE

Open out the triangle and cut scallops along the base, echoing the curves of the leaf-shaped cutouts.

Chain Reaction

Experiment with different paper edger blades to create some extraordinary paper chain results! Results can vary from the plain and simple to dizzyingly complex-looking effects. Chains can be crafted in different styles and period looks. For example: Fiskars Lightning pattern blades make V-shaped chain links; the Victorian pattern makes ornate links; and the Peaks pattern has a distinctly Art Deco feel. More intricate designs call for greater care and may require extra pressure while cutting.

10. MARK AND CUT CHAINS ON THE OTHER TRIANGLES

Use the triangle you have just finished as a template. Trace the cutout border design onto the back of the five remaining triangles. Next, fold and cut the triangles as for steps 7–9, but align your cuts with the traced outlines. This ensures that the triangles will fit together perfectly when they are glued side by side on the box lid.

11. CUT THE RUST-COLORED CHAINS

To embellish the box, you must cut the paper chains into smaller link strips. For each triangle, cut two links of the rust chain. For each side panel, cut four rust links. Trim the ends of each link strip into a leaf-tip shape. There are six triangles and six side panels.

12. PUNCH OUT THE DECORATIVE CIRCLES

Use the 1/4" (6mm) hole punch to cut decorative circles for the box lid and sides from the rust-colored paper. You need a total of seventy-two rust-colored circles. Position the punch on the printed paper pattern so that a particular area of the design falls on the circle. You also need to punch out one green circle and a 1" (25mm) flower from the rust-colored paper.

TIP

If you accidentally smudge a bit of glue stick on the box, remove it with a kneaded eraser while the glue is fresh.

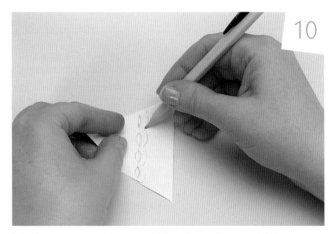

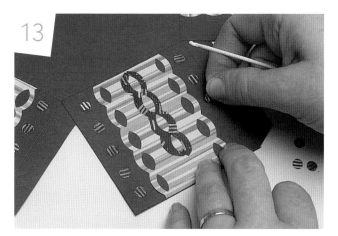

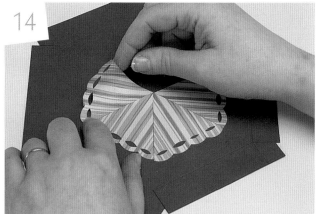

"Eyelet Lace"

For papercrafted "eyelet lace," thread a narrow ribbon of ¹⁄₁₆" or ¹⁄₈" (2mm or 3mm) in and out of the chain links. Use white paper with pastel ribbon— charming on new baby cards, romantic on wedding cards.

13. DECORATE THE BOX SIDES
- -

Glue the side panels onto the base of the box using a dry glue stick. Center a panel on each side. In the center of each panel, glue on four rust-colored chain links, as shown. Finally, glue on the dots to the sides of each panel using crafter's glue applied with a toothpick.

14. GLUE ON THE TRIANGLES
- -

Glue the triangles onto the lid with a dry glue stick. Glue the tip of each triangle at the center of the lid. Position the triangles side-by-side, like pizza wedges.

15. DECORATE THE LID
- -

Use a dry glue stick to attach the lid decorations. Glue the flower on at the center, then glue the rust-colored links onto each triangle. Align the rust links horizontally so they meet up to form a continuous chain around the lid. Glue on the circles using crafter's glue. Glue on the green circle for the flower center.

16. FOLD THE LID

Crease the sides of the lid along the scored lines. Remember to fold the little tabs.

17. GLUE THE LID TOGETHER

Use crafter's glue, applied with a toothpick, to glue the lid together. Apply glue to the top of each little flap, then glue the flaps under. Use masking tape to hold the lid in place until the glue dries.

18. DECORATE THE SIDE OF THE LID

Apply the green paper chain to the side of the box lid using a dry glue stick. You will need both strips of green chain. The end links of the two strips can be glued side by side. Trim off any excess links.

19. ASSEMBLE THE BOX

Fold the box base along the scored lines. Glue the sides together using crafter's glue. Again, a piece of tape will hold the box together while the glue dries.

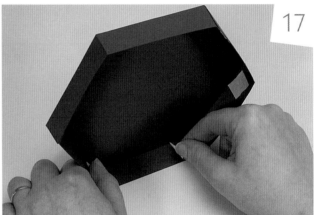

Enlarge the
patterns 200%.

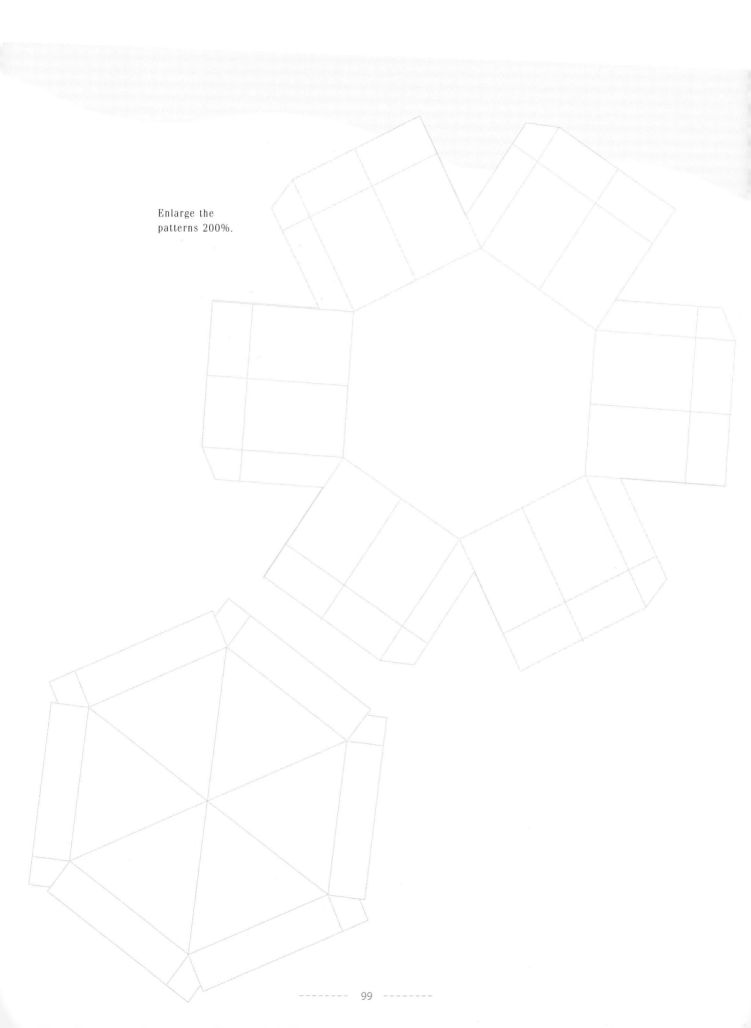

etched-glass photo frame

This pretty "etched-glass mirror" photo frame has the quaint, charming appearance of a bygone era. The frame makes a beautiful—mailable—gift presentation for a commemorative photograph and is perfect for special family occasions, such as anniversaries, birthdays or Mother's Day. Send it in place of a card: You can inscribe the frame back with your good wishes! Designed to fit a standard 4" × 6" (10cm × 15cm) snapshot, the frame can be used in either portrait or landscape direction.

For our frame, we chose matte-finish silvery pearlescent cardstock for a lustrous, quietly classy look—but you can go for glitz with highly reflective mirrored card!

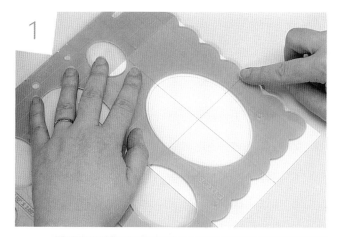

1. CUT OUT THE OVAL FRAME

Enlarge the frame pattern (see page 105) and make a pattern tracing (there are three pieces: the frame, the backing, and the strut). On the back of the silver cardstock (the white side), mark the 5" × 7" (13cm × 18cm) frame rectangle and the crisscross positioning lines. Cut out the frame rectangle using a craft knife held against a ruler. Position the frame behind the oval template. The size of the oval is 3" × 4" (8cm × 10cm), centering the crisscross lines on the oval template. Cut out the oval using a shape cutter tool.

2. TRIM THE CORNERS

Use the corner edgers to cut the decorative corners of the frame. To do this, inspect the edgers and check that the blades are on the correct side to cut a convex (inward-facing) scallop. Next, open the edgers and slide the corner of the cardstock underneath the guide slot until the cardstock is flush with the edges of the guide. Cut the corner, then repeat for the remaining three corners.

3. BOND A PEARLESCENT STICKER

Use a dry glue stick to glue the white pearlescent paper to the self-adhesive mailing label. Glue the matte side of the pearlescent paper to the paper side of the sticker. Make three stickers in this way.

4. PUNCH OUT THE LARGE HEARTS

You need to make two outline heart stickers for the frame. To begin the outline heart, punch a $\frac{1}{2}$" (13mm) heart out of the pearlescent sticker. Next, center a 1" (25mm) heart punch over the smaller heart-shaped cutout. Use the heart punch on the back so you can see how to position it. Punch out the heart. Repeat to make a second outline heart.

5. PUNCH OUT THE OTHER PEARLY STICKERS

In addition to the two outline hearts (above), you also need to punch two more 1" (25mm) hearts. Cut these in half vertically using small scissors. Also punch out sixteen small hearts and two $\frac{1}{4}$" (6mm) circles from the pearly stickers. Cut four of the small heart stickers in half.

6. TRACE THE DECORATIVE PATTERN

Tape your pattern tracing over the silver side of the frame using masking tape. Next, use a stylus to impress small dots to mark the position of each heart sticker. Make a dot at the point and the "valley" of each heart. Also mark the position of the pearly dots.

7. ADD THE HEART STICKERS

Peel off the backing from each heart sticker and, using the impressed dots as a guide, smooth the hearts onto the frame where indicated. Use the pattern tracing as a "map" to show the placement of each sticker (for example, which direction each heart faces). Also affix the two $\frac{1}{4}$" (6mm) circles.

TIP

No need to mark the heart outlines on the frame. The placement dots work just as well and are less likely to show when the stickers are covering them.

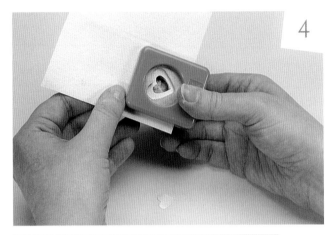

4

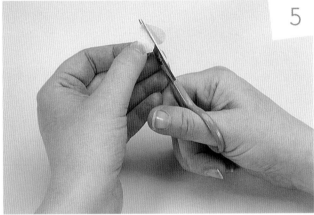

5

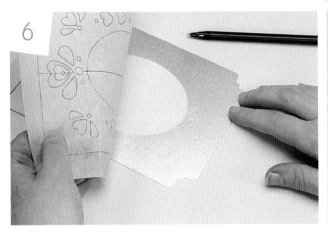

6

7

8. ADD THE SMALL CIRCLES

Use the ⅛" (3mm) hand punch to cut out sixteen small circles from the pearlescent paper. Use crafter's glue to apply them to the frame at the marked dots. Use a toothpick to apply the glue sparingly. These circles are glued on because they are too small to make as stickers.

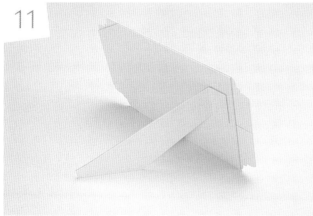

9. ADD THE BACKING

Using the pattern, trace and cut out the backing card and the strut from illustration board. The backing is the same size as the frame, with the corners trimmed so that the backing does not show beyond the frame. You may also need to trim the top for easy picture insertion. Glue the frame to the backing. Use a toothpick to sparingly apply crafter's glue around three of the straight sides of the backing. Leave one of the short sides unglued, as this is the picture opening.

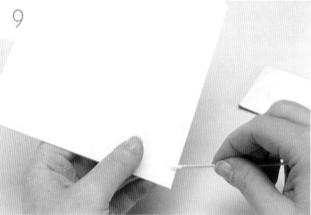

10. GLUE ON THE STRUT

Score the strut tab, but not too deeply, as the strut must support the frame. Once done, use crafter's glue to apply the strut to the back of the frame. Glue the strut onto the backing. The bottom of the strut should just touch the edge of the frame, and the tab is glued just below the open edge of the backing, to the left of backing center. To finish, gently slip the photograph into the frame opening.

11. OPEN THE STRUT

To display the frame, just open the strut and place it on the table. You may have to make a few adjustments to the strut to get the angle of the picture correct. The frame can be displayed both horizontally and vertically.

❀ VARIATION IDEA: THE FRAME GAME

For a different, but equally striking frame design, go floral. This is easy to do using flower and leaf punches. Arrange the floral stickers in garlands around the frame.

Or, you can change shape cutter templates to alter either the frame shape or the shape of the window aperture. How about the sophisticated elegance of an oval frame? A heart-shaped window is the ideal choice for a Valentine's gift.

Or make a smaller frame for wallet-sized pictures to add a touch of elegance to all your photos.

Enlarge the pattern 118%.

button box

Crafty person that I am, one of my favorite childhood playthings was the family button box. To me, it was a treasure chest! The magical contents of that button box—and my lifelong love of sewing—have inspired this cheerful paper collage box, suitable for storing sewing knickknacks in.

The button box would make a thoughtful gift for a sewing enthusiast of any age and will house a treasure trove of sewing notions. Maybe the gift will—in a small way—bring happy memories to a budding crafter.

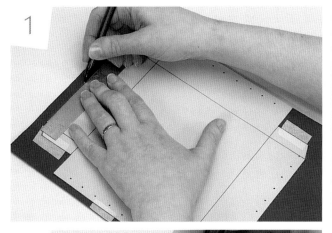

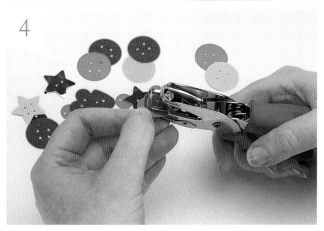

TIP

For the smaller paper buttons, you may find it easier to punch the holes in the cardstock first, then punch the shape out around the holes. To do this, hold the paper punch upside down and look through the cutout to position the shape over the holes.

1. TRACE THE BOX LID

Enlarge the box lid template on page 113. Transfer it onto a piece of light-colored cardstock and cut it out with a craft knife and ruler. Tape the template onto the back (the smooth side) of the blue basketweave corrugated cardboard. Use a stylus to impress the pattern outlines into the cardboard (see page 18). Remember to mark the fold lines, as well as the stitching holes along the box lid edges.

2. CUT OUT THE BOX LID

Use a craft knife and ruler to cut out the box lid. Be sure to cut the angle corners on the flaps. Cutting corrugated cardboard requires special care. Use a fresh blade in your knife and don't apply much pressure—or the paper could catch and tear. Next, use the ¹⁄₁₆" (2mm) punch to make the stitching holes.

3. PUNCH OUT THE LARGE BUTTONS

Using the 1" (25mm) circle punch, punch out four circles each from red, green and yellow cardstock. Make a graph paper template, marking dots for the four center holes in each button. With the stylus, use the template to mark indentations on each paper button to indicate hole placement. Keep placement uniform for all buttons.

4. PUNCH OUT THE HOLES IN EACH BUTTON

With the ¹⁄₁₆" (2mm) circle punch, punch out the four holes on all of the large buttons. Use the star, heart and small circle punches to cut out a variety of smaller paper buttons. Make four or five in each color and from mirrored cardstock. Punch two holes in the smaller-size buttons.

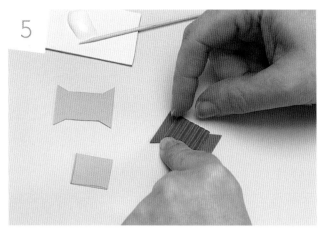

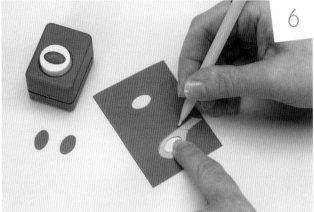

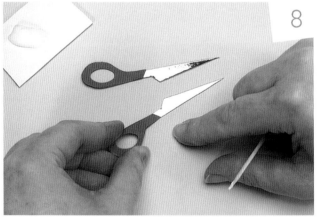

5. MAKE THE SPOOLS OF THREAD

Trace the cardstock template for the spool shape. Next, trace and cut out five spools from orange cardstock using a craft knife and ruler or scissors. Cut rectangular spool sized pieces of corrugated cardboard to fit the spools you just cut, making sure the ridges run horizontally across the width. This will be the thread. Cut thread rectangles in white, yellow and green—enough for all the spools. Glue the corrugated thread onto the spool.

6. TRACE THE SCISSORS' HANDLES

Cut out a cardstock template for the scissors' handles. Punch out two ½" (13mm) ovals from a piece of orange cardstock. Place the handle template over one punched oval and trace around it. Flip the template over to trace the other handle so that you have a right-facing and a left-facing handle.

7. TRACE THE SCISSORS' BLADES

Cut out a cardstock template for the scissors' blades. On the reverse side of the mirrored cardstock, trace the blade template. Flip the template over and trace a second blade.

8. ASSEMBLE THE SCISSORS' BLADES

Cut out all the scissors pieces with a craft knife and ruler for the straight lines and small scissors for the curves. Glue a handle onto each blade, as shown. Make sure the right and left sides are glued correctly. You may need to trim the base of the orange handle to fit the blade.

9. ASSEMBLE THE SCISSORS

Cross the left blade over the right blade and apply glue at the intersection. Next, punch out a ⅛" (3mm) circle from mirrored cardstock and glue it onto the cross point.

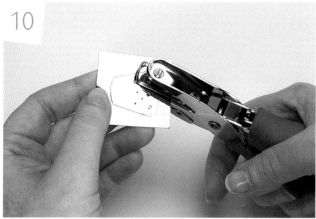

10. MAKE THE THIMBLE

Impress the thimble outline onto the back of the mirrored cardstock, marking dots for the thimble dimples. Use the $1/16$" (2mm) punch to punch out the thimble holes. Then cut out the thimble with scissors.

11. GLUE THE SPOOL AND SCISSORS

Using crafter's glue, glue the white spool of thread and the scissors onto the top of the box lid. Do not glue the uppermost blade of the scissors. With a tapestry needle, pierce a hole at the base of the spool.

12. ATTACH THE THREAD

Cut a piece of white velvety cord and knot the end. Push the cord up through the hole, pull it tight, then place the cord under the uppermost scissor blade so it resembles thread. Arrange the thread so it falls in a gentle curve. Glue the end of the thread onto the box, then glue down the tip of the uppermost scissor blade.

13. GLUE ON THE EMBELLISHMENTS

Glue the other embellishments onto the box lid. They should form a balanced arrangement of shape, size and color. For instance, on each box lid side, you should have one spool of thread and at least one large button. After all the buttons have been glued onto the box lid, take a tapestry needle and pierce the holes in the buttons through the box lid.

TIP

If desired, knitting yarn can be substituted for the velvety cord.

14. STITCH THE BUTTONS

Use the tapestry needle to sew velvety cord through the holes in the buttons. The cord color should contrast with the button. Sew a cross-stitch through the large red buttons. Knot thread ends on the underside of the box lid.

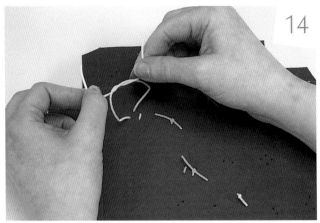

15. ASSEMBLE THE BOX LID

Crease the box lid on all the fold lines. One at a time, apply glue to the textured surface of the angled side flaps and glue them under each box side. Use a bit of masking tape to secure the flap until the glue dries. Make sure the cord knots clear the flaps.

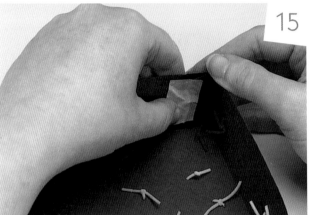

16. LACE THE LID BORDER

Thread a tapestry needle with 14" (36cm) of yellow cord. Lace the thread through the holes using an overcast stitch (that is, sewing around and around the box edge). When you run out of cord, tie on a new piece on the front of the box, then continue lacing. When you have stitched around the box, tie the cord ends together. Trim the cord ends by each knot.

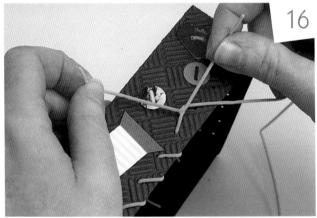

17. ASSEMBLE THE BOX BASE

Enlarge the box base pattern (on page 113) and make a cardstock pattern. Trace the box base onto a piece of red cardstock; cut it out using a craft knife held against a straightedge. Score the fold lines. Next, crease the box base along the folds. Apply glue to the flaps, and glue them behind the box base sides. Use masking tape to hold the box base in place as the glue dries. When the glue is dry, slide the box lid over the base to complete the button box.

Real Buttons

For a realistic touch, you can sew genuine buttons onto the box lid instead of the paper ones. Choose lightweight plastic buttons, or the lid will become too weighty.

This needle book is an attractive and convenient holdall for sewing and embroidery needles. With a felt liner to hold your needles,
there will be no more sticking needles into
thread spools for storage. (Ouch!)

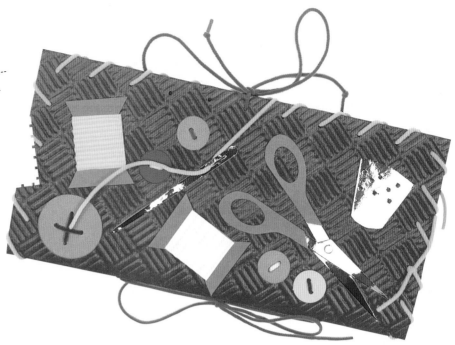

1

1. CUT OUT AND DECORATE THE NEEDLE BOOK

Enlarge the needle book pattern on page 113.
Trace it onto the smooth side of a piece of dark
red basketweave corrugated cardboard, as for
step 1 of the Button Box. Decorate the front cover
of the needle book with embellishments (thread
spools, buttons, scissors, thimble) as for the
Button Box. Next, trace the needle onto the back
of mirrored cardstock. Cut it out using a craft
knife. Then use the craft knife to cut out the eye
of the needle. Thread yellow cord through the eye
of the needle, then lace the edge of the needle
book, as for step 16 of the Button Box—only
leave the last few lacing holes unstitched on the
front cover (as if it is a work in progress). Glue
the free end of the cord inside the needle book.

TIP

*Do not use paper edgers to cut out the felt.
They are not strong enough for the job. Use
pinking shears that are made for fabric use.*

2. CUT OUT THE FELT LINER

The needle book is lined with a piece of felt. This will hold the needles. Enlarge the liner template and tape it onto a piece of blue felt. Use pinking shears to cut out the felt rectangle.

3. ATTACH THE FELT LINER

With a tapestry needle, pierce three holes, as marked on the center fold of the needle book. Cut 18" (46cm) of blue cord. Thread a tapestry needle with the cord. Lay the felt on the back of the needle book. Sew the cord through the two end holes, so it catches in the felt and makes one long stitch across the fold on the right (basketweave) side of the needle book. On the felt side, adjust the cord ends so they are equal in length. Next, sew the cord ends through the center hole, bringing one end out to either side of the long stitch. Make a knot in the end of each cord, then tie the cord ends into a bow.

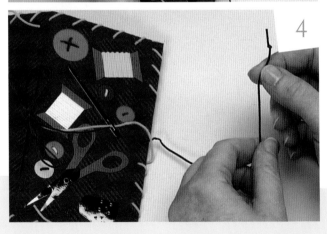

4. ATTACH THE TIES

Cut two 8" (20cm) pieces of blue velvet cord. Knot the end of each piece of cord. Thread a piece of cord through the center lacing hole on the front cover of the needle book. Thread the other cord through the center lacing hole on the needle book back. Make a decorative knot at the end of each cord. To fasten the needle book, tie the cords in a bow.

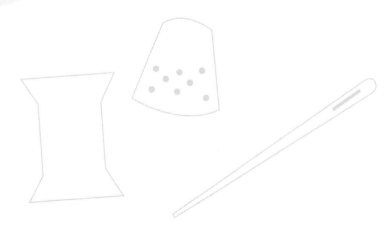

These patterns appear at full size.

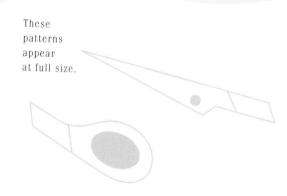

LINER

Enlarge the patterns 250%

LID

NEEDLEBOOK WITH LINER

★ MATERIALS LIST

PAPER

One sheet of cardstock (for pattern template)

12" × 12" (30cm × 30cm) sheets of printed scrapbooking paper in the following patterns: blue-on-white floral print, white-on-blue floral print, small green checks, small blue checks

8½" × 11" (22cm × 28cm) sheets of pearlescent cardstock: one sheet in blue and one sheet in green

One sheet of plain white paper (for box lid grid)

A scrap of matte gold paper

ADDITIONAL SUPPLIES

One 6" (15cm) square papier-mâché box

Acrylic craft paint in light blue

Small round gold beads: one each ¼" (6mm) and ⅛" (3mm) diameter

Gold wire thread

Self-adhesive mailing label

12" (30cm) of ⅛" (3mm) wide metallic gold taffeta ribbon

Dry glue stick

Crafter's glue

Paintbrush

Pencil

Metallic gold marker (fine point)

Paper towel

Toothpicks

Kneaded eraser

Craft knife

Cutting mat

Metal ruler

Right triangle

Tapestry needle

Sewing needle

Hand punch: ⅛" (3mm) circle

Small scissors

folded star gift box & tag

T he kaleidoscopic starburst design gracing the box lid is inspired by Folded Star patchwork, a needlework technique in which multilayered starbursts are built up using folded triangles of fabric.

There is a secret to constructing the seemingly intricate starburst configuration. By gluing a paper grid onto the box lid, positioning the triangles is a piece of cake and the starburst can be assembled in minutes!

This gift box is a shining example of how printed scrapbooking papers can be used to create realistic patchwork-style projects. The papercrafted Folded Star patchwork is a dead ringer for its fabric-crafted "cousin."

TIP

*The following instructions are for a 6"
(15cm) square box. If you are using a larger or smaller box, you may have to adjust
the measurements to fit.*

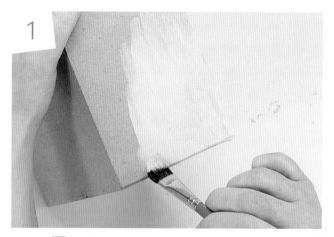

1. BASECOAT THE BOX

Use light blue acrylic paint to basecoat the
box. Add a little bit of water for a creamy
consistency. Paint the entire box: inside and
outside, base and lid. It may take two to three
coats to cover the dark color of the papier
mâché box. Make sure nothing shows through.

2. TRACE THE PATTERN PIECE

Cut a rectangular pattern template measuring
$1\frac{1}{2}$" × $\frac{3}{4}$" (40mm × 20mm) out of cardstock.
Use a pencil to trace around the template on
the back of the printed scrapbooking paper.
Mark twenty-one rectangles on the green
checked paper, sixteen on the blue-back-
ground floral, and twenty-four on the white-
background floral.

3. CUT OUT THE RECTANGLES

Cut out the rectangles using a craft knife
held against a metal ruler.

4. FOLD THE TRIANGLES

Fold the rectangle in half crosswise; then fold the top corners to meet at the bottom of the center crease, forming the triangle. Crease the folds sharply. Fold so the back of the paper is on the inside.

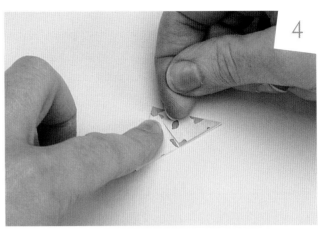

TIP

Store like-colored triangles together in small plastic bags—makes for speedy selection when gluing.

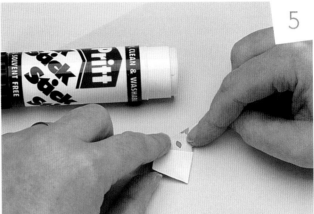

5. GLUE THE TRIANGLES

Apply a dry glue stick to the bottom edge of each triangle to seal it. You will have to open out each triangle and then refold it to do this. Glue all the triangles in this way.

6. CUT OUT THE BASE FOR THE BOX LID

Mark a 5" (13cm) square on the pearlescent blue cardstock. Use a right triangle to make sure the corners are square. Cut out the square using a craft knife and ruler.

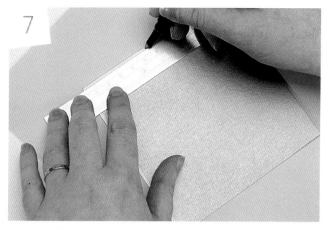

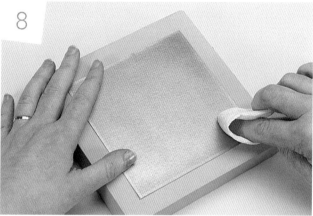

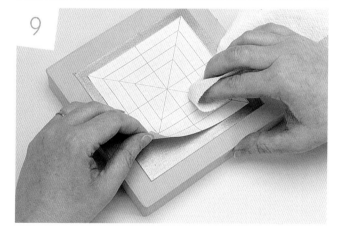

7. OUTLINE THE EDGES IN GOLD

Use the metallic gold fine point marker to outline the edges of the blue square. Draw against a straightedge to ensure straight lines. Wipe the straightedge clean after you mark each side.

8. GLUE THE BASE ONTO THE BOX LID

Measure a $\frac{5}{8}$" (15mm) border around the box lid. With a dry glue stick, glue the base onto the box lid within the border. Smooth the base in place to prevent bubbles in the paper.

9. GLUE ON THE PATTERN GRID

Trace the pattern grid template (given on page 125) onto a piece of plain white paper, marking the concentric squares and the diagonals. Adjust the size of the pattern, if necessary, using a photocopier. Mark a $\frac{3}{8}$" (10mm) border around the edge of the base. Cut out the pattern grid square, and glue it onto the base with a dry glue stick. Smooth the grid in place with a paper towel.

Circular Starbursts

To create round—rather than square—starburst designs, fold your triangles from semicircles of paper. Crease each semicircle in half, then fold the sides to the center, creating a "pizza slice" wedge. Glue the wedges onto a pattern grid made of concentric circles.

10. APPLY GLUE TO THE TRIANGLES

Use the following gluing technique for all the paper triangles: On the back of the triangles use a toothpick to place a dab of glue near the tip of the triangle and also apply a line of glue sparingly along the base.

11. APPLY THE CENTER TRIANGLES

For the first round of the design, glue on four green triangles, one on each side of the square in the center of the grid. The triangle tips face the grid center, and each base is placed on the first grid line.

12. START THE SECOND ROUND

To begin the second round, glue on four blue triangles. The point of each triangle belongs on the center line of each side, and the base belongs on the second grid line.

Tea Bag Paper Extravaganza

For a fantastic, superdeluxe kaleidoscope effect, make your starburst triangles out of tea bag folding papers with "engineered" border designs. Position the printed paper differently for the triangles of each round.

10

11

12

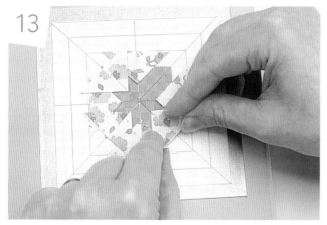

13. COMPLETE THE SECOND ROUND

To finish the round, you need four more blue triangles. Glue a blue triangle diagonally across each corner. The tips of corner triangles should be placed at the same level as those glued on in the previous step.

14. GLUE THE THIRD ROUND

For the third round, you need twelve green triangles, three evenly spaced on each side. Start with the left-hand triangle on each side. Glue it so that its left-hand edge is on the corner diagonal and its base is on the third grid line. Overlap the next triangle, gluing it so that the left-hand tip lies at the midpoint of the previous triangle, and its center lies at the center of the grid side. Lap the third triangle over the second triangle to complete the side. The right-hand side of the triangle should align with the corner diagonal. Work your way around the grid, gluing the triangles in a counterclockwise direction until the third round is complete.

15. GLUE ON THE FOURTH ROUND

You need sixteen white triangles for the fourth—and final—round of the starburst. Glue the triangles as you did for the previous round, overlapping each successive triangle, but use four on each side. Along the baseline, position the left-hand tip of each triangle at the midpoint of the previous triangle. Work in a counterclockwise direction to complete the round.

16. OUTLINE THE EDGE

Use the gold marker to decoratively outline the edges of the starburst. This will conceal any ragged edges. Use a straightedge to keep the lines crisp and even. Wipe the straightedge clean after each side.

17. PIERCE A HOLE

For the beads, use a tapestry needle to pierce a hole through the center point of the starburst, penetrating the box beneath. The papier-mâché is pretty soft, and you will be able to work the needle through. If one is handy, a bradawl would be a more effective tool for the job. Place a piece of kneaded eraser underneath to catch the point.

18. THREAD THE BEADS

Thread the ⅛" (3mm) bead on the gold wire by hand and place it at the center of the wire. Next, thread both wire ends through a sewing needle and draw it through the ¼" (6mm) gold bead.

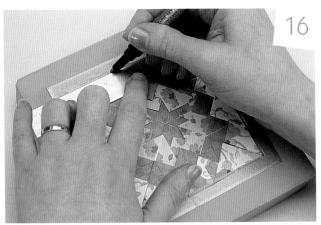

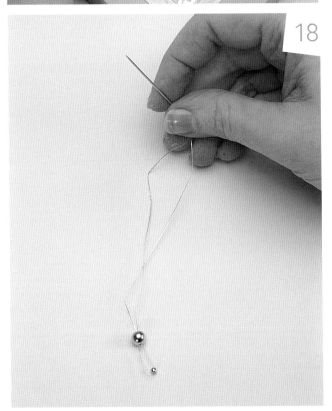

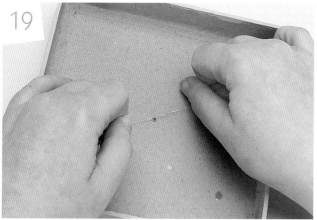

19. ATTACH THE BEAD

Draw the bead wire through the hole in the box, pull it tight, then knot it in place several times.

20. SECURE THE BEADS

Spread the bead wire open, ends apart, then apply crafter's glue to the underside of the bead hole. Affix a self-adhesive label over the hole, then trim off the gold wire thread, letting it extend a little beyond the label.

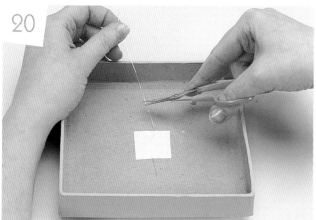

21. OUTLINE THE TOP EDGES OF THE LID

With the gold marker, rule decorative lines on the top edges of the box lid. Do this on all four sides. Wipe the straightedge clean after each side.

22. DECORATE THE LID SIDES

Decorate the box lid sides by gluing on a border of overlapping triangles. You need six triangles for each side, two in each color. Each left-hand triangle tip should touch the center line of the previous triangle. Make sure the triangles fill the entire lid side; you might have to fudge the spacing a little to ensure this. When the border is complete, use a ruler to make a gold marker line along the bottom edge.

23. CREATE THE BOX BANDS

Cut out four bands from pearlescent blue cardstock, each measuring ¾" (20mm) wide by 5¾" (15cm) long—the length of the box side. Line the top and bottom on each band with gold marker.

24. ATTACH THE BANDS

Measure up ¾" (19mm) from the bottom of the box. Use crafter's glue to attach a band onto each side of the box. Make sure the bands fit the box sides; trim them if necessary. Use a paper towel to smooth the band down.

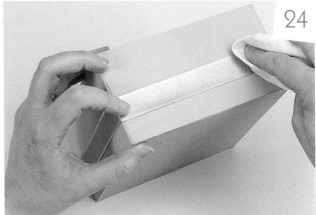

Patchwork Gift Tag

The following steps are for making a patchwork gift tag for your box, but this tag certainly isn't just for this box. It will make an excellent addition to any gift packaging you do, from presents to gift bags!

1. MAKE THE GIFT TAG

Measure and cut out a 3⅛" (8cm) square from the green pearlescent cardstock. Outline the tag edges with gold marker.

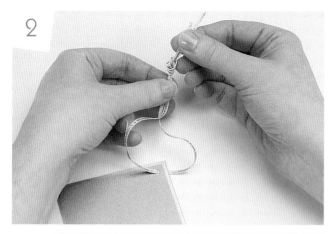

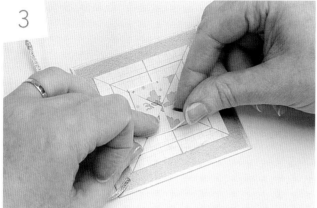

2. ATTACH THE RIBBON

Punch a ⅛" (3mm) hole in the corner of the tag. Cut a 12" (30cm) piece of ⅛" (3mm) wide gold taffeta ribbon; thread it through the hole and knot the ends together. Trim off the ribbon ends.

TIP
Create a grid for the gift tag pattern by reducing the grid for the Folded Star Gift Box by 25% and trim the grid so that you are using only three rounds.

3. GLUE ON THE PLACEMENT GRID

Glue the grid onto the tag, placing it ⅜" (10mm) from the tag edges. The triangles for the tag are folded from rectangles 1¼" (30mm) long by ⅝" (15mm) wide. You need four blue triangles, eight blue-check triangles and nine white triangles. Glue on the first round of blue triangles, as for step 11.

4. FINISH THE STARBURST

Continue gluing triangles to complete the pattern. Attach round 2 (blue checks), as for steps 12–13. Attach round 3 (the final round), as for step 14. Use white triangles. The gift tag starburst has only three rounds.

5. DECORATE THE TAG

Use the gold marker to outline the edges of the starburst. Punch a ⅛" (3mm) dot from matte gold paper and glue it onto the starburst center.

❀ VARIATION IDEA: NESTED BOXES

A set of boxes in graduated sizes—like Russian dolls—makes a charming gift. Papier-mâché boxes come in standard sizes of 4" (10cm), 6" (15cm) and 8" (20cm). The pattern should be reduced 25% for the smaller box. The small and large starbursts are constructed in exactly the same way as for the illustrated project (the medium-size box); only, the triangles should be enlarged 50% for the large box. The starburst for the small box lid is the same as for the gift tag; it has just three rounds of triangles.

Small box: 4" (10cm)
Lid base: 3⅛" (8cm) square
Side band: ½" (13mm) wide by 3¾" (10cm) long,
  ½" (13mm) above box base

Large box: 8" (20cm)
Lid base: 7" (18cm)
Side band: ⅞" (22mm) wide by 7¾" (20cm) long,
  1" (25mm) above box base

The details for the medium box are given in the project instructions.

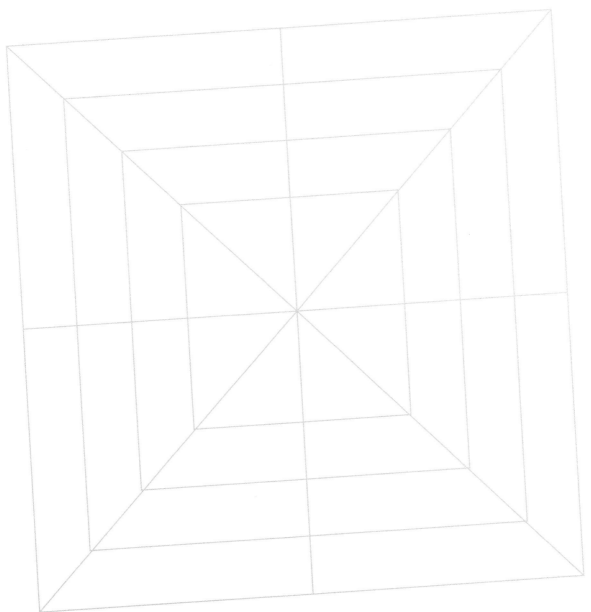

The following pattern is for the large
box. Reduce by 50% for the medium box.

The following pattern
is for the medium
size box.

Resources

Artbase

88 North Street
Hornchurch
Essex RM11 1SR
UK
Tel: 01708 457 948
www.artbasehornchurch.com

* Mail-order suppliers of
scrapbooking materials. They
stock DMC Fantasy Velvet craft
cord.

Creative Xpress!!

295 West Center Street
Provo, UT 84601
Tel: (800) 563-8679
www.creativexpress.com

* Mail-order suppliers of craft
materials, including scrapbooking supplies and the Coluzzle
cutting system.

Daler-Rowney USA

2 Corporate Drive
Cranbury, NJ 08512-9584
Tel: (609) 655-5252
www.daler-rowney.com

* Manufacturers of artists'
materials, including Canford
colored paper and card stock.

EK Success

Clifton, NJ
Tel: (800) 524-1349
www.eksuccess.com

* Manufacturers of scrapbooking supplies, including Paper
Shapers punches and Zig
Memory System archival quality markers. Product info only.

Fiskars Brands, Inc.

7811 West Stewart Avenue
Wausau, WI 54401
Tel: (800) 500-4849
www.fiskars.com

* Manufacturers of Fiskars
paper-cutting products, including paper edgers, hand punches
and the ShapeCutter. Web site
includes how-to tips and project ideas.

Olfa

33 South 6th Street
Terra Haute, IN 47807
Tel: (800) 962-OLFA
www.olfa.com
* Manufacturers of cutting
tools; craft knives, compass-
style circle cutter.

Origami 4 You

Tel: +44 (0) 7966 071 765
www.origami4you.co.uk

* Mail-order origami resource.

Paper Adventures

935 South 5th Street
Milwaukee, WI 53204
Tel: (800) 727-0699
www.paperadventures.com

* Manufacturers of acid-free
scrapbooking papers. No shopping from the Web site, but an
inspirational browse!

Pilot Pen Corporation

60 Commerce Drive
Trumbull, CT 06611
Tel: (203) 377-8800
www.pilotpen.com

Manufacturers of gel ink pens, Super Color Gold markers and more.

Phrazzle Card Limited

Phrazzle House
29 Hest View Road
Ulverston
Cumbria LA12 9PH
UK
Tel: +44 (0) 1229 588880
www.phrazzlecard.co.uk

Mail-order supplier of pearlescent paper and corrugated cardboard.

Sakura of America, Inc.

30780 San Clemente Street
Hayward, CA 94544
Tel: (800) 776-6257
www.gellyroll.com

Manufacturers of archival-quality pens, including Pigma Micron pens.

USArtQuest, Inc.

7800 Ann Arbor Road
Grass Lake, MI 49240
Tel: (517) 522-6225
www.usartquest.com

Manufacturer and mail-order supplier of acid-free, archival-quality and nontoxic Perfect Paper Adhesive.

Uchida of America, Corp.

3535 Del Amo Boulevard
Torrance, CA 90503
Tel: (800) 541-5877
www.uchida.com

Manufacturers of craft supplies, including craft punches. Can buy direct from the Web site.

Xyron, Inc.

15820 North 84th Street
Scottsdale, AZ 85260
Tel: (800) 793-3523
www.xyron.com

Manufacturers of laminating machines. Web site includes how-tos and project ideas.

new Ideas in
Ribboncraft

new Ideas in

Ribboncraft

Susan Niner Janes

NORTH LIGHT BOOKS

CINCINNATI, OHIO

table of contents

it's a ribbon wonderland

ibbon is one of life's affordable luxuries—a little touch of something elegant that turns the everyday into the exception.

Ribbon and special occasions go hand in hand—an oversized bow on a birthday gift, the delicate streamers trailing from a bride's bouquet, a blue-ribbon prize. A ribbon is just a narrow band of fabric, but it is nearly always made of something special, whether it is shimmering satin, gossamer taffeta or luxurious velvet. These special fabrics mark special times, and it only takes a small bow to make a noticeable difference.

One of the most exciting things about ribboncraft is the amazing variety of ribbons available. Your local craft store is a ribbon wonderland! So many different widths, fabrics and textures to choose from: satin, sheers, grosgrain, velvet, jacquard, wire-edge, rat-tail cord, ready-made ribbon rosebuds. Ribboncraft encompasses an amazing spectrum of activities from weaving and embroidery, to lacing and flower-making. Ribbons can dress up garments, decorate home furnishings, make greeting cards unique and transform gifts into treasured keepsakes.

So, what can you expect to find in this book? Something for everyone, whether you are a skilled crafter or an eager beginner. You'll find three chapters: Home Accents shows you ways to decorate towels, placemats and lampshades; Gifts and Keepsakes includes a Snowflake Holiday Stocking and a Beaded Penny Rug Purse; and Wedding and Baby is filled with projects to commemorate the two most exciting events of your life.

Remember, the ribboncrafts you produce help to make special days more memorable. And the pleasure of crafting with ribbon can make an ordinary day special. Pretty good for a narrow band of fabric....

Happy Ribboncrafting!
—Susan Niner Janes

The ribbons used in this book are woven-edge ribbons or narrow bands of fabric with selvages—tightly woven edges that prevent unraveling—on both sides. Because the edges are finished, woven-edge ribbons can be washed repeatedly and are therefore suitable for long-lasting craft projects, such as clothing or home accents.

Here is a list of the most commonly used ribbons that you will use for the projects in this book.

all about ribbon

Satin

Nothing can compare to the lustrous sheen and texture of satin ribbon. The good news is that it's also easy to care for since polyester satin can be machine-washed and dried, and usually requires no ironing. Many of the projects in this book use satin ribbon, which comes in an amazing range of widths and colors, making it suitable for all sorts of projects, from ribbon embroidery to gathered flowers.

There are two types of satin ribbon: single-face satin, which has one lustrous and one matte surface; and double-face satin, which is lustrous on both sides. When should you use each? If you are tying a bow, choose double-face satin, since both sides of the ribbon will show. Double-face satin is thicker, so it is more suitable for glued projects (the glue is less likely to seep through). Single-face satin is ideal for stitched trims in which only the top side of the ribbon shows. Single-face satin is also slightly less expensive, so to save money, use it whenever possible.

Feather-Edge

Also known as picot-edge, this satin ribbon has wispy loops along its edges. Use it on trims for feminine projects, such as sachets.

Velvet

Velvet ribbons have a luxurious pile finish, which makes them weighty. Nylon velvet is washable and crease-resistant. Velvet ribbon is stunning during autumn and winter, especially for the holidays, because of its deep, rich colors.

Sheer

Translucent ribbons, such as organdy, are perfect for romantic, whimsical effects. Some sheer ribbons, such as the ones used in the wedding projects, combine satin stripes with the sheer effect.

Rat-Tail

Not quite ribbon because it isn't flat, rat-tail cord is very useful and attractive, despite its name. This silky cord is often used for beading. It comes in handy when making drawstrings and bag straps. Also, rat-tail cord is often braided or used when making tassels.

Grosgrain

Grosgrain is a strong, tightly woven ribbon recognizable by its narrow cross-wise ridges.

Jacquard and Brocade

Jacquard ribbon has woven patterns, and brocades are jacquards with raised patterns. Multi-colored jacquards have an embroidered look.

Taffeta

Taffeta is a crisp, tightly woven ribbon, available in solids, plaid and moiré effects. It makes great bows that retain their shape well.

Wire-Edge Ribbon

This ribbon has narrow wires woven into its selvages. The wires are flexible so the ribbon can be bent into formations that hold their shape, such as a ribbon rose (see page 26) or large bows.

Novelty Ribbons

This is a catch-all category to cover the staggering array of specialty ribbons that are available. Novelty ribbons include metallics, printed ribbons, gingham checks and plaids.

Ribboncraft is so versatile because you can use it in many different types of craft projects and pair it with many types of materials. This makes for very dynamic, creative projects, but it also means that you'll have to stock up on other craft materials such as papercraft and sewing supplies. The small investment is well worth it, however, because the results are so rewarding!

materials & supplies

✳ ADHESIVES

Keep the following adhesives, sealants and protectants on hand when creating your unique ribbon projects. Not only are they necessary for constructing the project, but they also seal the ends of ribbons to prevent fraying.

Craft Glue

Craft glue is handy for sealing ribbon ends and gluing non-washable ribboncraft projects, especially those involving paper. It dries clear and flexible.

Clear Nail Polish

Although this is not an adhesive, it is a quick-drying sealant for ribbon ends. Be careful—it is flammable, so do not use it for projects you will place near a heat source.

Fabric Glue

Use fabric glue to seal ribbon ends on washable projects, and for gluing ribbon to fabric. You can find this at your local craft or fabric store.

Liquid Seam Sealant

A liquid seam sealant, such as Fray Check, seals ribbon ends so they won't unravel. It is available at your local fabric store.

Glue Stick

A glue stick is very useful when working with paper punches and other paper-based decorative embellishments that you can add to your ribboncraft projects.

Fusible Web

Fusible web is an iron-on adhesive that permanently bonds two layers of fabric together. It comes on a paper backing and is very easy to use. You can find it in craft and fabric stores.

Masking Tape

Masking tape is indispensable for attaching templates to project surfaces.

SHOPPING ADVICE:

Fabric stores stock woven-edge ribbons and paper stores stock craft ribbons, but hobby superstores carry both. Craft ribbons, also known as cut-edge ribbons, are stiffened strips of fabric, plastic or paper with unfinished edges. They are used by florists and for gift wrapping—projects for temporary use. Do not purchase them by mistake. Make sure that you are buying the right stuff!

Adhesives seal ribbons and prevent fraying, keeping your projects clean and finished.

You can find a wide assortment of decorative papers as well as embellishments like paper punches, hole punches and pre-cut designs at your local craft store.

✳ PAPER

Several different types of paper are used in this book. Check out your local art, scrapbooking or paper supply store to see the wide variety of papers available for craft projects.

Corrugated Cardboard

Corrugated cardboard has fluted ridges that make it very flexible. It comes in several colors and is excellent for use in paper ribboncrafts because it is sturdy and durable.

Cardstock

Cardstock is another very strong surface to use for paper ribboncrafts. It is widely available in a multitude of colors at your local craft store.

Handmade Paper and Giftwrap

Giftwrap is soft and supple, and is suitable for covering boxes. Use handmade papers with visible fibers for added texture.

Pearlescent Paper

Papers with pearly or iridescent finishes are a recent trend in crafts. They are available in a wide range of colors and are ideal for festive occasions.

Vellum

Vellum comes in a large selection of colors and weights. It is ideal for lampshades or mobiles.

✳ PAPER TOOLS

Paper punches are a great way to add a simple decorative touch to your ribboncraft projects. They are available in a multitude of sizes and shapes, suiting your own personal style. These items can be found at your local craft or scrapbooking store.

Hand Punches

Hand punches enable you to make uniformly sized holes quickly, and are suitable for use on either paper or felt. The $1/16$" (1.6mm) circle punch is used extensively in this book to punch holes for ribbon lacing. Other useful sizes are the $1/8$" (3mm) circle and the $1/4$" (7mm) circle.

Paper Punches

These punches are inexpensive and add a polished finish to your paper ribboncrafts. Press-down punches are available in a wide range of die-cut shapes. For this book, you will need small and large heart punches, and a large flower-shaped punch.

Metal Ruler

Use rulers when cutting or scoring paper, as well as for measuring.

Craft Knife and Cutting Mat

Use a craft knife for cutting and scoring paper and cardboard. It will give you accurate, professional results. Use a self-healing cutting mat whenever you use a craft knife.

✳ SCISSORS

All the scissors that you'll need for this book are listed in this section. Remember to keep papercraft scissors for paper use and sewing scissors for fabric use. Never mix them up—you'll dull the blades!

Nail Scissors

Whether you choose straight or curved nail scissors is your own preference. They are indispensible for crafts and ideal for fine cutting. Keep a pair expressly for papercraft projects.

Paper Edgers

Paper edgers are like pinking shears, but are made expressly for papercraft use. A variety of decorative blade patterns are available fairly inexpensively, so collecting them can become an obsession. For this book, I used Fiskars Clouds, Scallop and Wave paper edger patterns.

Needlecraft Scissors

These scissors are about 5" (12cm) long, a handy size for ribboncraft projects. The pointed blades are ideal for snipping threads and angling ribbons. They are also used to cut felt or fabric.

Pinking Shears

Use pinking shears for cutting patterned edges on fabrics, such as tulle or felt. They are longer and heavier than paper edgers. Pinking shears are now available with scalloped blades, in addition to the traditional zigzag pattern.

❋ SEWING SUPPLIES

Even if you have never tried to sew before, you will learn how simple ribboncraft projects can be. Here are some sewing supplies that you should have available before starting any of the projects in this book.

Iron-On Interfacing

Use iron-on interfacing to strengthen and stabilize fabrics and prevent puckering. Interfacing is available in fabric stores.

Machine-Washable Felt

Felt is a fabric made from fibers that have been compressed and tangled to produce a soft, fuzzy surface. The advantage of felt over other fabrics is that its edges, when cut, will not fray, and require no finishing. This is a great timesaver, especially for beginners. In the past, felt could not be washed, so it was used for cheap and cheerful cut-and-glue crafts. Today, machine-washable felt is available in a wide assortment of colors and styles, and will give your projects a longer lifespan. I used Kunin Rainbow Classic Felt for the projects in this book.

Iron

Keep an iron and ironing board handy when you begin working on fabric ribboncrafts. Not only will you want to press your ribbons and fabrics for a crisp, finished project, but you will need the heat from an iron to bond interfacing and fusible web.

Needles

For this book, you will need both sewing needles and embroidery needles. The embroidery needles required are a chenille needle (large eye, pointy tip) and a tapestry needle (large eye, blunt tip). Embroidery needles are used for ribbon embroidery and must be large enough to accommodate a $^{1}/_{8}$" (3mm) wide ribbon. You may also use a tapestry needle when piercing holes in paper ribboncraft projects.

Straight Pins

Straight pins are suitable for most sewing projects. Use them for temporarily holding fabrics together during the construction process.

HAND-SEWING VS. USING A SEWING MACHINE:

The projects in this book use basic sewing techniques that you can easily learn. For some of the projects, this is a basic hand-stitch. For other projects, light use of a sewing machine is recommended. All of the projects that I suggest you use a sewing machine for are clearly marked at the beginning of the instructions. The sewing machine work is a very simple, straight stitch, but should you choose not to use a machine, you may hand-stitch those steps as well.

Basic sewing supplies are all you need to easily create a decorative finish to your ribboncraft projects.

Silk Pins

Use silk pins when working with delicate fabrics like satin and sheers because they will not mark the fabrics. You will need to use them for the wedding projects in this book.

Tape Measure

Use a fabric tape measure to measure lengths of ribbon and fabric. They are usually available in 60" (150cm) lengths.

✷ SEWING NOTIONS AND EMBELLISHMENTS

A well-chosen finishing touch can transform a nice ribboncraft project into a breathtaking one. Buttons, beads, pearl beading, charms, machine-embroidered appliqués and ribbon roses add texture, color and shape to your projects. Remember, an embellishment should contribute to, but not overpower, a project.

Buttons

Add a sweet touch to a project by attaching a button with $1/8$" (3mm) ribbon. Look for buttons in novelty shapes and interesting textures.

Beads

You can find frosted, glass, plastic and semi-precious stone beads. They are available in a multitude of sizes and shapes. Also try using beads in graduated sizes.

Charms

Charms come in themed shapes (for example, baby motifs) and various metallic finishes. They are sewn onto projects through the top loops. Try sewing them on with ribbon, then tie a bow.

Pearl Beading

Pearl beading is available by the yard. To sew a cascading string of pearls onto your project, just catch the beads onto the background fabric with a few strategically placed stitches.

Machine-Embroidered Appliqués

Using ready-made embroidery is a real time-saver. Look for dainty florals because they look great with satin ribbon.

Ribbon Roses

Pre-formed ribbon roses are sold either individually or in packs. They are a great time-saver whenever a large quantity of roses is required.

How To Use The Patterns In This Book:

Project patterns are given whenever necessary in this book. You will have to enlarge most of them using a photocopier. Then transfer the pattern onto tracing paper, and finally onto your project. Applying self-adhesive plastic, such as clear Contact paper, makes the pattern durable and suitable for repeated use.

"Impressing" the design with a stylus (or a dry fine-point pen) is an easy way to transfer the design onto the surface of the project, leaving no pencil marks to erase. Use masking tape to secure the pattern in place.

When making a large quantity of one project, it is helpful to make templates of the pattern on heavy cardstock or poster board and cut them out with a craft knife.

Crafting with ribbons is easy to do, but there are a few tips and techniques that will help you to achieve top-notch results every time. Note also that the ribbons used in this book are woven ribbons—not nonwoven craft ribbons—and the techniques shown apply specifically to them. You'll also need to be familiar with a few basic sewing techniques—these begin on page 144.

basic techniques

[RIBBON TECHNIQUES]

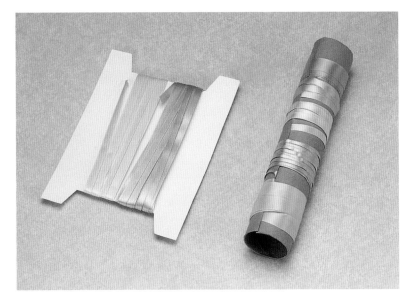

✳ STORING RIBBON

Many crafters are packrats, and who can blame them? After all, you never know just when you might need that beautiful piece of ribbon for a last-minute gift. Unfortunately, ribbon scraps can accumulate into a tangled mess. The image at the right shows a few suggestions for ribbon storage.

One option (ABOVE) is to cut U-shaped notches in either side of cardboard, then wind ribbon around it. Cut vertical slits to catch the ribbon ends securely. Ribbon stored this way packs flat, but may require ironing when you use it.

The second storage idea (ABOVE) is to use a cardboard tube. Slit the tube lengthwise, then tuck the ribbon tails into the slit. Ribbon kept in this way requires no ironing when it is unwound. Empty thread spools and ribbon bolts are also excellent ways to store ribbon.

✳ CUTTING AND FINISHING RIBBON EDGES

It is important to carefully finish the ribbons that you cut to prevent frayed edges and unraveling projects! While this may seem like an unnecessary step, your projects will look neater and last longer if you follow these simple guidelines.

Cutting Ribbon Edges

Ribbon tails should always be neatly cut, whether straight or on the diagonal. Use this method for ensuring crisp edges every time.

Cut against a piece of masking tape. You can position the tape at exactly the angle you want. The tape edge provides a straight cutting guide.

Finishing Ribbon Edges

Scruffy-looking frayed ribbon tails can ruin the look of a fabulous project. To eliminate this problem, seal ribbon ends with craft glue.

Apply the glue to the edges in a thin line. The glue dries clear and is non-toxic. Use for non-washable projects. Ribbon ends can also be sealed with clear nail polish. Ribbons sealed with nail polish are machine-washable. Nail polish, however, is flammable, so never use it on projects that will be placed near a heat source. The best choice for washable ribbon projects is to purchase a liquid seam sealant, such as Fray Check, to prevent unraveling.

Glue down the ends on the back side of your work. You do not have to tie knots; plus the glue dries leaving a smooth finish to your work.

Finishing Ribbon Papercrafts

Ribbon papercrafts are simple to finish because you do not have to knot and tie them off, as with ribbon fabric crafts.

❋ KNOT-FREE SEWING

Making a thread loop is a handy way to cut down on the number of knots in your sewing, since knots can look lumpy and messy.

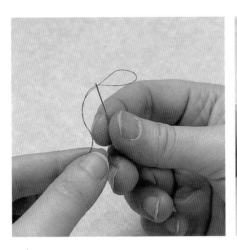 

1 *Fold thread in half, making a loop. Thread the loop and make a small stitch through fabric. Remove the needle from the loop.*

2 *Bring the thread tails through the loop and pull tight. Then re-thread the needle with the tails. Continue sewing as normal.*

❋ TAILOR'S TACKS

Short thread loops are called tailor's tacks, and are used as a method of marking fabric without chalk or carbon paper (see Rose Garland Makeup Bag, page 222).

❋ BASTING

Basting is a way to sew two fabrics together temporarily until you can join them in a more permanent way. Basting is more precise than pinning.

❋ TACKING

Tacking is another simple stitch, connecting two pieces together. Often, you will tack ribbons together, tack ribbons and fabric together, or reinforce a bow by tacking it with a stitch.

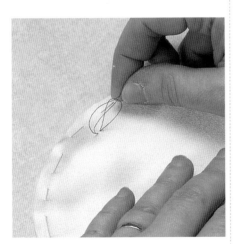 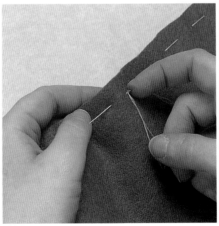 

To make tailor's tacks, fold your thread in half and thread the loop end in your needle. Make a stitch through the fabric, then pull the tails through the loop and trim.

To baste two fabrics together, sew a widely spaced running stitch (in and out, repeat) through the fabrics you are joining. Remove the basting after the sewing has been completed.

Tacking is a simple technique, accomplished by making small stitches about the same length, very close together. Thread your needle, make the stitches and tie off with a knot on the back side of your project.

✳ FISH LOOP

A fish loop is a simple way of making a hanging loop out of ribbon. This can be used as a decorative hook to hang your project, as in the Snowflake Holiday Stocking, on page 204. Why is this called a fish loop? Just view the loop sideways!

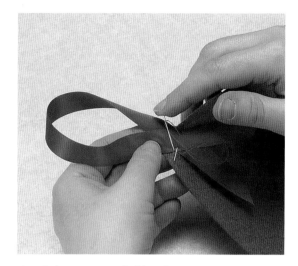

Simply loop a piece of ribbon by crossing its tails, pin the cross-point and stitch it in place. Be sure to pin the ribbon flat; do not twist the ribbon and pin opposite sides together.

✳ RIBBON FRINGE

Adding fringe to your project is a quick and simple technique, but it really adds to the overall appeal. You can create this polished look by using ⅛" (3mm) wide satin ribbon that matches the colors in your project.

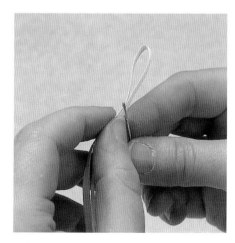

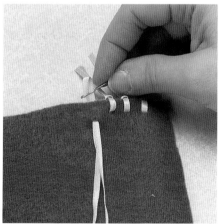

1 *To make a decorative fringe, start with a piece of ⅛" (3mm) narrow ribbon, about 8" to 10" long (20cm to 25cm). Fold the ribbon in half to form a loop and thread the loop through the eye of an embroidery needle.*

2 *Pass the ribbon tails through the loop and pull tight. You've now made one fringe loop. Repeat the process if you'd like more.*

You will definitely want to familiarize yourself with the stitches in this glossary. They are all simple embroidery stitches, easy to learn and execute. In no time, you will be creating fabulous ribboncraft projects!

stitch glossary

RIBBON EMBROIDERY

Satin ribbon is a natural for embroidery, but working with ribbon is slightly different from working with thread. First of all, it is best to keep your stitching simple, so that you can best appreciate the smooth satin surface and luster of the ribbon. Remember to keep the ribbon flat and untwisted as you stitch, and examine each stitch as you go.

You will need a needle with an eye large enough to fit the width of the ribbon. A chenille needle is used for stitching tightly woven fabrics, while a tapestry needle is suitable for loosely woven fabrics, or when stitching through prepunched holes (such as on the Granny Patchwork Pillow on page 168).

✳ CROSS STITCH

This familiar X-shaped stitch can be used to make decorative borders, or to fill in large areas. To make the stitch efficiently, sew a line of diagonals and then back-track in the other direction to complete the X.

 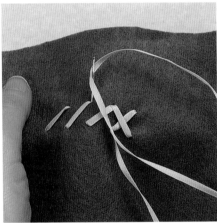

1 Sew a row of diagonal stitches.
Working from left to right, sew equally spaced diagonal lines. Stitch from lower left to top right, bringing the needle down vertically, as shown.

2 Back-track to complete the Xs
When you reach the end of the row, double back and sew the diagonal stitches from lower right to top left, as shown. Use the same holes as the first row of diagonals.

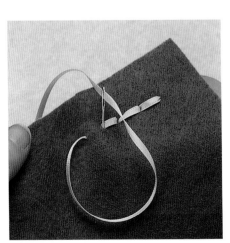

✳ BACK STITCH

This stitch is used for outlining. Back stitches are excellent for adding borders, lettering or creating pattern designs.

Bring the needle up a short distance from the previous stitch. Bring the needle down, in the hole of the previous stitch. Repeat these steps until you have completed your outlining.

✳ SLIP STITCH

This stitch is an almost-invisible way to join two fabrics together. Great for hems and appliqués—whenever a folded edge is present!

✳ BLANKET STITCH

A blanket stitch is a decorative method of finishing an edge. As you might guess, woolen blankets are often finished in this way. A blanket stitch is a widely spaced version of a buttonhole stitch.

✳ BEADED BLANKET STITCH

Beaded borders are ideal in situations where weight is desired—such as tablecloth borders.

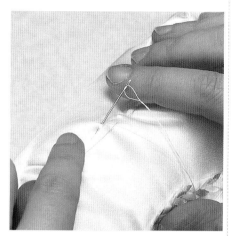

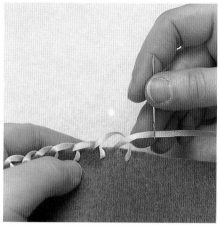

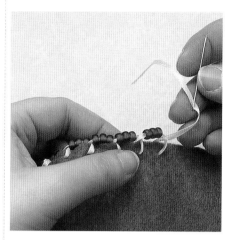

Bring the needle up through the folded edge. Catch a thread from the backing fabric. Re-insert the needle into the fold, and slide it along. Bring the needle out, pull the thread taut, and then repeat the catch-and-slide sequence.

Bring the needle through the loop, then down into the fabric, a little away from the edge of the fabric. Bring the needle through the loop just formed. Repeat the cycle.

Bring the needle through the loop. Thread the beads onto the needle and slide them onto the ribbon. Put the needle through the edge of the fabric and repeat.

✳ FRENCH KNOT

This stitch creates a decorative knot that is ideal for flower centers. It gives your work dimension and texture.

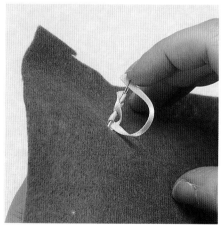

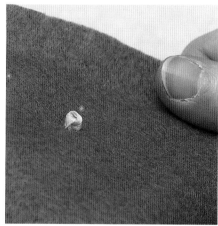

1 *Bring a piece of threaded ribbon about 10" (25cm) long up through the fabric. Spiral the ribbon around the needle five times. Push the needle back down through the fabric and pull taut.*

2 *The finished knot forms a ball on the right side of the fabric. Tie the ribbon ends together on the wrong side of the fabric. Trim the ends close to the knot.*

Most often associated with prize-giving, a pin-on rosette bow can add decorative emphasis to all sorts of home furnishings. To make a rosette, ribbon loops are arranged in a fan-like circular formation and stitched onto a felt base. Two types of rosettes are shown. The flat-looped style is more tailored and sedate than the dramatic petal-looped rosette. Try making both types. You can easily change the styles to suit your mood or the occasion.

decorative bows

Ribbon

- 2¹/₂ yards (2.3m) of ⁷/₈" (23mm) wide single- or double-face satin ribbon
- 2 yards (2m) of 1¹/₂" (39mm) wide double-face satin ribbon

Supplies

- one 9" x 12" (23cm x 31cm) rectangle of machine-washable felt
- fusible web
- large decorative button
- needle and thread
- straight pins
- safety pin
- craft glue
- tape measure
- iron

1 | Make the Rosette Base

The rosette requires a thick base because it must support many layers of ribbon. Cut two small pieces of felt and sandwich fusible web in between. Bond the felt together following manufacturer's instructions. Cut a felt circle with a 3" (8cm) diameter for the base.

2 | Add the Ribbon Loop

Mark the center of the circle with a piece of thread. Cut eighteen 4" (10cm) pieces of ⁷/₈" (23mm) ribbon for the rosette spiral. Seal the ribbon ends with glue. Finger-press (flatten or "press" with your finger or fingernail) the first piece of ribbon in half and pin the loop onto the felt. Using doubled sewing thread, catch the corner of the loop to the felt.

3 | Continue Adding Loops

Pin the ribbon loops onto the felt, angling and overlapping them as shown. Pin them in a clockwise spiral, until the circle is complete. Tuck the last loop under the first. Stitch a circle around the ribbon at the center of the rosette, through all layers.

4 | Stitch the Loops to the Felt

Using doubled sewing thread, sew around the wrong side of the rosette, catching each ribbon loop to the base. Make sure the stitching does not show on the front of the rosette.

5 | Sew a Button in the Center

Stitch a decorative shank-style button onto the rosette center using doubled sewing thread.

6 | Secure the Backing

Cut an 18" (45cm) piece of ⅞" (23mm) ribbon for the tail. Fold it in half and flatten the loop end into a V-point. Sew the point down. Trim the tail ends diagonally and seal them with glue. Sew the tail onto the rosette back. Sew a safety pin onto the rosette back. Make sure you stitch down the non-opening side of the safety pin.

You can easily pin this decorative bow to anything from a curtain tieback to a very special gift.

2 Petal-Looped Rosette Bow

Ribbon

- 2¼ yard (2.1m) of ⅝" (15mm) wide double-face satin ribbon
- 1¼ yard (1.2m) of ½" (12mm) wide metallic nylon taffeta ribbon

Supplies

- one 9" x 12" (23cm x 31cm) rectangle of machine-washable felt
- fusible web
- faux jewel button
- needle and thread
- straight pins
- safety pin
- craft glue
- tape measure
- iron

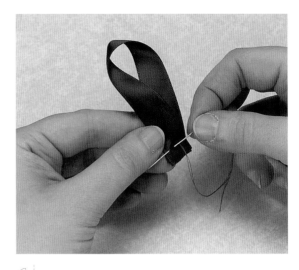

1 Make the Petal Loops

Cut fourteen 5½" (16cm) strips of satin ribbon. Seal the ends with craft glue. Fold each strip in half, then slide the left end over the right. Stitch the base of the loop together.

2 Add the First Loop

Cut two 3" (8cm) felt circles and join them to make a felt base with fusible web (see Flat-Looped Rosette Bow, step 1, page 148). Pin, then stitch, the first loop onto the base, sewing the left-hand corner.

3 Add the Loops Onto the Base

Pin, then stitch, the loops onto the base in a circular fashion.

4 Secure the Loops

On the back of the rosette, catch each ribbon loop to the base, using doubled sewing thread.

5 Add Smaller Loops

Cut fourteen 3" (8cm) strips of metallic taffeta ribbon. Seal the ends and make petal loops, just like you did in step 1. Pin and stitch the loops, forming a smaller circle.

6 Sew a Button in the Center

Using doubled sewing thread, stitch the button onto the center of the rosette.

7 Secure the Backing

Stitch a safety pin onto the back of the rosette. Make sure that you stitch the non-opening side of the pin.

Turn a rosette into a curtain tieback with 2 yards (2m) of 1¹/₂" (39mm) wide ribbon for the sash. Tie it in a bow around the curtain. Sew a curtain ring behind the bow. Slip the ring over a cup hook attached to the wall. This will prevent the tie-back from slipping down the curtain. Pin the rosette onto the bow. Or dress up a plain moiré pillow with an ambassador-style sash. Wrap a band of wide ribbon around a pillow, then pin a rosette onto the sash.

Flowers made from spiralled pieces of wired ribbon have a generous "cabbage rose" appearance, and they

couldn't be simpler to make. Fine lengths of wire are woven into the ribbon edges, giving it resilience and

"memory." Pin this rose onto a dress or coat, or use it as a curtain tie-back, an embellishment on a special gift

or to top a padded lingerie hanger or keepsake box. You'll really enjoy working with this fun ribbon!

ribbon rose

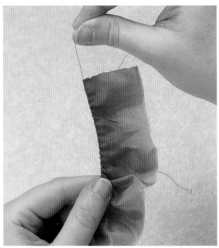

Ribbon

- ⅝ yard (50cm) of 1½" (39mm) wide hombre (shaded from light to dark) wire-edge taffeta ribbon
- ¾ yard (70cm) of ⅝" (15mm) wide green wire-edge taffeta ribbon

Supplies

- needle and thread
- safety pin
- craft glue
- wooden toothpick

1 Seal the Ends

Cut a piece of ribbon about 20" (50cm) long. Tease the end of the wire on what will be the inner edge of the rose. Seal the edges by applying craft glue with a toothpick.

2 Pull the Wire

Grasp the wire and gently push the ribbon down its length, forming gathers.

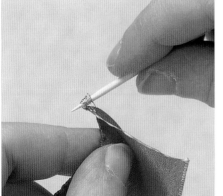

3 Coil the Exposed Wire

Wind the wire end around a wooden toothpick to form a small coil, then remove the toothpick. This will prevent you from pulling through the whole length of wire.

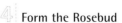

4 Form the Rosebud

Wind the ribbon end around the toothpick several times to form the bud. Remove the toothpick. With doubled sewing thread, catch the base of the coil with a few stitches.

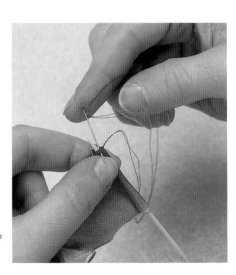

5 | Spiral the Ribbon

Begin to form the rose by winding the gathered ribbon in a loose spiral. Reinforce this shape with overcast stitches on the bottom edge as you go.

6 | Finish the Bloom

When you reach the end of the ribbon, fold it diagonally, as shown. Stitch the short end onto the base of the rose.

7 | Begin the Double-Leaf Pair

Cut two 12" (30cm) pieces of ⁵/₈" (15mm) wide wire-edge ribbon. Seal the ends with glue. Fold one piece of the ribbon in half so the ends meet at the center. Open out and flatten the ribbon, forming points at each end. Using matching sewing thread, stitch each point to secure it into position. Repeat for the other piece.

8 | Bind the Leaves in the Center

Cut a 3" (8cm) piece of green ribbon and seal the ends. Wrap it around the double-leaf pair at the center, catching the ends of the ribbon. Stitch the center wrap to itself on the wrong side of the leaves.

9 | Sew Leaves to the Rose

Center the leaves on the back of the rose and stitch them into place. Stitch along each side of the center wrap. With doubled thread, stitch the non-opening side of a safety pin onto the back of the rose.

If you use hombre ribbon, which is shaded from light to dark along its length, then you can choose to make either a predominantly light-colored or a predominantly dark-colored rose from the same piece of ribbon. Gather the light side for a dark rose, or the dark side for a light rose. They'll complement each other perfectly.

home accents

splash of color, a hint of texture, a glint of shimmering satin...

These thoughtful details help make a house a home and are part of fond, cherished memories. A touch of ribbon can perk up and personalize your home décor for the kitchen, bed or bath. Add charm to store-bought purchases, and create a friendly, welcoming atmosphere.

Ribbons are both pretty and practical, giving high style and low maintenance. Satin floral trims on a towel or pillowcase, grosgrain appliqués on table linen, or a velvety bow on a pillow or curtain tieback are luxurious extras that family and friends will appreciate at your home. The best part is, all of these fabric projects can be machine washed and no-iron if you label-check the ribbon bolt for easy-care features when you shop.

This section includes a mix of projects using a variety of easy and enjoyable ribboncraft techniques. Try your hand at simplified ribbon weaving with our Amish heart placemats, lace a leaf-motif lampshade, or decorate a dish towel with colorful ribbon flowers.

Projects

Nosegay Towel

Give plain towels a new look by adding a ribbon

border and floral corsage. Sewing on ribbon borders is

simple. Making the pin-on bouquet is also quick and

easy when using purchased ribbon rosebuds. When it's

laundry time, remove the nosegay from the towel. To wash

the nosegay, put it in a mesh laundry bag. Nosegay towels

make delightful housewarming gifts. Make some for

yourself, too—no need to save them only for guests.

Ribbon

- 1¼ yards (1.2m) of 1" (25mm) wide lilac single-face satin ribbon
- ¼ yard (20cm) of ⅛" (3mm) wide violet double-face satin ribbon
- ½ yard (50cm) of ¼" (7mm) wide violet double-face satin ribbon
- ¼ yard (20cm) of 1½" (4cm) wide scalloped white lace
- satin rosebuds, 3 lilac, 3 violet and 1 white

Supplies

- 1 white terrycloth washcloth
- iron-on interfacing
- fabric glue or liquid seam sealant
- small safety pin
- needle and thread
- iron
- straight pins

SEWING MACHINE REQUIRED

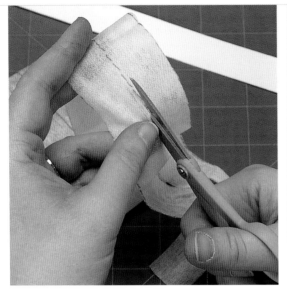

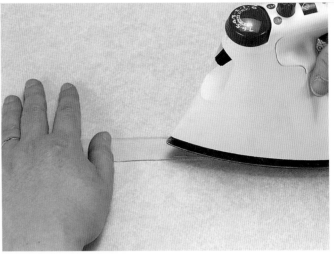

1 Cut Interfacing Strips

To prevent the ribbon from puckering when it is sewn, iron-on interfacing must be applied. Start by cutting strips of interfacing that are $1/8$" (3mm) narrower than the actual ribbon width. To do this, cut out a cardboard template to the required width. Trace the strips onto the interfacing, then cut them out.

2 Iron Interfacing Onto the Ribbon

Following the manufacturer's instructions, iron the interfacing strips onto the wrong side of the ribbon.

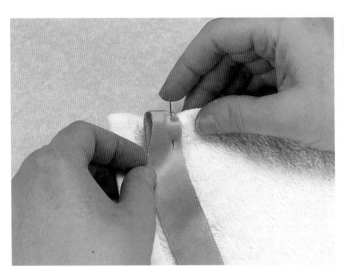

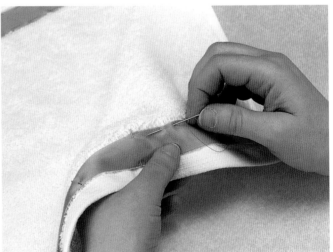

3 Pin the Ribbon Onto the Washcloth

Cut two 9" (23cm) pieces of 1" (25mm) wide lilac ribbon. Pin the ribbon onto the washcloth, covering the woven bands at either side. Tuck the ribbon under $3/4$" (2cm) at both ends.

4 Baste the Ribbon

Baste stitch the ribbon close to the edges of the washcloth, then remove the pins.

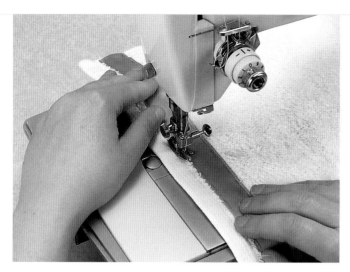

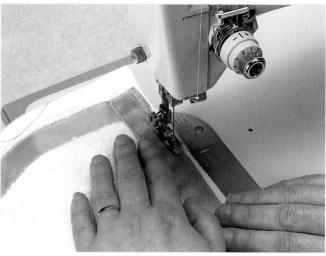

5 Stitch the First Ribbon Border

Use a sewing machine to sew each ribbon close to the edge. Knot the thread on the wrong side and trim close to the knots.

6 Continue to Sew Ribbon Borders

Pin, baste, then sew the two remaining ribbon borders onto the washcloth.

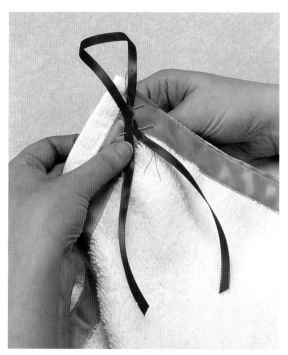

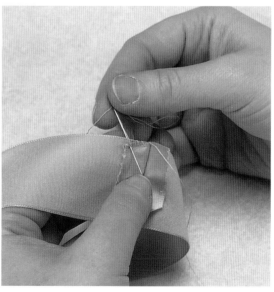

7 Pin a Hanging Loop in the Corner

With 18" (46cm) of ¼" (7mm) wide violet ribbon, pin a loop and stitch the loop to the towel where the ribbon intersects. Trim and seal the ends.

8 Make a Loop for the Rosette

Cut an 8" (20cm) piece of 1" (25mm) wide ribbon. Machine-stitch the short ends of the ribbon together to secure the loop, using a ½" (12mm) seam. Finger-press the seam open. Stitch across the seam so it lies flat. Trim the seam bottoms diagonally and seal the cut edges.

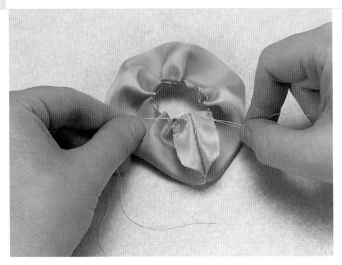

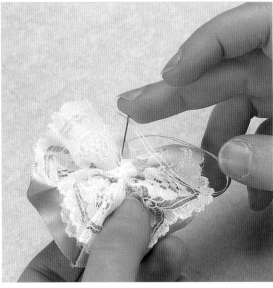

9 Gather the Loop

With doubled thread, stitch around the top of the loop. Gently pull up the gathers to form the rosette. Knot, then trim, the thread ends.

10 Make a Lace Rosette

Follow steps 8 and 9 to make a rosette out of lace. Place it on top of the ribbon rosette, with centers and seams matching. Sew the rosettes together through the centers.

IT'S A GIFT

Want to make a great gift? Add a ribbon nosegay and trim to a gift basket. Simply glue a wide band of ribbon onto a purchased straw basket. Pin a nosegay onto the band. Line the basket with handmade paper, tissue paper or a paper doily. Fill with scented gift soaps or other small gifts. For presentation, wrap the gift basket in cellophane and tie it with a bow.

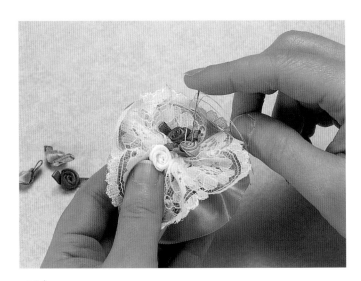

11 Sew on the Ribbon Rosebuds

Use matching sewing thread to sew on the rosebuds. Place a white rosebud in the center, then alternate lilac and violet around the center rosebud. Sew through the rosebud spirals.

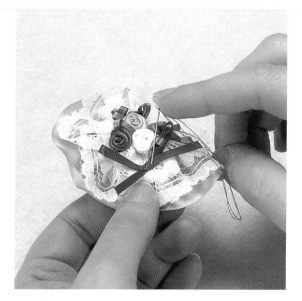

12 Sew on a Bow

Make a bow using 9" (23cm) of ⅛" (3mm) wide violet ribbon.
Seal the ribbon ends. Sew the bow onto the nosegay, stitching
through the bow's knot.

13 Sew a Safety Pin Onto the Back

Stitch the non-opening bar of the safety pin onto the back of
the rosette.

*Try creating a coordinated set
of towels. They're even easier to
make—you only have two borders
to sew. Choose ribbon wide enough
to conceal the towel band. Enlarge
the rosette to match the towel's
size. You'll need 11" (28cm) of 1½"
(4cm) wide satin ribbon for the
rosette, and the same quantity of
white scalloped lace.*

Laced-Leaf Lampshade

This store-bought lampshade makeover yields great

results quickly and inexpensively. It's amazing what a

few paper cut-outs and a bit of simple stitching can do.

When the lamp is switched on, the translucent portion of

the leaves glows softly. This project features a shade for a

table lamp, but you could just as easily decorate a wall

sconce or an ordinary hanging shade. While you're at it,

why not make a matching window shade border?

Ribbon

Ribbon quantities depend on shade dimensions. Here's how to calculate your needs:

- For the top lacing, you need 3 times the top circumference of the shade.

- For the bottom lacing, you need $2^{1}/_{2}$ times the bottom circumference of the shade.

- For each leaf, use $^{3}/_{4}$ yard (70cm) of $^{1}/_{8}$" (3mm) wide satin ribbon.

For the 10" x 10" (25cm x 25cm) shade shown in this project, use these ribbon quantities:

- $4^{1}/_{8}$ yards (3.8m) of $^{1}/_{8}$" (3mm) wide moss green double-face satin ribbon for the top and bottom lacing

- 9 yards (8.4m) of $^{1}/_{8}$" (3mm) wide forest green double-face satin ribbon for the leaves

Supplies

- 1 large sheet of green watercolor paper

- 1 large sheet of green vellum

- 10" x 10" (25cm x 25cm) square paper or fabric-covered plastic lampshade

- two frosted seafoam green glass beads

- paper edger scissors, wave pattern

- tapestry needle

- needle and thread

- craft glue

- glue stick

- tape measure

- pencil

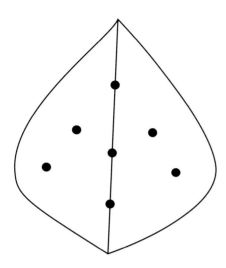

Use this template to make the leaves for the Laced-Leaf Lampshade. It appears here at full size.

1 Make a Paper Pattern

Because your lampshade may be different from mine, plan the design on paper. Trace around the outline of the shade onto a piece of paper. Using the leaf template to the left, plan the placement of the leaves and the top and bottom lacing holes on the tracing. To mark the leaf positions on the shade, place the pattern over the shade and pierce the shade at the top and bottom of each leaf with a tapestry needle. Also, pierce a hole for the stem bottom, about $^3/_4$" (2cm) below the leaf bottom.

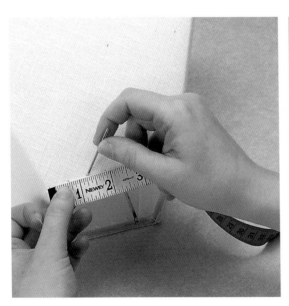

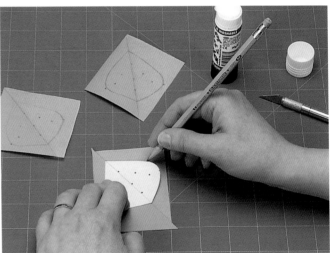

2 Pierce the Lacing Holes

Measure across the shade top and bottom edges. With a tapestry needle, pierce holes at regular intervals, approximately $^5/_8$" (1.5cm) apart.

3 Prepare the Leaves

For each leaf, you need a two-toned piece of paper slightly larger all around than the leaf template. To make the two-toned paper, use a glue stick to glue a right triangle measuring $3^1/_2$" (9cm) tall and $2^1/_2$" (6cm) long of watercolor paper onto a $3^1/_2$" x $2^1/_2$" (9cm x 6cm) rectangle of green translucent paper. Using the leaf template above, cut a leaf out of cardstock and pierce the dots with a tapestry needle. Center the cardstock leaf on the two-toned paper and pencil around it, also marking the dots. Pierce dots in the two-toned paper using a tapestry needle. Use paper edgers to cut out the top half of the leaves, and plain scissors to cut out the bottom edges. Cut out as many leaves as required for the shade. This shade requires twelve leaves.

4 Glue the Leaves Onto the Shade

Only glue the bottom half of each leaf (the opaque portion) onto the shade. Position each leaf on the shade, using the shade holes you pierced in step 1 as guides. After each leaf is glued, use a tapestry needle to pierce the lacing holes inside each leaf. Insert a needle through the pierced holes in each paper leaf, penetrating the lampshade material underneath.

5 Start Lacing

Fold a 27" (70cm) piece of 1/8" (3mm) forest green ribbon in half and tie a knot at the center. Thread a tapestry needle with the ribbon doubled. Sew the knot through the top leaf hole.

6 Lace the Leaf

Re-thread the needle with one strand of the ribbon. Make the long stitch at the top of the leaf, then backstitch the vein to the right. Continue stitching the righthand side of the leaf.

7 Stitch the Stem

Make the long stitch that extends from the leaf onto the shade. Then bring the needle back up through the hole at the leaf base. Remove the ribbon from the needle as shown.

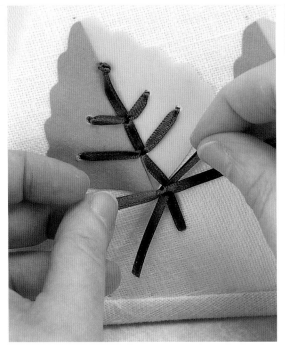

8 Finish Stitching the Leaf

Re-thread the needle with the remaining ribbon length, then backstitch the lefthand side of the leaf. Bring the ribbon out at the bottom leaf hole, then tie the ribbon ends in a bow. Stitch through the knot with matching sewing thread. Lace all the leaves in this way.

9 Lace the Top Border

Starting at a corner, lace the top of the shade. Thread the ribbon through the corner hole, leaving a 16" (40cm) tail extending outside the shade. Stitch the ribbon through the holes, angling the stitches.

10 Complete the Lacing

Work around the top of the shade, bringing the last stitch out through the first hole. Leave a ribbon tail.

11 Tie a Bow

Pull the ribbon tails tightly and tie them into a bow. To secure the bow, make a stitch through the knot with matching thread.

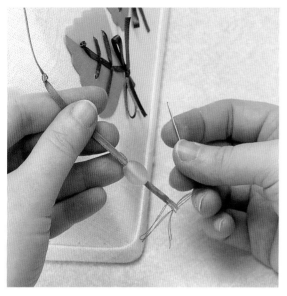

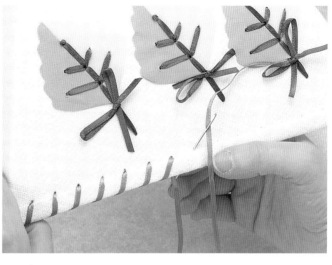

13 Lace the Bottom of the Shade

Stitch the bottom edge of the shade, just as you did for the top of the shade, but omitting the ribbon tails. To finish, knot the ribbon ends inside the shade, and then trim the ribbon.

12 Add the Frosted Beads

Knot each ribbon tail to mark the level of each bead. Sew a loop of sewing thread on the ribbon tail and pull it tightly. Re-thread the needle and add one bead. Slide the bead onto the ribbon. The ribbon should pass easily through the bead hole. Knot the ribbon below the bead. Trim the excess ribbon. Repeat for the other bead.

variation idea

How about an autumn leaves shade to complement the springtime version? Simply change the color scheme for an entirely new project. Try using a round shade for variation as well. To make a pattern tracing of a cylindrical shade, roll the shade along a piece of tracing paper, penciling along the top and bottom edges. A curved pattern will result. Use the pattern to plan the leaf and lacing placement.

This lampshade gives off a soothing glow and is perfect to complement your springtime décor.

Granny Patchwork Pillow

If you want to put a new spin on a traditional idea,

then this is the project for you. Fun and easy to make, this

pillow is a great way to use up small quantities of ribbon

and felt. This is a unit-pieced project. That is, the individual

hexagons build up to form the big center medallion. The

pillow is made of machine-washable felt, which comes in a

vast and sophisticated range of colors. You could also

make a luxury version of the pillow in faux suede.

Ribbon

- 15" (38cm) pieces of $^5/_8$" (15mm) wide satin ribbon, one of each color: dusty rose, burgundy, cream, lilac, purple and moss green
- 47" (1.2m) pieces of $^1/_8$" (3mm) wide satin ribbon for the blanket stitching, one of each color: dusty rose, burgundy, cream, lilac, purple and moss green
- 8" (20cm) pieces of $^1/_8$" (3mm) wide satin ribbon, one of each color: dusty rose, burgundy, cream, lilac, purple and moss green
- $4^1/_4$ yards (4m) of $^1/_8$" (3mm) wide satin ribbon in moss green

Supplies

- one 9" x 12" (23cm x 31cm) rectangle each of assorted felt in Leaf Green, Deep Rose, Lavender and Wheat (I chose Kunin Rainbow Classic Felt)
- 1 yard (1m) of Ruby felt
- 1 yard (1m) of 12oz. (340g) polyester batting
- fusible web
- $^1/_{16}$" (1.6mm) circle hand punch
- craft knife and cutting mat
- tapestry needle
- masking tape
- needle and thread
- straight pins
- iron

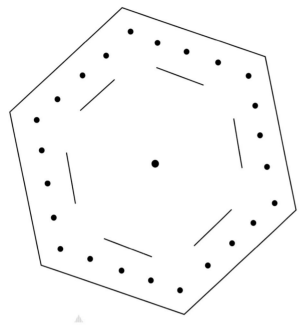

Use this template to make the Granny Patchwork Pillow. Enlarge 111% for the patches. Enlarge 200%, then 200%, then 120% for the pillow cover.

1 | Fuse a Double Layer of Felt

The hexagons require double-thick felt. Cut all the felt rectangles in half, crosswise. Following the manufacturer's instructions, sandwich fusible web between two pieces of like-colored felt and bond with a hot iron. Do this with all the hexagon colors.

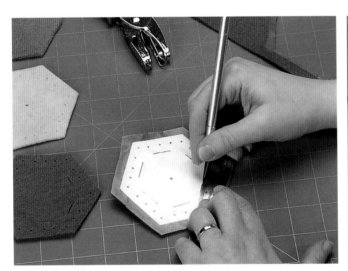

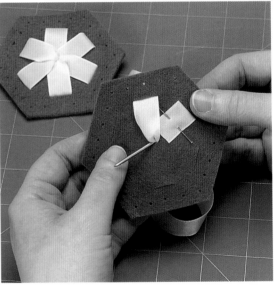

2 | Cut Out the Felt Hexagons

Use the hexagon pattern above, and cut hexagons from the double-thick felt: two rose, two lavender, two green and one wheat. To do this, tape the template onto the felt and cut it out. With a craft knife, cut six slits where marked on the template. Next, punch the holes along the edges of the hexagon with a circle hand punch. Use a tapestry needle or nail to pierce the center hole (the hand punch won't reach). Make sure that the center hole is generously sized. You can use small scissors to enlarge it slightly.

3 | Make the Pinwheel Design

Slide a 15" (38cm) piece of ⁵⁄₈" (15mm) satin ribbon through any slit and pin the end down. Thread the tapestry needle with the free end of the ribbon. Working in a counter-clockwise direction on the wrong side of the hexagon, thread the ribbon up through center hole, then down through the corresponding slot, progressing in a spiral motion. Make sure the ribbon lies flat. When the pinwheel is complete, overlap the ribbon ends and sew them down. Remove the pin.

  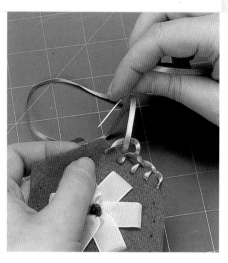

4 Embroider a French Knot

Bring an 8" (20cm) length of ribbon up through the center hole, then remove the needle. Make five spiral wraps around the needle with the ribbon.

tip *You may want to use a button or bead instead of a French knot to add texture to the pillow.*

5 Complete the French Knot

Insert the needle tip in the center hole. Thread the needle, then gently push the needle through to the other side. Knot and trim the ribbon ends on the wrong side of the hexagon. To prevent the knot from slipping through the center hole, take a few stitches through the knot in matching sewing thread. Catch in all the layers—knot, ribbon and felt.

6 Create a Blanket Stitch Border

Thread the needle with 47" (1.2m) of ⅛" (3mm) wide satin ribbon in a contrasting color. Bring the needle up through a corner hole. Take the needle down through the next hole, then up through the left side of the loop. Continue stitching in this way around the hexagon.

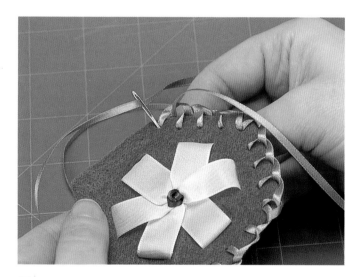

7 Double Stitch the Corners

Stitch twice through the corner holes. This creates a V-formation.

BALANCING THE COLORS

Here's how to arrange ribbon colors successfully within the pillow: Match light hexagons with dark blanket stitching and dark hexagons with light blanket stitching. Ribbon color should contrast sufficiently with the felt hexagon color. Do not place two identical (or very similar) colors next to each other. You may wish to plan the color arrangement on paper before you begin stitching the patchwork together.

8 Connect the Hexagons

Seven hexagons make up the front of the pillow—six surround the center hexagon. Note the color sequence: lilac, green, pink, repeat (wheat in center). To start, you only need to sew the corners at the base of each surrounding hexagon onto the center hexagon. Make tacking stitches (see page 18) using matching doubled sewing thread. Knot and trim the thread on the wrong side.

9 Finish the Patchwork

After the hexagons have been sewn onto the center, join them side to side at their top corners.

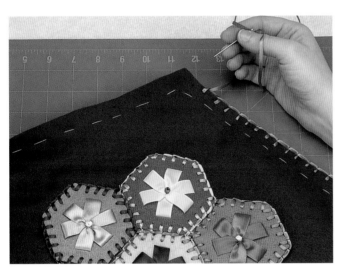

10 Blanket Stitch the Pillow Cover

Enlarge the hexagon pattern on page 170. Cut out two hexagons in Ruby felt. Punch 18 border holes per side, spaced $1/2$" (12mm) apart and $1/4$" (6mm) from the edge. Sew the medallion, centered, onto one piece of felt. Baste the two felt hexagons together on top of each other with edges matching. Blanket stitch through both layers of felt, leaving just over one side of the hexagon unstitched.

11 Make Your Own Pillow Form

Use the pillow cover pattern to cut three layers of batting. Stack the batting hexagons on top of each other and baste the edges. Stitch the edges of the batting to complete the pillow form. Remove the basting. This is an easy method to make pillow forms in any shape you need.

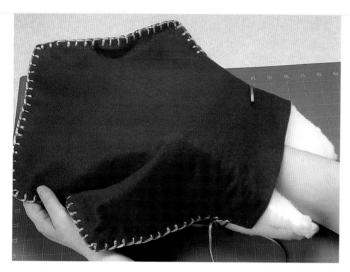

12 | Stuff the Pillow

Insert the pillow form into the felt cover, matching the corners. Blanket stitch the remaining side of the cover. To finish blanket stitching, knot the ribbon on the wrong side of the pillow, then poke the knot through to the inside.

variation idea

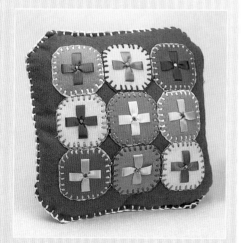

Instead of making a hexagon pillow, create a square pillow with square patchwork. The basic technique is the same as for the hexagon, only you use a total of nine patches. The corners of the square have been trimmed away, which allows the backing fabric to peek through attractively when a group of squares are joined.

This decorative patchwork pillow will make a beautiful addition to any room.

Flowerpot Kitchen Towel

Transform a plain kitchen towel into a decorative

accent using easy, low-sew ribbon appliqués. This towel

features five ribbon flower styles, all made in the same

way, with slight design variations. Simply string the

ribbon petals, then pull up the gathers to complete each

flower. Make it easy. Choose a plaid or checked kitchen

towel for your project—the grid simplifies appliqué

placement, making ribbons easy to space and align.

Ribbon

- $^1/_2$ yard (50cm) of $^5/_8$" (15mm) wide blue double-face satin ribbon
- $1^1/_8$ yards (1m) of $^3/_8$" (9mm) wide blue double-face satin ribbon
- $^5/_8$ yard (50cm) of $^1/_4$" (7mm) wide leaf green double-face satin ribbon
- $^3/_4$ yard (60cm) of $^3/_8$" (9mm) wide leaf green double-face satin ribbon
- $1^3/_4$ yards (1.5m) of $^5/_8$" (15mm) wide terra cotta double-face satin ribbon
- $^1/_2$ yard (40cm) of $^5/_8$" (15mm) wide yellow double face satin ribbon
- $^5/_8$ yard (50cm) of $^3/_8$" (9mm) wide yellow double-face satin ribbon

Supplies

- 20" x 30" (50cm x 75cm) plaid or checked kitchen towel
- three yellow and two white $^1/_4$" (7mm) diameter round plastic beads
- needle and thread
- fabric glue or liquid seam sealant
- tape measure
- straight pins

1 Begin the Open-Loop Flower

Cut eight 2³/₄" (6.5cm) strips of ³/₈" (9mm) wide satin blue ribbon. Seal the ends of each strip to prevent fraying (see Finishing Ribbon Edges, page 143). With doubled thread, make a stitch through one end of the ribbon strip.

2 Make a U-Shaped Loop

Sew through the opposite end of the ribbon strip in the same way, forming a U-shaped loop.

3 String the Ribbon Loops into a Ring

To make the flower petals, string all eight ribbon loops together like beads. The rounded side of the loops is the right side. When all eight loops are threaded, turn them to the other side. Sew the last loop to the first loop to complete the circle. Stitch through the base of the first loop.

4 Complete the Flower

Pull the thread tight and knot it securely on the wrong side of the flower. Trim the thread close to the knot.

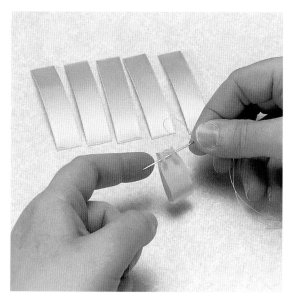

5 Create the Flat-Petal Flower

Cut six 2¹/₂" (6cm) strips of ⁵/₈" (15mm) wide satin yellow ribbon. Seal the strip ends. Fold a strip in half horizontally, to make a loop. With doubled thread, sew three small stitches across the base of the loop: under, over, under.

6 Join the Loops to Form a Ring

Sew all six loops in the same way, and string them like beads as shown. Turn the petals over, then stitch through the first loop to form a ring.

7 Gather and Knot the Petals

Pull the thread tightly, knot it securely and trim the thread close to the knot. The right side of the flower has outwardly-curved petals.

8 Begin the Pinwheel Flower

Of all the flowers, the pinwheel has the most complicated petal shape, but it is easy to make if you take it one step at a time. Cut six 2⁷/₈" (7cm) strips of ⁵/₈" (15mm) wide satin blue ribbon. Crease a strip in half horizontally.

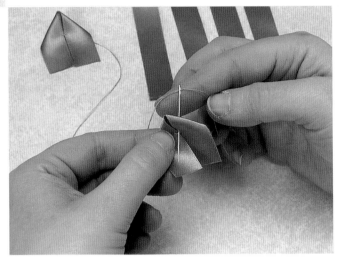

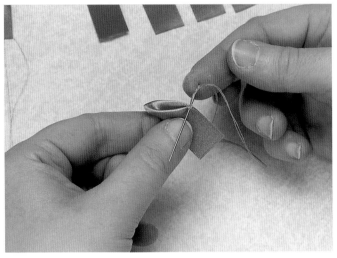

9 Fold into an Inverted V

Open the folded strip, creasing angles at the top to form an inverted V point. Take a few small stitches at the midpoint of the V, catching all of the layers—the right and left sides of the ribbon, plus the layer underneath. The V will now hold its shape permanently.

10 Stitch the V Closed

Finger-press the V in half, and stitch the outer corners together to make the angled petal shape. Make five more petals in this way.

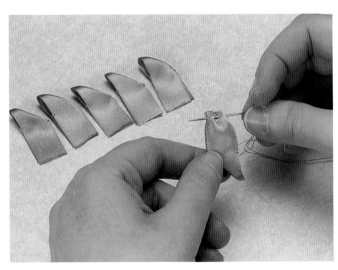

11 Sew Across the Petal Base

Using a doubled piece of thread, make three small stitches across the base of the ribbon loop, as in step 5. String all six petals onto the thread like beads, making sure that the points all face the same direction.

12 Complete the Flower

Sew through the first petal to make a ring. Pull the thread tight to gather the flower, then knot it securely to finish.

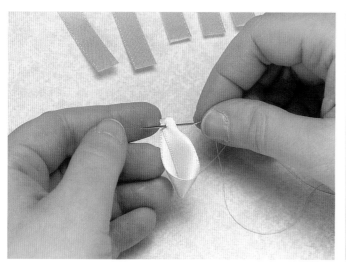

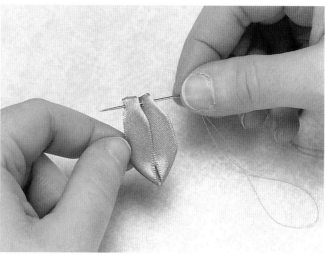

13 Create the Cross-Loop Flower

Cut seven 2³/₄" (7cm) long strips of ³/₈" (9mm) wide satin yellow ribbon. Fold the ribbon into an inverted V, but do not stitch down the point. Slide the righthand ribbon end over the lefthand ribbon end, so that the ends overlap completely. With doubled thread, make a stitch across the overlapped ribbons, as shown. String seven petals together and finish the flower.

14 Create the Starburst Flower

Cut six 2⁷/₈" (7cm) strips of ³/₈" (9mm) wide satin blue ribbon. Fold and stitch an inverted V petal, as in steps 8 and 9. String all six petals and complete the flower.

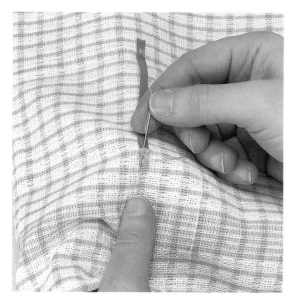

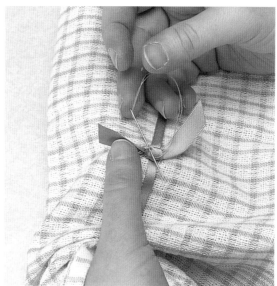

15 Sew Stems on the Towel

Measure across the base of the towel and mark the position of five equally-spaced flower stems with pins. (These stems were spaced 2" [5cm] in from each end and 4" [10cm] apart.) For each stem, cut 3³/₄" (9.5cm) of ¹/₄" (7mm) leaf green satin ribbon, and seal the ends. Pin each stem onto the towel, starting ³/₄" (2cm) above where the flowerpot base will be. Sew each stem onto the towel with tacking stitches at the top and bottom.

16 Add the Leaves

For each pair of leaves, cut 5" (12cm) of ³/₈" (9mm) wide satin leaf green ribbon. Make a center knot. Trim the leaves at an angle, about 1" (2.5cm) to either side of the knot. Seal the ribbon ends. Pin the leaves over the midpoint of the stem. Sew the leaves on the towel, stitching both sides of the knot.

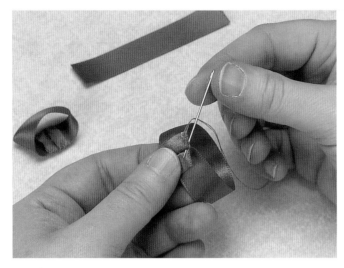

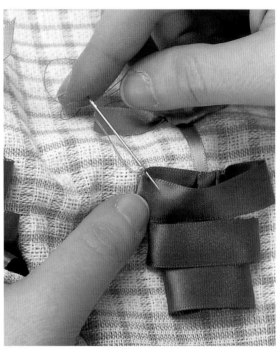

17 | Make Flowerpot Loops

Each flowerpot consists of three ribbon loops in graduated sizes. Each flowerpot requires three strips of $^5/_8$" (15mm) wide satin terra cotta ribbon in $4^7/_8$" (12cm), 4" (10cm) and $3^1/_4$" (8cm) lengths. Seal ribbon ends, then stitch the short ends of each ribbon strip, taking a $^1/_4$" (7mm) seam allowance. Finger-press each seam open, then stitch the top and bottom edges of the seam allowances down.

18 | Sew on the Flowerpots

Finger-press each loop flat, with the seam at the center back, and pin the stacked flowerpot formation onto the towel, covering the base of each stem. Center all of the loops, going from smallest to largest, as shown. To sew each loop onto the towel, stitch the top and bottom corners.

19 | Sew on the Flowers

Pin each flower onto the towel, concealing the top of each stem. Stitch each flower onto the towel through the center. Attach a bead to the center at the same time.

20 | Sew Petals Onto the Towel

Catch the ends of each petal with a few stitches to anchor each flower in place.

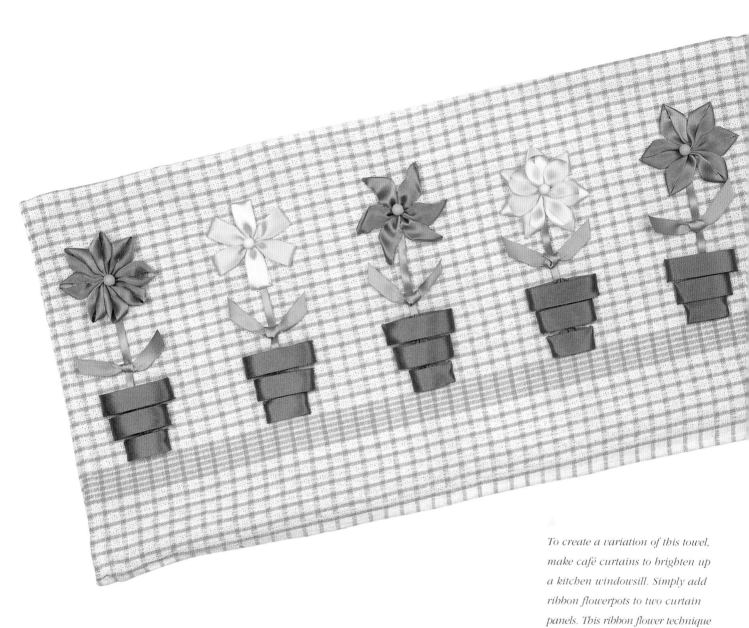

To create a variation of this towel, make café curtains to brighten up a kitchen windowsill. Simply add ribbon flowerpots to two curtain panels. This ribbon flower technique can also be used to decorate children's clothing.

Amish Place Setting

This Amish heart design is applied to woven-ribbon

appliqués, which add a touch of folk art charm and a

splash of color to table accessories. Grosgrain ribbon,

with its subtle crosswise ribs, has been chosen to add

surface texture. It contrasts nicely with the chunky

ridges of the rough-weave placemat. The traditional

Amish colors, brights on a dark background, will add

personality and warmth to your tablesetting.

Ribbon

- 1¹⁄₈ yards (1m) each of 1" (25mm) wide polyester grosgrain ribbon in blue and magenta
- 1¹⁄₄ yards (1.2m) each of ⁵⁄₈" (15mm) wide polyester grosgrain ribbon in blue and magenta
- ⁵⁄₈ yard (60cm) of ⁷⁄₈" (23mm) wide lilac double-face satin ribbon
- 1¹⁄₈ yards (1m) of ¹⁄₄" (7mm) wide lilac double-face satin ribbon
- 3³⁄₄ yards (3.2m) of ¹⁄₈" (3mm) wide lilac double-face satin ribbon

Supplies

- 18" x 13" (45cm x 33cm) navy blue placemat
- 15" x 15" (38cm x 38cm) navy blue napkin
- straw basket with 8¹⁄₂" (22cm) diameter opening
- needle and thread
- straight pins
- fabric glue or liquid seam sealant
- tape measure

▶ MATERIALS ARE FOR ONE PLACEMAT, ONE NAPKIN RING AND ONE BASKET.

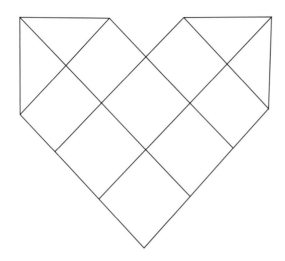

Use this template to make the hearts for the Amish Place Setting. Enlarge 143%.

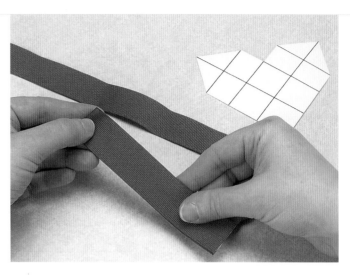

1 Cut Two Ribbon Strips

Copy the heart template below. Cut one 10" (25cm) piece of magenta 1" (25mm) wide ribbon, and one 10" (25cm) piece of blue ribbon. Fold the blue strip in half crosswise.

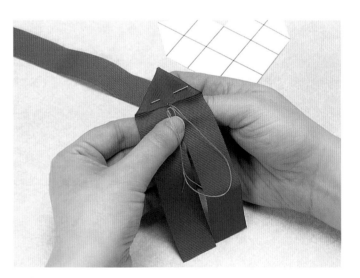

2 Fold the Ribbon Points

Open the ribbon loop, creasing angles at the top to form an inverted V. Finger-press it flat, and pin it into place. Stitch through the point, catching both ribbon tails and the base of the triangle. Repeat steps 1 and 2 with the magenta ribbon.

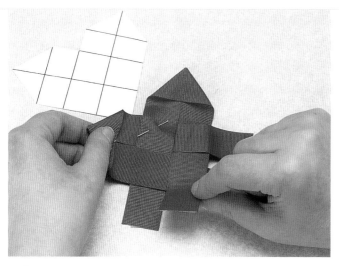

3 | Weave the Ribbon Heart

Weave the two ribbon pairs over, under, under, over, as shown. Hold the woven ribbon against the template to check ribbon positions. Pin the completed weaving.

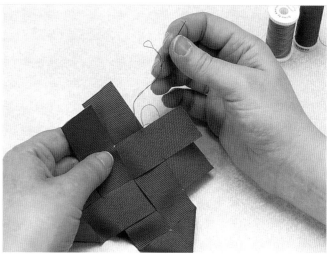

4 | Stitch the Outer Edges of the Weaving

Secure the cross-points of the ribbon to the outer edges by making a few stitches through all layers in matching thread. For clean, knot-free sewing, begin stitching with a thread loop, as shown (see page 144).

5 | Complete the Stitching

Pull the ribbon tails through the thread loop, as shown, then re-thread your needle and continue sewing. Knot the thread on the back of the heart, and trim the thread ends.

6 Sew Down the Ribbon Tails

Fold the ribbon tails onto the wrong side of the heart. Pin them in place, then stitch the edges down. Make sure the stitching does not show on the heart front.

7 Add a Lilac Bow

Tie a bow with 10" (25cm) of 1/4" (7mm) ribbon. Trim and seal the ends. Sew it onto the center of the heart. A few stitches at the knot corners will secure it. Make three more woven-ribbon hearts in the same way.

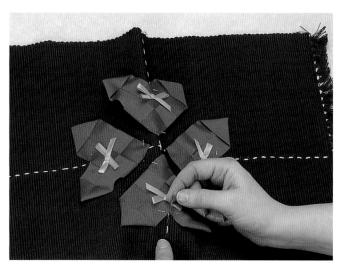

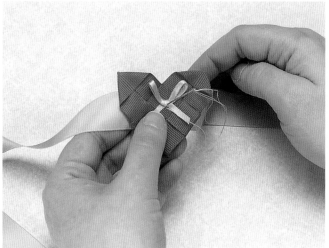

8 Sew the Hearts Onto the Placemat

Mark the vertical and horizontal center of the placemat with two lines of running stitches. Pin the hearts onto the placemat, points facing center. Make sure they are evenly spaced. Stitch the hearts onto the mat. You only need to stitch the hearts at the points and corners.

9 Make a Napkin Ring

For a tie-style napkin ring, make a small woven heart and sew it onto the center of a 22" (56cm) strip of 7/8" (23mm) wide lilac ribbon. To make a small woven heart, use 6" (15cm) each of 5/8" (15mm) wide magenta and blue grosgrain. Sew on a bow using 8" (20cm) of 1/8" (3mm) lilac satin.

10   Attach the Hearts to the Basket

For the basket, make six small woven hearts, as you did for the napkin ring in step 9. Sew a 12" (30cm) piece of ⅛" (3mm) lilac ribbon onto the back of a small woven heart. Knot the ribbon at its midpoint, then stitch through the knot. Thread the ribbon tie through the woven straw of the basket. Repeat for each heart, spacing them apart evenly. Tie bows on the inside of the basket to secure the ties.

You can make an entire coordinated tabletop ensemble using the Amish heart appliqués. Sew them onto napkins, a tablecloth or a table runner. Consider creating festive Christmas ornaments using red and green grosgrain.

Ribbon Embroidered Desk Set

Capture the look of smocking by doing a few simple ribbon

embroidery stitches on corrugated cardboard. This desk set

combines the ease of papercrafting with the elegance of

needlework. The ridges of the corrugated cardboard teamed

with the pre-pierced stitching holes make spacing your

stitching simple. A variety of stitches are used for this project,

so think of it as a ribbon embroidery sampler. This pretty,

pastel desk set would look great in a girl's bedroom.

1 Ink Blotter • *page 190*

Ribbon

- 1 yard (90cm) of $^1/_8$" (3mm) wide cream double-face satin ribbon
- 4 yards (3.8m) of $^1/_8$" (3mm) wide lavender double-face satin ribbon
- 1$^1/_4$ yards (1.1m) of $^1/_8$" (3mm) wide pink double-face satin ribbon
- 2$^3/_8$ yards (2.1m) of $^1/_8$" (3mm) wide turquoise double-face satin ribbon

Supplies

- 13$^1/_4$" x 6" (33.5cm x 15cm) cream corrugated cardboard
- 18" x 13" (46cm x 33.5cm) cream illustration board
- 1 sheet each of pink and turquoise pearlescent cardboard
- 11$^5/_8$" x 15$^1/_2$" (30cm x 39cm) pink blotter paper
- paper edger scissors, clouds pattern
- 1" (2.5cm) diameter flower-shaped hand punch
- craft knife and cutting mat
- tapestry needle
- needle and thread
- craft glue

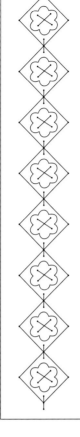

Use this template to make the Ink Blotter. Enlarge 200%.

1 Prepare the Blotter Strips

Using the template provided, cut two strips of cream-colored corrugated cardboard to 13¼" (33.5cm) long, cutting one long edge with paper edgers. On the smooth side of the cardboard, pierce holes along the scalloped edge. Also, pierce the remaining stitch holes as shown on the pattern.

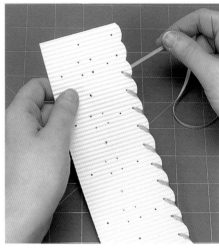

2 Stitch the Scalloped Edge

Thread the tapestry needle with 24" (60cm) of turquoise ribbon and stitch the scalloped edge, spiralling ribbon from the center hole over the scallop. Repeat on the second blotter strip. When finished, apply a dab of craft glue to the end of the ribbon and smooth the ribbon onto the back of the blotter strip.

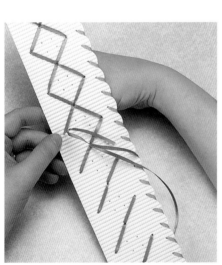

3 Embroider the Lattice Pattern

Thread a tapestry needle with 2 yards (1.9m) of dark lavender ribbon. Work the stitches through the holes in diagonal pairs, going first in one direction, then reversing to complete the diamond lattice. Repeat for the other blotter strip.

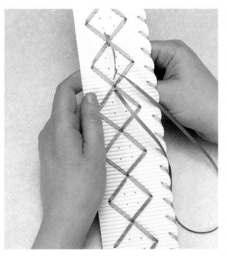

4 Stitch the Lattice Intersections

Thread the needle with 22" (56cm) of pink ribbon. Back stitch over each lattice intersection (see page 146). Repeat on the other blotter strip.

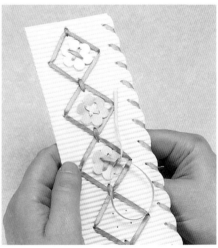

5 Sew on the Flowers

Punch out eight turquoise flowers and eight cream flowers from pearlescent paper. Pierce four centered "buttonholes" in each. Make a cross stitch in each flower, using turquoise ribbon for pink flowers and pink ribbon for turquoise flowers. Glue the ribbon ends onto the back.

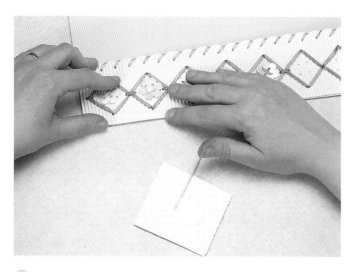

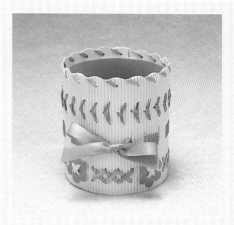

6 Assemble the Blotter

For the blotter backing board, cut a piece of cream-colored illustration board measuring 13" x 18" (33 x 45.5cm). Glue the three straight edges of each blotter strip to the board. Press along the glued edges and weight the blotter with books as it dries. Cut a piece of blotter paper to 11$\frac{1}{2}$" x 15$\frac{1}{2}$" (29 x 39.5cm) and slip it in place.

The finished Ink Blotter stands on its own as a fashionable project, or works well with other pieces in the desk set.

variation **idea**

Why not make a ribbon-embroidered desk set consisting of several pieces? A plastic cylinder, for example, can easily be transformed into a decorative pencil holder by adding the same design elements as the Ink Blotter. The coordinating pieces will look great in any little girl's room.

2 Picture Frame

Ribbon

- 1⁵/₈ yards (1.5m) of ¹/₈" (3mm) wide cream double-face satin ribbon
- 2¹/₂ yards (2.2m) of ¹/₈" (3mm) wide pink double-face satin ribbon
- 1³/₈ yards (1.2m) of ¹/₈" (3mm) wide turquoise double-face satin ribbon

Supplies

- 8" x 10" (20cm x 25cm) sheet of lilac corrugated cardboard
- one sheet of cream pearlescent cardboard
- 19" x 23" (48cm x 58cm) sheet of white illustration board or heavyweight cardboard
- paper edger scissors, clouds pattern
- 1" (2.5cm) diameter flower-shaped hand punch
- craft knife and cutting mat
- tapestry needle
- needle and thread
- craft glue

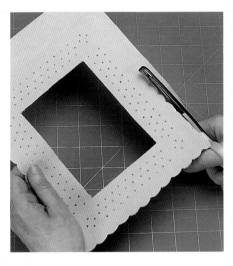

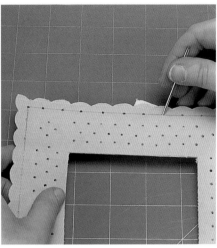

1 Cut Out the Frame and Design

Enlarge template A and copy it onto tracing paper. Tape the pattern onto the smooth side of a piece of corrugated cardboard (on the right side, ridges should run horizontally across the frame). Using a tapestry needle, poke holes at both ends of the marked lines. With a craft knife, cut out the window, and use paper edgers to cut out the frame.

2 Pierce Holes

Using a tapestry needle, pierce holes at the dots and at either end of the marked lines. Also, pierce holes at the scallop mid-point, ³/₈" (1cm) below the scallop peak.

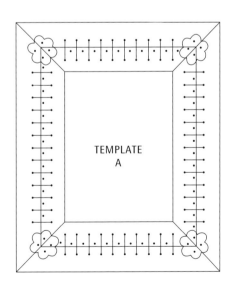

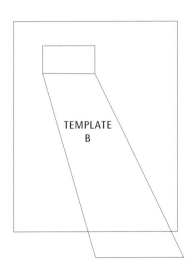

Use template A for the Picture Frame front and surround. Enlarge 200%.

Use template B for the Picture Frame backing piece and strut. Enlarge 200%.

TEMPLATE A

TEMPLATE B

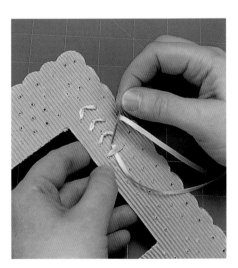

3 Add the Fishbone Embroidery Stitch

Thread a needle with pink ribbon. For each short side of the frame, use 40" (1m), and for each long side, use 48" (1.2m) of ribbon. Starting from a hole near the window cut-out, make a horizontal stitch, left to right. Bring the needle up above the stitch at the center hole. Loop the ribbon under and around the horizontal stitch. Bring the ribbon back down the same center hole. Continue on all four sides of the frame.

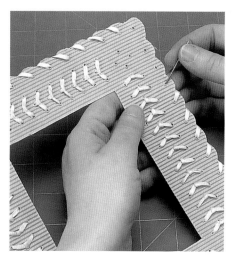

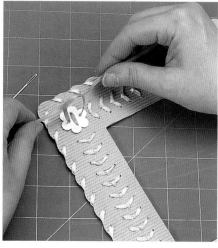

4 Stitch the Frame Edges

Thread the needle with cream ribbon. Stitch around the frame edges, spiralling ribbon from the center hole of each of the scallop valleys. Work in a counterclockwise direction. Glue the ribbon tails down on the wrong side of the frame.

5 Tie on the Corner Bows

Punch four flower shapes from pearlescent cardboard. Pierce four "buttonholes" in each flower, as indicated on the pattern. To sew on each flower, thread a needle with 12" (30cm) of turquoise ribbon. Sew the flower onto the frame, using a diagonal stitch from top right to bottom left of the buttonholes. Sew the ribbon ends through the remaining buttonholes. Tie a bow and secure it with a stitch through the knot with matching sewing thread.

6 Cut Out the Frame Pieces

Enlarge templates A and B and cut out the frame surround, backing piece and strut from cardboard using a craft knife and metal ruler. Score the strut near the top, as marked. Glue the strut top onto the backing piece. Next, apply glue around three edges of the backing piece, leaving the top glue-free so a photo can be inserted. Glue the backing piece onto the frame surround. Glue the corrugated cardboard onto the front of the frame surround, matching the edges. Weight the frame with books as the glue dries.

This photo frame has been designed to fit a snapshot measuring 4" x 6" (10cm x 15cm). Just slip the photo into the slot at the top. The frame can be used in either portrait or landscape direction. Tie the button-bows to face the direction of use.

gifts and keepsakes

S ay the word gift, and what images spring to your mind?

A ribbon-tied box with a magnificent bow. Ribbons and gift-giving go hand in hand because using ribbon is a simple way to add a festive touch to a special gift or treasured keepsake. When you invest time in crafting a gift, you want it to be special and unique.

This section includes ribboncraft ideas for everyone on your gift-giving list. Some of the projects can be produced quickly and in large quantities as party favors, like the Pomander Sachet. Others, such as the Snowflake Holiday Stocking, are more involved keepsake projects that could be displayed for many years to come.

You'll be inspired by the folk art style of the Amish Papercrafts, and brush up on an Early American tradition with the Beaded Penny Rug Purse. Plus, the Rose Garland Makeup Bag will glamourize your beauty accessories with style and simplicity.

Keepsake Sachets

Transform an ordinary handkerchief into a

dainty sachet. Pretty and practical, these fragrant

sachets loop over a doorhandle to scent your bathroom,

bedroom, or linen closet. There are three different

styles to choose from: the Drawstring Purse Sachet,

the Strawberry Sachet, and the Pomander Sachet.

They all have easily-refillable pouches that hold an

abundance of fragrant potpourri.

1 Drawstring Purse Sachet • *page 198*

Ribbon

- ³⁄₈ yard (30cm) of ¹⁄₄" (7mm) wide mint green double-face satin ribbon
- ⁷⁄₈ yard (80cm) of ¹⁄₈" (3mm) wide mint green double-face satin ribbon
- 2¹⁄₈ yards (2m) of ¹⁄₄" (5mm) wide pink polyester gingham ribbon
- 5 red ribbon rosebuds

Supplies

- 10" x 10" (25cm x 25cm) floral-print handkerchief
- 2 clear red plastic beads
- potpourri
- needle and thread
- straight pins
- small safety pin
- fabric glue or liquid seam sealant
- tape measure

SEWING MACHINE REQUIRED

1 Fold and Stitch the Handkerchief

Fold the hankie so the triangular points meet in the center. Pin it in place. Machine stitch around all four sides of the hankie. Sew two parallel lines of stitching, one close to the folded edge and the other ⁵/₈" (1.5cm) from the folded edge.

2 Thread the Drawstrings

Cut two pieces of gingham ribbon, each measuring 22" (58cm) long. Pin a small safety pin to one end of a ribbon. Use the pin to guide the ribbon through the stitched channel and across the gap between two sides. When you have threaded the first ribbon, insert the other ribbon through the remaining two sides of the handkerchief.

3 Pull Up the Gathers

Pull the drawstring ribbons to gather the handkerchief into a pouch.

4 Add Beads and Knot Ribbons

On each side of the pouch, thread both ribbon ends through a tapestry needle, then thread on a bead. Hold all four ends of the drawstring together and knot them about 2¹/₂" (6cm) from the tops of the ribbons. Trim the ribbon ends at an angle and seal them.

5 Add a Bow

Make a bow from 10" (25cm) of ¹/₄" (7mm) mint green ribbon. Pin it in place, and sew it onto the knot. Sew a ribbon rose onto the bow center.

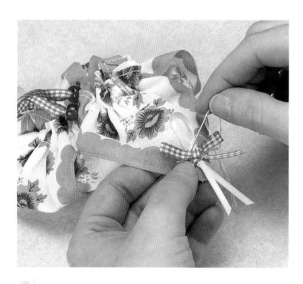

6 Decorate the Handkerchief Points

Cut the ¹/₈" (3mm) mint green ribbon into four 8" (20cm) lengths. Make a fish loop out of each piece and pin one onto each corner (see page 145 for Fish Loop instructions). Cut four 8" (20cm) pieces of gingham ribbon. Tie bows and sew them over the fish loops. Sew purchased rosebuds near the top corners of the handkerchief points.

Fill the pouch with potpourri and hang it on a bedroom door or place it in a lingerie drawer.

2 Strawberry Sachet

Ribbon

- 1 yard (90cm) of ¹/₄" (5mm) wide pink polyester gingham ribbon
- ³/₈ yard (30cm) each of ¹/₈" (3mm) wide double-face satin ribbon in pink, green and white
- 1 red ribbon rose

Supplies

- ¹/₄ yard (30cm) of tulle
- 10" x 10" (25cm x 25cm) floral-print handkerchief (border print works best)
- 2 clear red plastic beads
- potpourri
- paper edger scissors
- pinking shears
- needle and thread
- straight pins
- small safety pin
- fabric glue or liquid seam sealant
- tape measure

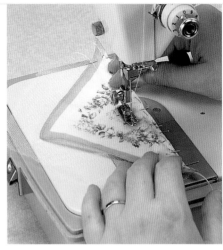

1 Cut and Pin the Pattern

Enlarge the provided templates. Pin the sachet pattern onto a double layer of tulle. Using pinking shears, cut out the tulle. Use the handkerchief point pattern below to cut two opposite corners off the handkerchief. Baste under the seam allowance on the long edge of the hankie and trim off the extending corners. Place the handkerchief corner exactly on top of the pointy end of a tulle piece. Pin it in place.

2 Sew a Drawstring Path

Fold the corners of the tulle and handkerchief to the front and pin down. Machine-stitch a drawstring path across the top. Stitch two parallel lines, one close to the edge, the other with a ⁵/₈" (1.5cm) seam allowance. Stitch only on the handkerchief area—stitching should not extend onto the tulle. Repeat for the other piece of the sachet.

3 Finish the Thread Ends

Thread a needle with the thread ends on the top side of the sachet. Bring the ends to the wrong side. Knot, then trim the thread.

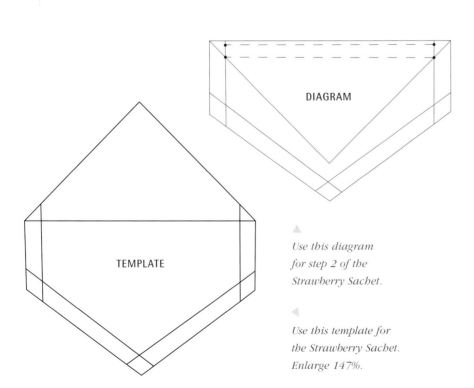

DIAGRAM

TEMPLATE

Use this diagram for step 2 of the Strawberry Sachet.

Use this template for the Strawberry Sachet. Enlarge 147%.

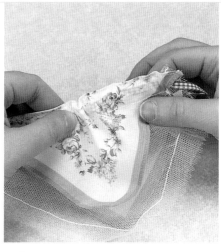

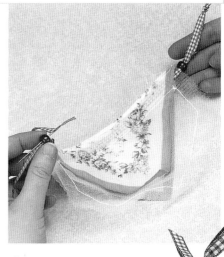

4 Stitch the Sachet

With the wrong sides together and edges even, stitch the sachet front to back. Use a ⅝" (1.5cm) seam allowance. Be sure to begin the stitching below the drawstring path.

5 Thread the Ribbon

Cut the pink gingham ribbon into two 18" (45cm) pieces. Fasten a safety pin to one end of the ribbon, then use it to guide the ribbon through the handkerchief. Repeat on the other side.

6 Thread on the Beads

On each side of the sachet, add a bead, then knot the ribbon ends together. Trim the ends at an angle, then seal them (see page 143).

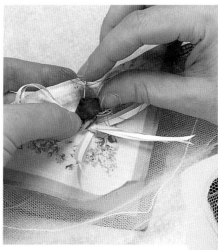

7 Make a Triple Bow

Cut three 10" (25cm) pieces of ⅛" (3mm) wide ribbon in white, pink and green. Tie a bow, treating all three strands as a single thickness. Fluff the bow.

8 Sew on the Bow

Stitch the bow onto the center top of the sachet. Sew a ribbon rose over the knot.

Fill the sachet with pot-pourri. To make a more economical Strawberry Sachet, use only tulle.

3 Pomander Sachet

Ribbon

- ³/₈ yard (30cm) of ⁵/₈" (15mm) wide cream double-face satin ribbon
- 15" (50cm) of ³/₈" (9mm) wide lilac double-face satin ribbon
- 18" (40cm) of ¹/₄" (7mm) wide lilac double-face satin ribbon
- 1¹/₄ yards (1.1m) of ³/₁₆" (5mm) wide pink feather-edge, double-face satin ribbon
- ³/₈ yard (30cm) of ¹/₈" (3mm) wide pink double-face satin ribbon

Supplies

- ³/₈ yard (30cm) of tulle
- potpourri
- paper edger scissors
- needle and thread
- straight pins
- craft glue

1 Pin Ribbons Onto the Net

Enlarge the template and cover it with tulle. Cut three 7" (18cm) strips of ³/₁₆" (5mm) wide pink feather-edge ribbon. With matching thread, sew the ribbons onto the tulle at the intersecting point and at the end of every piece. Cut out the tulle using paper edgers.

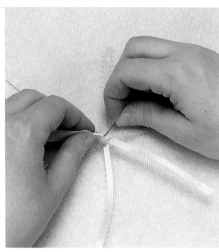

2 Attach the Hanging Loop

Cut a 20" (50cm) piece of ³/₈" (9mm) wide lavender ribbon for the handle. Fold it in half and knot the ends to make a loop. Sew the knot onto the inside center (on the wrong side) of the tulle circle.

3 Sew on the Ribbon Tails

Cut two 15" (38cm) pieces of ¹/₄" (7mm) wide lavender ribbon for the streamers. Put one piece of ribbon on top of the other. Sew the streamers, at their midpoints, onto the outside center of the net circle.

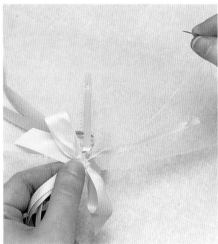

4 Add a Bow

Make a bow from 10" (25cm) of ⁵/₈" (15mm) wide cream satin ribbon. Sew it onto the folded ribbon tails.

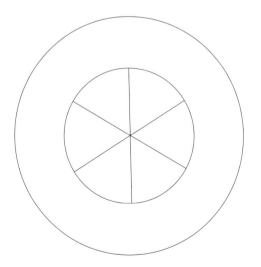

Use this template to make the Pomander Sachet. Enlarge 200%, then 125%.

5 Begin the Drawstring Stitch

Add a running stitch around the "inner circle" of the tulle (stitch just outside the feather-edge ribbon ends). Center the potpourri on the tulle circle. Gently pull up the running stitch thread to gather the tulle, and tie the pouch.

6 Conceal the Gathering With a Bow

Wrap a 12" (30cm) piece of ³/₈" (8mm) wide pink ribbon around the neck of the pouch. Tie the ends into a bow.

Hang this Pomander Sachet from a bedroom door. You may also reduce the template and make a smaller version for a drawer pull.

Snowflake Holiday Stocking

This stocking features an easy-stitch version of net embroidery, the needlecraft in which delicate stitchery is worked on openwork mesh fabric. Because the tulle is backed with felt, the mechanics of your needlework are kept hidden (where they belong). The border stitch, a streamlined version of the closed buttonhole stitch, saves time, too! The embroidery requires a fair amount of ribbon, but your investment will surely pay off.

Ribbon

- ⁵/₈ yard (50cm) of ⁵/₈" (15mm) wide red double-face satin ribbon
- ¹/₂ yard (40cm) of 1¹/₂" (4cm) wide plaid ribbon
- 20 yards (20m) of ¹/₈" (3mm) wide white double-face satin ribbon

Supplies

- ³/₈ yard (30cm) of machine-washable red felt
- ³/₈ yard (30cm) of white tulle or net
- eighteen ¹/₄" (7mm) diameter frosted white glass beads
- ¹/₁₆" (1.6mm) circle hand punch
- chenille needle and tapestry needle
- needle and thread
- straight pins
- black fabric marker
- fabric glue or liquid seam sealant
- tracing paper

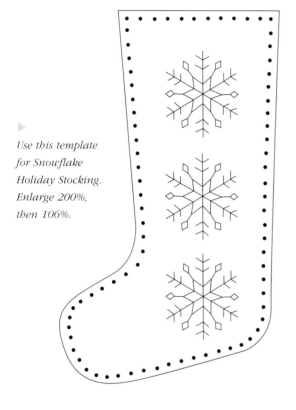

▶ *Use this template for Snowflake Holiday Stocking. Enlarge 200%, then 106%.*

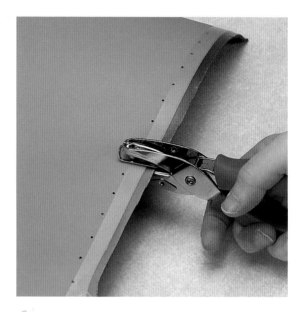

1 Cut the Stocking Out From Felt

Enlarge the stocking pattern to the left. Make a stocking template in heavyweight paper, with dots marked around the edge. Tape the pattern onto red felt, and cut it out roughly. Punch holes at the dots with a $^1/_{16}$" (1.6mm) circle punch. Cut the stocking shape out of felt. Cut out another felt stocking in the same way (for the stocking back).

2 Mark the Snowflakes on the Tulle

From the stocking pattern, make a tracing paper pattern with the snowflake outlined. Cut a piece of tulle to fit over the tracing. Tape or pin the pattern under the tulle. Outline the snowflakes on the tulle with a black fabric marker. Use a ruler to keep lines straight.

3 Embroider the Snowflake Spokes

Lay the tulle over the felt stocking. Baste around the edges and trim the excess tulle. Thread an embroidery needle with $^1/_8$" (3mm) wide white satin ribbon. Back stitch (see page 146) the snowflake spokes. Make sure your stitching conceals the black outlines, and that the ribbon does not twist. Each snowflake requires about $3^3/_4$ yards (3.5m) of ribbon.

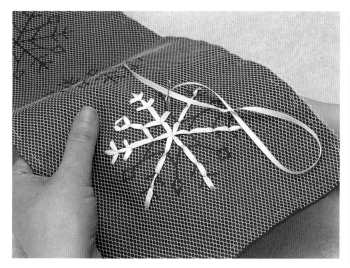

4 Stitch the Snowflake Details

After the spokes are completed, back stitch the details. Work around each snowflake, one spoke at a time. When stitching is finished, knot and trim the ribbon ends on the wrong side.

tip *When embroidering with ribbon, it is crucial to make sure that the ribbon lies flat. Smooth out any twists before moving on to the next stitch.*

5 Sew on the Beads

Stitch on a bead just above the tip of each diamond-top spoke (alternate spokes). Using doubled sewing thread, take several stitches through each bead and knot on the wrong side.

6 Outline the Back

Thread a tapestry needle with ribbon, and with the stocking toe pointing left, stitch the top edge of the back piece. To begin stitching, take a diagonal stitch from the upper lefthand corner down into the righthand hole. Bring the stitch up in the lefthand loop.

Continue by bringing the ribbon down the lower righthand hole again. Pass the ribbon through the loop, then repeat the cycle across the top edge of the stocking, keeping an even tension.

7 Stitch the Stocking Front to Back

With ribbon, stitch across the top edge of the stocking front, same as for the stocking back (steps 6 and 7), but with stocking toe pointing right. Next join the stocking front to back. Place stocking front on top of the stocking back, with wrong sides together and edges even. Align the holes and stitch all around the stocking, through both layers of felt. Knot the ribbon ends and poke them inside the stocking.

8 Sew on a Hanging Loop

Cut a piece of ⅝" (15mm) wide red satin ribbon measuring 14" (35cm). Pin a diagonal fish loop in the lefthand corner of the stocking. Sew the loop where the ribbon intersects, stitching through all of the layers of ribbon and stocking. Trim the ribbon ends diagonally and seal with craft glue.

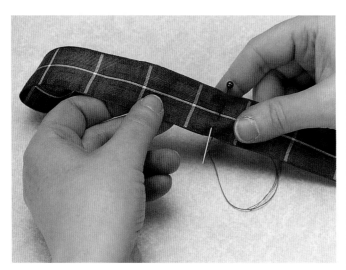

9 Begin the Bow With a Loop

Cut an 18" (45cm) piece of plaid ribbon. Fold it in half to make a loop. Pin the ribbon together 6" (15cm) below the fold. Back stitch across the width of the ribbon through both layers and remove the pin.

10 Gather the Bow Center

Open the loop and flatten it out with the seam centered. Thread a needle with doubled sewing thread. Take three small stitches—under, over, under—then pull the stitches tightly to gather the ribbon. Knot the thread on the wrong side.

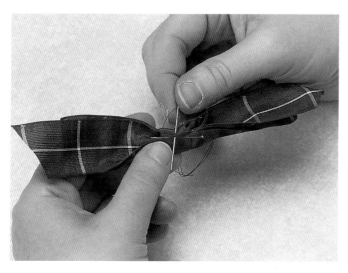

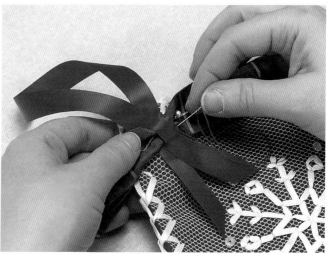

11 Add a Loop Around the Center

Cut a 6" (15cm) piece of red ribbon. Wrap it tightly around the bow center, folding the end under on the wrong side. Stitch the seam. Trim the bow ends diagonally and seal them with craft glue.

12 Sew the Bow Onto the Hanging Loop

Pin the bow onto the hanging loop, concealing the loop's cross points. Sew the bow to the stocking, stitching at the corners of the center loop.

Make a stocking for every family member, and hang them on the mantle for a one-of-a-kind holiday decoration.

Amish Papercrafts

Amish patchwork, prized for its combination of

vibrant, contrasting colors and bold geometric designs,

is the folk art inspiration for this project. The bookmark

provides a simple introduction to ribbon weaving,

along with an opportunity to play with fun papercraft

tools. The notecard features a jumbo version of the

friendship heart motif, and surrounds it with a

hand-stitched, ribbon-laced border.

1 Amish Heart Bookmark • *page 212*

Ribbon

- $^5/_8$ yard (60cm) each of $^1/_4$" (7mm) wide single-face satin ribbon in red and purple
- $^5/_8$ yard (50cm) of $^3/_8$" (9mm) wide double-face satin red ribbon

Supplies

- 1 sheet of black cardstock
- 1 sheet each of red and purple paper
- $^1/_2$" (12mm) heart-shaped paper punch
- $^1/_8$" (3mm) circle hand punch
- craft knife and cutting mat
- needle and thread
- craft glue
- glue stick
- masking tape
- rounded corner edgers (optional)

Use this template for the Amish Heart Bookmark. Enlarge 200%.

1 Trace and Cut Out the Bookmark

Enlarge the template to the left, and trace the pattern. Cut out a piece of black cardstock measuring 8" x 2¹⁄₂" (20cm x 6cm). Tape the tracing over the black card and impress the pattern outlines with a dry fine-point pen. Cut out the three windows with a craft knife and ruler. Round off the top corners with corner edgers. Punch a ¹⁄₈" (3mm) hole at the top center of the bookmark.

2 Add the Paper Cut-Outs

Punch out two purple hearts and one red heart from the red and purple paper. Using the bookmark tracing, mark and then cut out three ⁷⁄₈" (23mm) diameter red semi-circles and three purple ones. Apply a glue stick to the wrong side of each cut-out and smooth the cut-outs in place over the impressed pattern outline.

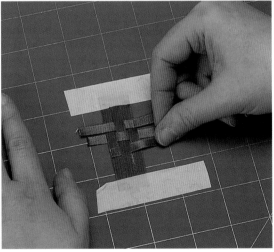

3 Weave the Ribbon

For the woven center, cut six 2¹⁄₂" (6.5cm) strips of ¹⁄₄" (7mm) wide ribbon, three red strips and three purple. Tape three vertical red strips directly onto the cutting mat. Position the strips face (shiny side) down, side-by-side, with no gaps. Weave the purple ribbons horizontally through the red ribbon. Apply overlapped strips of clear tape to cover and reinforce the weaving, then cut off the masking tape with scissors. Make three woven centers in this way.

4 Add the Weaving

Position each of the three weavings behind its window, sticky tape side down, and glue it in place. Make sure each weaving fits behind its window squarely. Cut out a backing to exactly match the front of the bookmark and glue it to the wrong side of the bookmark. Punch a top hole in the backing, in the same position as the bookmark front.

5 Loop a Ribbon Tail

Cut a 10" (25cm) piece of ³/₈" (9mm) wide red ribbon for the top tail. Fold the ribbon strip in half, push the loop through the punched hole from front to back. Next, thread the tails through the loop and pull tight to make a "half-hitch" knot. Cut angled edges at the ends of the ribbon. Seal the ribbon edges.

tip When making papercrafts with ribbon, buy your ribbon first, then match paper colors to the ribbon. Staple ribbon swatches onto a piece of neutral-colored paper for at-a-glance shopping convenience.

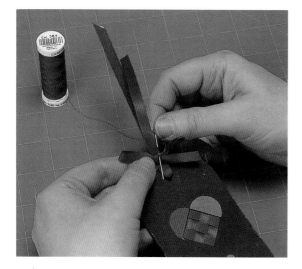

6 Add a Final Bow

Cut a 10" (25cm) piece of ³/₈" (9mm) wide red satin ribbon. Tie it into a bow, adjust the loops to equal size, then trim and seal the bow ends. Sew a few stitches at the top and bottom of the bow knot to attach the bow to the ribbon tail.

The bright and bold colors on this Amish patchwork heart make a stunning bookmark that you could give as a gift, along with a favorite book, to your family or friends.

2 Amish Heart Notecard

Ribbon

- ½ yard (40cm) each of ⅝" (15mm) wide single-face satin ribbon in red and purple
- 2 yards (1.7m) of ⅛" (3mm) wide red double-face satin ribbon
- ⅛ yard (20cm) of ⅛" (3mm) wide lilac double-face satin ribbon

Supplies

- 2 sheets of lilac parchment-look cardstock
- 1 sheet each of red and purple paper
- 1" (2.5cm) heart-shaped paper punch
- ⅛" (3mm) circle hand punch
- craft knife and cutting mat
- tapestry needle
- needle and thread
- craft glue
- glue stick
- rounded corner edgers (optional)

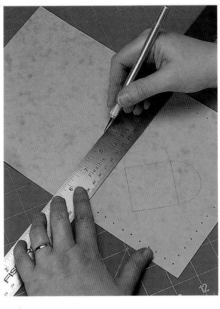

1 Transfer the Template

Enlarge the notecard pattern for the card front given below and trace the pattern. Tape the tracing over lilac cardstock, and impress the pattern outlines with a dry fine-point pen. Use a ruler for the straight lines. Lightly score the center fold of the card, using a craft knife against the ruler.

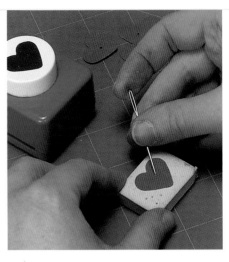

2 Cut Out the Paper Buttons

The heart-shaped buttons must be sturdy, so use a glue stick to mount a small piece of the purple paper onto a piece of the thicker lilac parchment paper. Punch out four hearts. Pierce a center hole in each heart using a tapestry needle.

Use this template for the Amish Heart Notecard. Enlarge 200%, then 125%.

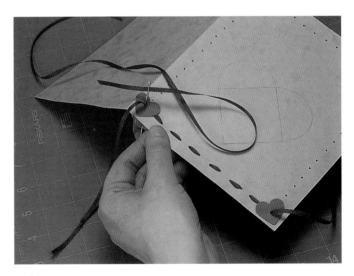

3 Lace the Ribbon Border

Pierce holes as marked along the front edges of the card using a tapestry needle, as in the previous step. Cut two 16" (40cm) pieces of red double-face satin ribbon for the top and bottom edges of the card, and two 18" (45cm) pieces of ⅛" (3mm) wide red double-face satin ribbon for the sides of the card. Thread a tapestry needle with a piece of ribbon. Starting at a corner hole, thread on a heart button and sew a running stitch, bringing the needle under and over to complete each side. Thread on a button at each corner. The ribbon tails at each corner should be equal in length. Tie, seal and secure the bows at each corner.

4 Weave the Center Square

Cut out the window opening, and then cut out and glue the paper semi-circles in place to create the heart shape. Weave the center square, using the technique described in step 3 of the bookmark project on page 212. For the woven square, you need four 4" (10cm) strips each of ⁵⁄₈" (15mm) wide red and purple ribbon.

5 Glue the Weaving and the Backing

Position the ribbon weaving behind the window and glue it in place, as for the bookmark in step 4, page 213. For a clean finish, cut a piece of lilac cardstock as a backing. Glue it over the back of the card front. You only need to glue around the edges of the backing card.

tip You are investing your precious free time in making ribbon papercrafts, so be sure to purchase acid-free, archival-quality papers and adhesives from craft or scrapbooking retailers. Remember to also inscribe the card using archival-quality inks.

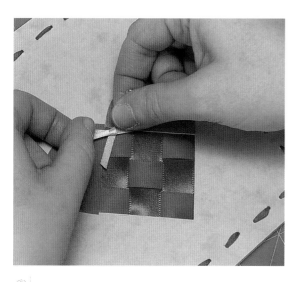

6 Add a Contrasting Bow

Tie a bow using 8" (20cm) of pale lilac ribbon. Glue it onto the center top of the heart, using a dab of craft glue.

Apply this Amish patchwork heart to other paper gifts to show friends and family just how much you care.

Beaded Penny Rug Purse

This purse gives a pleasant update to a traditional

early-American needlecraft, the art of making

penny rugs. Concentric circles of felted wool, recycled

from old clothes, were blanket stitched onto background

fabric, and coins were used as circle templates.

Penny rugs were most often used as table coverings,

so their name is a bit misleading (penny mats

would be more accurate).

Ribbon

- 1⅝ yards (1.5m) of ⅛" (31mm) wide blue double-face satin ribbon
- ¾ yard (60cm) of ⅛" (3mm) wide forest green double-face satin ribbon
- ⅜ yard (30cm) of green rat-tail cord
- 1⅛ yards (1m) of gold rat-tail cord
- 6½ yards (6m) of ⅛" (3mm) wide golden yellow double-face satin ribbon

Supplies

- one 9"x12" (23 x 30cm) sheet of felt in each of the following colors: Cashmere Tan, Royal Blue and White (I used Kunin Rainbow Classic Felt)
- one package each of ¼" (5mm) frosted glass beads in golden yellow, royal blue and turquoise
- ¹⁄₁₆" (1.6mm) circle hand punch
- tapestry needle and chenille needle
- needle and thread
- straight pins
- craft glue or liquid seam sealant
- tape measure

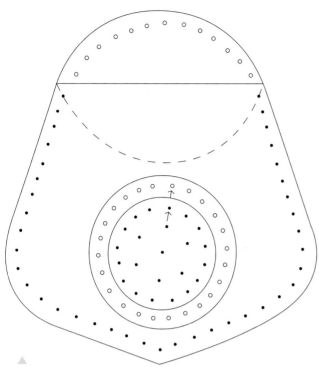

*Use this template to make the
Beaded Penny Rug Purse.
Enlarge 200%.*

1 Transfer the Template to the Felt

Transfer the pattern templates (purse front, purse back/flap, large circle and small circle) onto heavyweight paper. Tape the templates onto felt and cut them out in the colors shown. Punch holes in the felt with either a tapestry needle or the hand punch. Draw an arrow on each circle to mark your start position; you will then know when you have punched all the way around.

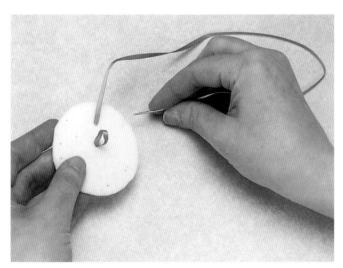

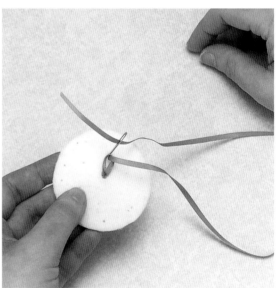

2 Begin Making a Lazy Daisy

The flower is made with a circle of ribbon-loop chain stitches. Thread a tapestry needle with 24" (60cm) of ¹⁄₈" (3mm) wide golden yellow ribbon. Bring the needle up at the circle center, make a loop, and bring the needle back down through the center hole. Bring the needle up at the hole directly above the loop.

3 Complete the Petal

Pass the ribbon through the loop, then bring it back down the hole it last emerged from.

4 Finish the Daisy with a Center Bead

Work six petals to complete the daisy. Knot the ribbon on the wrong side and trim. Bring a new piece of ribbon through the center hole. Thread on a blue bead. Bring the ribbon back down and knot on the wrong side.

5 Start the Beaded Blanket Stitch

Center the white felt circle on the tan and baste in place. Thread a chenille needle with 24" (60cm) of green ribbon. Bring the needle up at any hole on the white circle. Thread on three turquoise beads. Bring the needle down through the next hole to the left. Bring the needle up, through both thicknesses of felt and through the lefthand side of the loop. Continue until the circle is fully beaded. Bring the needle through the last loop and knot the ribbon ends on the back.

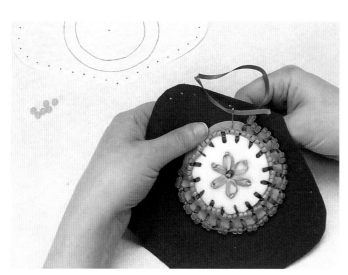

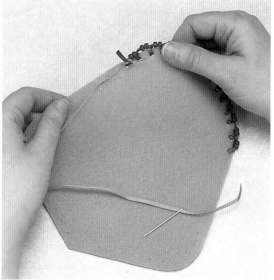

6 Bead the Front of the Purse

Center the two circles on the purse front and baste in place. Thread a chenille needle with 34" (86cm) of blue ribbon. Work the beaded blanket stitch all around the tan circle, this time threading only two gold beads on each blanket stitch (see page 147 for Beaded Blanket Stitch instructions).

7 Stitch the Purse Flap

Thread a tapestry needle with 24" (60cm) of blue ribbon. Work a beaded blanket stitch only on the top portion of the purse back piece—this is the flap of the purse. Add two blue beads per stitch. Leave 2" (5cm) ribbon tails on each side of the stitching.

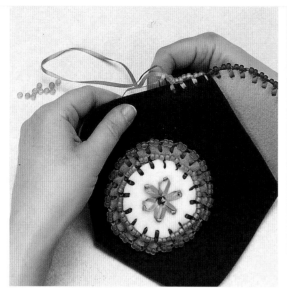

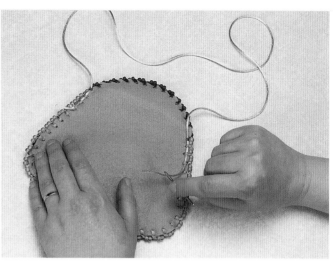

8 Stitch the Purse Front to Back

Cut a 64" (1.6m) piece of golden yellow ribbon. Knot it onto the blue ribbon and trim the ribbon ends. The side with the knot is now the inside of the purse. With holes aligned, join the purse front to back using a beaded blanket stitch, two turquoise beads per stitch. Make sure the knot falls inside the purse when you finish stitching.

9 Add the Shoulder Strap

Cut 38" (96cm) of silky gold cord. Seal the cord ends. Thread a tapestry needle with the cord. On the purse back, thread the cord through four stitch loops, then knot the cord end. Repeat for the other side.

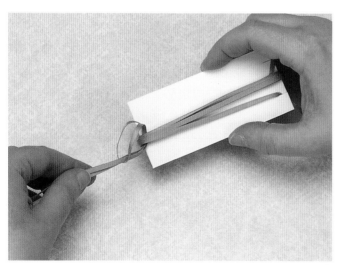

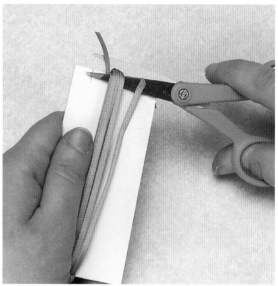

10 Make the Tassel

Cut a piece of cardboard measuring 4" x 2" (10cm x 5cm). Cut two slits in one short end. Cut 140" (3.6m) of gold ribbon. Insert the ribbon end in the slit. Wrap the ribbon around the length of the card sixteen times, then insert the free end in the other slit. Cut a 10" (25cm) piece of ribbon. Loop it through the gold ribbon at the top of the card (opposite of the slits) and tie it tightly.

11 Cut the Tassel

Cut across the bottom edge of the card to release the ribbon.

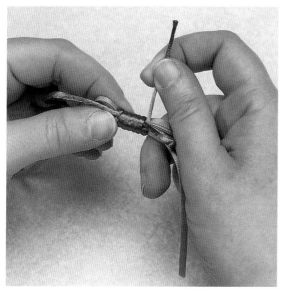

12 Wrap the Tassel Top

Secure the tassel by stitching through it with matching sewing thread. Knot the thread ends. Cut 10" (25cm) of green rat-tail cord. Next, wrap the tassel top. First, loop the cord, then hold the loop in place on the tassel, loop downward.

13 Attach the Tassel to the Purse

Wrap the cord around the tassel top downward. When you reach the bottom, thread the cord through the loop. Trim the cord so only about ³/₄" (2cm) extends. Slowly tug on the cord at the tassel top to conceal the tail. Tie the tassel onto the loop at the bottom point of the purse back. Trim the ribbon close to the knot and seal the ribbon ends with glue.

variation idea

Try this as an alternative to the beaded purse. You'll need 2¹/₂ yards (2.3m) of narrow ¹/₈" (3mm) wide ribbon for the blanket stitching around the outside edges, and twice as much ribbon for the double tassels. Use a jumbo bead to hold the flap shut.

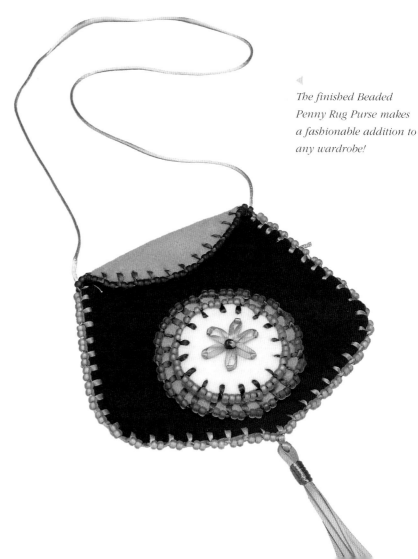

The finished Beaded Penny Rug Purse makes a fashionable addition to any wardrobe!

Rose Garland Makeup Bag

✳

Roses are just about the easiest ribbon flowers you

can make. Their simplicity does not make them any less

impressive, though. If you can sew a ribbon loop, then

you are well on your way to making these delightful

blooms. Using a sewing machine speeds things up, but

you can make them entirely by hand if you choose.

This duffel-style makeup pouch is pretty and practical,

with a vinyl lining to protect against spills.

Ribbon

- ³/₄ yard (60cm) of ⁷/₈" (23mm) wide apricot double-face satin ribbon
- ¹/₄ yard (20cm) of ⁵/₈" (15mm) wide apricot double-face satin ribbon
- ³/₄ yard (60cm) of ⁷/₈" (23mm) wide lilac double-face satin ribbon
- 1³/₈ yards (1.2m) of ⁵/₈" (15mm) wide lilac double-face satin ribbon
- ⁷/₈ yard (80cm) of ¹/₄" (7mm) wide mint green double-face satin ribbon
- 1³/₈ yards (1.2m) of ³/₈" (9mm) wide mint green double-face satin ribbon

Supplies

- ¹/₂ yard (40cm) of cream satin fabric
- ³/₈ yard (30cm) of frosted or clear vinyl
- 10 pearl beads
- 2 cream plastic hairbeads
- needle and thread
- straight pins
- fabric glue or liquid seam sealant
- tape measure

SEWING MACHINE REQUIRED

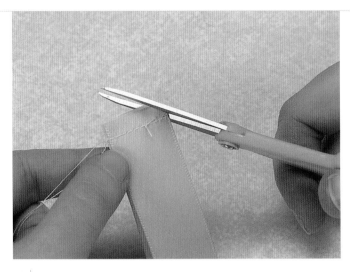

1 | Begin the Rose

Cut a 6" (15cm) length of $^7/_8$" (23mm) wide apricot or lilac ribbon. Seal the ribbon ends with craft glue. Stitch the short ends together to form a loop, using a $^1/_4$" (7mm) seam allowance. You can sew the seam either by hand or machine. Knot the thread ends and sew in the tails with a sewing needle. Trim the bottom of the seam diagonally. Seal the newly cut edges.

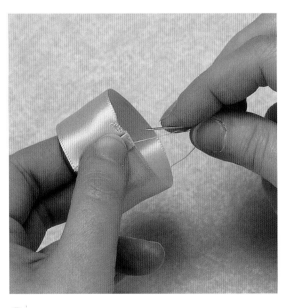

2 | Stitch the Seam Allowance

Finger-press the seam open. Stitch the top edges of the seam allowances to the ribbon loop, so they lie flat.

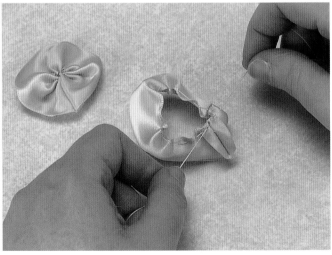

3 | Gather the Top of the Loop

Using doubled sewing thread, hand-sew a running stitch around the top of the loop. Use fairly large stitches. Begin and end at the loop seam. Gently pull up the gathers and knot the thread. For the makeup bag bottom border, make four apricot and four lilac roses.

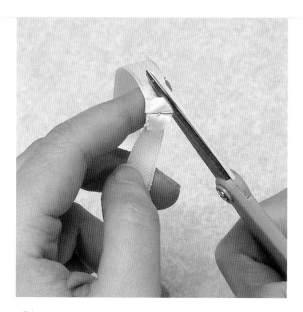

4 Begin the Double-Leaf

The double-leaf begins with a ribbon loop, just like the rose.
Cut a 6" (15cm) strip of ³/₈" (9mm) wide mint green ribbon.
Follow steps 1 and 2 for making the leaf loop. Finger-press the
leaf loop flat, so the seam falls at the loop's midpoint. Baste
the long edges of the loop together on one side of the flattened
loop—the side where the seam allowances are stitched down.

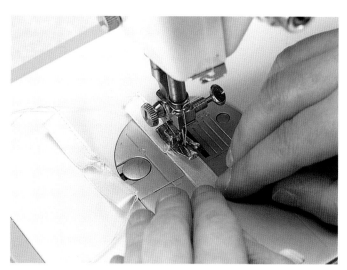

5 Sew the Long Edges

Seam the loop together, stitching very close to the edge. You can do this
by machine or hand. Knot the thread ends, but do not cut them off.

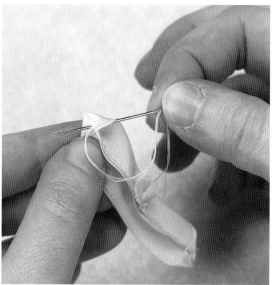

6 Turn the Leaf Tips to the Right Side

Spread open the seam and turn the ends to the right side.
Use a needle to pick out a nice crisp point. On the wrong side
of the leaves, thread a needle with thread ends. Sew the ribbon
onto the seam at either end.

7 Gather the Center of the Double-Leaf

Thread a needle with doubled sewing thread. Take three stitches across the center of the double-leaf—under, over, under, as shown.

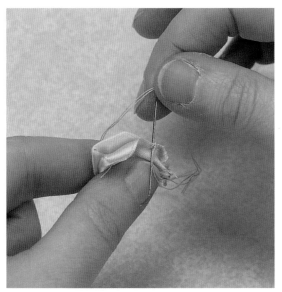

8 Stitch the Leaves Together

Pull up the gathers, then knot them on the wrong side of the double-leaf. Do not cut the thread. With right sides together, fold the leaves in half. Thread a needle with doubled thread and make several stitches through the folded edges of both layers, stitching upward from the leaf center.

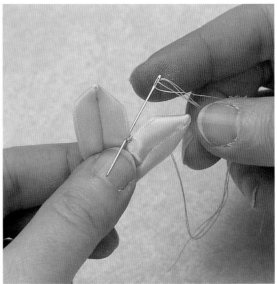

9 Open the Double-Leaf

Unfold the double-leaf. On the right side, make several stitches at the top end of the seam. Knot the thread on the back and cut it off. Make a total of eight leaves in this way.

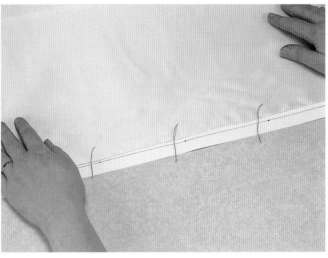

10 Cut Out the Base of the Bag

From the satin, cut out a circular bag base 6¹/₂" (17cm) in diameter. From the vinyl, cut out another circle the same size. Pin the vinyl circle to the matte side of the satin with edges matching. Baste around the edges of the vinyl, through both layers. Make tailor's tacks (see page 144) at the 12, 3, 6, and 9 o'clock positions on the circular bag base, ⁵/₈" (1.5cm) from the edge. These will correspond with the body of the bag.

11 Measure and Cut the Body of the Bag

Cut a 15" x 18¹/₂" (39cm x 47cm) piece of satin. Then cut a 11" x 18¹/₂" (28cm x 47cm) rectangle of vinyl. Mark a ⁵/₈" (1.5cm) seam allowance all around the body of the bag, then space tailor's tacks at 4¹/₄" (11cm) intervals along the bottom seam allowance. The tailor's tacks divide the base of the bag into quarters, not including the side seam allowances.

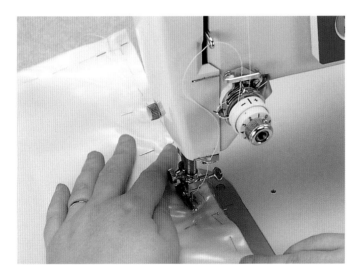

12 Sew the Bag

With the matte sides of the satin facing each other, pin the short sides of the bag rectangle together. Notice that the satin extends above the vinyl. Stitch a seam, with a ⁵/₈" (1.5cm) allowance. This forms the tube that is the body of the makeup bag. Turn the bag to the right side.

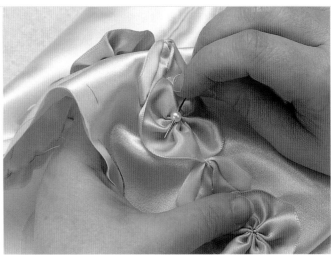

13 | Create a Finished Top Edge

Turn under the top edge of bag ⁵/₈" (1.5cm). Spread open and flatten the seam allowance of the bag side seam before you turn the top edge under. Baste down the folded edge. Fold the top of the bag body under 3¹/₂" (9cm), along the edge of the vinyl lining. Baste down the bottom edge of the turning, then machine-stitch it close to the edge. You now have a tube with a finished top edge.

14 | Add the Roses

Pin the flower garland 1¹/₂" (4cm) above the bag base. Start with a flower centered at the back seam. Alternate apricot and lilac flowers, with double-leaves in between. There are eight flowers and eight double-leaves in total. Sew a pearl bead to the center of each flower, catching in all layers (rose and bag). Stitch the flower garland down using matching sewing thread. Sew on the leaves at the leaf tips and center, and the flowers at opposite sides. To finish the body of the bag, turn the bag inside out and stitch all around the base ¹/₂" (12mm) from the edge. Cut the fabric close to the stitching at regularly-spaced intervals. With the right sides together, pin the bag base to the bag body, matching tailor's tacks. Baste in place, then stitch the bag base to the body using a ⁵/₈" (1.5cm) seam allowance.

15 | Add the Drawstring Loops

Cut four 6" (15cm) pieces of ¹/₄" (7mm) wide mint green satin ribbon. Fold the ribbon in half and knot 1" (2.5cm) below the loop. Trim the angled tails 1" (2.5cm) below the knot. Seal the ribbon ends. Repeat for the three remaining ribbon pieces. Hand-sew four equally spaced drawstring loops onto the right side of the makeup bag, along the horizontal stitching line around the bag. Place the first loop at the back seam. Sew on each loop through the knot.

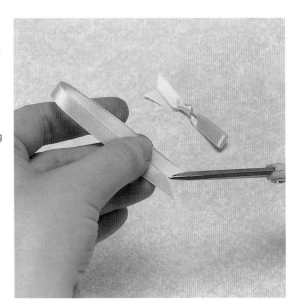

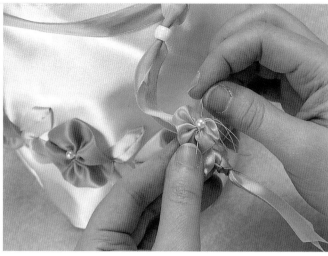

16 Add the Drawstring

Cut two 24" (60cm) pieces of lilac ribbon for the drawstring. Angle and seal the ends. Thread the ribbon through the carriers, one piece on each side of the bag. Thread on a bead at both sides of the drawstring, over the doubled ribbons. Knot each side of the drawstring about 2" (5cm) from the end. Make two mini-roses and double-leaves. Sew a rose and leaf onto each side of the drawstring, near the knot. Each mini-rose requires 4" (10cm) of ⁵⁄₈" (15mm) wide ribbon. (Take a ¹⁄₄" [7mm] seam when making the loops.)

variation idea

Once you start making rose garlands, it is difficult to stop. Why not make an entire bedroom ensemble? Pillowcases, sheets, nightgowns, slippers—almost anything can be decorated. The roses look especially delicate when you make them in graduated sizes. Simply vary the width of the ribbon and the length of the strips. You can also sew on the garlands in curved or circular arrangements.

Fill this elegant bag with your favorite cosmetics, or give it as a gift for someone special.

[s e c t i o n   t h r e e]

wedding and baby

*W*eddings and births are the two

happiest events of a lifetime…

and what better way to celebrate than with ribboncraft projects? Handmade wedding accessories have more

character than their mass-produced counterparts. You have taken the time to create unique mementos, and both

the time spent crafting and the objects themselves will be valued by the bride and groom.

The wedding projects in this section share a rose trellis theme. Ribbon roses, both purchased and handmade,

pearl beads, sheer ribbons and brocades all contribute to the opulent total effect. There are projects for the bride,

the ceremony, the reception and for preserving cherished memories. Projects include a ring bearer's pillow, a basket

for confetti, and memory boxes that resemble a tiered wedding cake.

The birth of a baby is another milestone, and a heartfelt way to celebrate

the miraculous occasion is to welcome the new arrival. A ribbon-trimmed baby

blanket is a quick makeover for a store bought fleece blanket. The nursery mobile

made out of an embroidery hoop, ribbons and pearlescent cardboard will

fascinate and delight the baby.

Ribboncraft is not only a way to embellish ordinary days. It is also a fabulous

way to mark special occasions. You will enjoy creating these projects and cele-

brating life's wonderful moments!

Projects

Wedding Cake Memory Boxes

A wedding is the event of a lifetime. Cherished wedding memorabilia merits a very special home of its own. These tiered "wedding cake" boxes store treasured wedding keepsakes in style. The biggest boxes are spacious enough to hold items such as the bridal veil, while the smaller containers are just right for snapshots, cards and other keepsakes. Organize these precious memories by writing the contents of each box on the heart-shaped index tags.

Ribbon

- $2^5/_8$ yards (4cm) of $1^1/_2$" (39mm) wide lilac double-face lilac satin ribbon
- $1^3/_8$ yards (1.2m) of $1/_8$" (3mm) wide lilac satin ribbon
- $5/_8$ yard (50cm) of $1/_8$" (3mm) wide moss green satin ribbon
- 8 yards (7.2m) of $1/_8$" (3mm) wide white satin ribbon
- $1^3/_8$ yards (1.2m) of $5/_8$" (15mm) wide white sheer-stripe ribbon
- $1^3/_8$ yards (1.2m) of $1/_8$" (3mm) wide lilac satin ribbon
- $1/_2$ yard (50cm) of $5/_8$" (15mm) wide lilac double-face satin ribbon
- $3/_8$ yard (30cm) of 1" (25mm) wide bridal white sheer stripe ribbon
- $3/_8$ yard (30cm) of 1" (25mm) wide bridal white satin ribbon
- 55 lilac satin rosebuds

Supplies

- 4 round pâpier-mâché boxes, in graduated sizes in the following diameters: 10" (25cm), 8" (20cm), $5^1/_4$" (13cm) and 4" (10cm)
- lilac cardstock
- off-white handmade paper giftwrap
- $4^1/_2$ yards (4.2m) of pearl beading
- 1 pack of $3/_{16}$" (4mm) diameter pearl beads
- off-white acrylic paint and paintbrush
- $1/_{16}$" (1.6mm) circle hand punch
- tapestry needle
- needle and thread
- craft glue
- gluestick
- tape measure

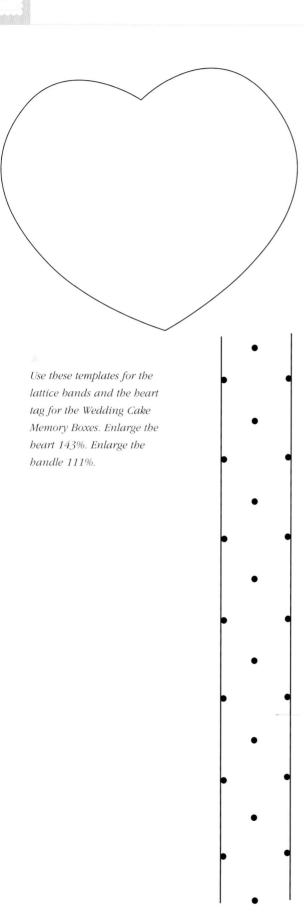

Use these templates for the lattice bands and the heart tag for the Wedding Cake Memory Boxes. Enlarge the heart 143%. Enlarge the handle 111%.

1 **Paint the Box and Lid**

Paint the box and the lids with off-white acrylic paint to cover up the brown pâpier-mâché color. A second coat may be needed.

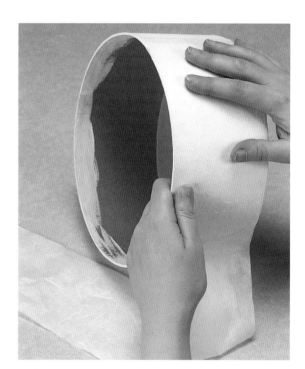

2 **Cover the Box with Giftwrap**

Trace around the lid onto the back of the handmade gift wrap and cut out the circle. For the lid side pattern, cut a strip $3/4$" (2cm) longer than the box's circumference and $1/8$" (3mm) wider than the lid's height. Cut a piece of gift wrap for the box base. Measure it in the same way as for the lid. Apply the glue stick to the wrong side of the handmade paper. Smooth the circle onto the box top. Apply the side strip by aligning the paper overlap with the seam in the lid.

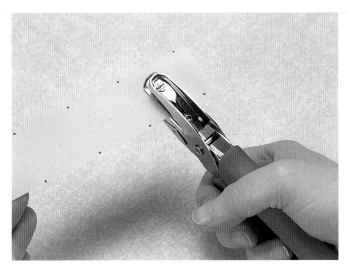

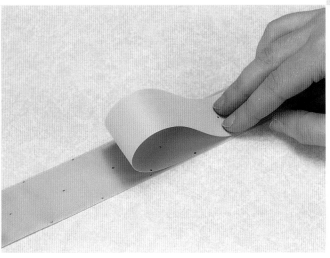

Make a Guide for the Lattice Bands

Copy the pattern on page 234 onto a piece of stiff paper. Cut out a paper strip to size, mark dots along sides and punch center holes as marked.

Transfer the Lattice Design Onto the Ribbon

For each box, cut a band of 1¹/₂"(39mm) wide lilac ribbon measuring 2¹/₂" (6cm) longer than the box circumference. Seal the ribbon ends with glue. Carefully transfer the lattice design onto the lilac ribbon. You will use this as a guide to keep your latticework consistent and even. The dots on the lilac ribbon show you where to place the narrow ribbon in order to create the criss-cross design.

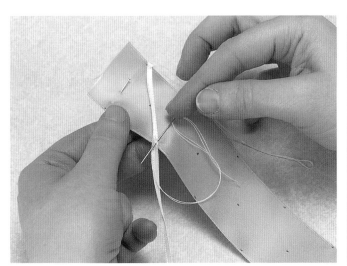

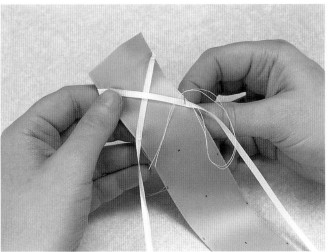

Begin Stitching on the Lattice

Cut a piece of ¹/₈" (3mm) wide white ribbon three times the length of the lilac band. Fold the white ribbon in half, and pin the folded end behind the lilac ribbon, close to one end. Fold the narrow ribbon diagonally, right to left, matching dots. Sew the ribbon to the lilac ribbon at the dots with matching thread.

Fold the Opposite Diagonal

Cross the ribbon over, from left to right. Sew at the markings, just as in the previous step.

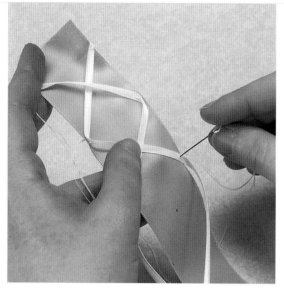

7 Continue Making the Lattice Design

Pick up the righthand ribbon and fold it to the left. Sew as shown. Repeat with the lefthand ribbon, and continue the design all the way down the lilac ribbon.

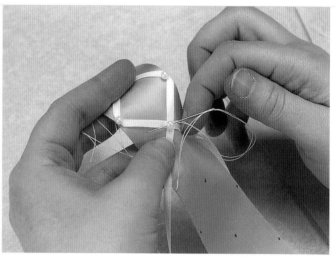

8 Sew on the Pearl Beads

Sew on pearl beads at all the diamond points. Leave the last inch or two on one end of the band unbeaded for the underlap. Mark a line on the box about 1/2" (1cm) above the box bottom.

9 Glue the Lattice to the Boxes

Glue the lattice band onto the box at the marked level, starting with the bead-free end. Align the short end of the band with the giftwrap seam on the box. Apply craft glue onto wrong side of the ribbon. Glue a small portion at a time.

tip It is a good idea to test-glue the lilac ribbon before making the lattice band. If glue soaks through, you'll need to interface the ribbon. (See the Nosegay Towel project, page 158, steps 1 and 2.)

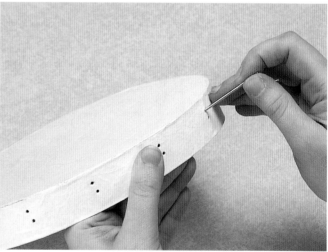

10 Measure the Lid for the Beading

Measure the lid circumference and divide it into equal segments of about 2" (5cm). Mark around the lid, 1/4" (7mm) below the lid top and 2" (5cm) apart. Mark a second dot 1/4" (7mm) below each one. Use a tapestry needle to pierce holes at the marked dots. The pâpier-mâché is soft and easily pierced.

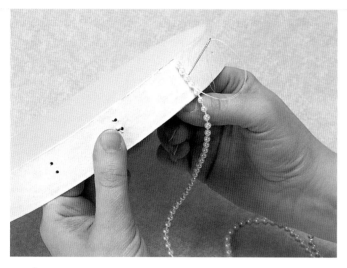

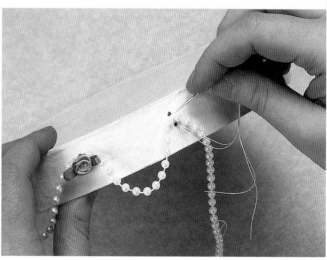

11 Attach the Beading

Cut the beading to the required length. For the smallest box, you need 2¹/₂" (6.5cm) of beading per segment. For all other box sizes, you need 3¹/₄" (8.5cm) per segment. (Multiply the segment length by the number of segments to get the total length of beading.) Pre-measure the beading segments and tie on a piece of doubled thread to mark each one. You can then thread the needle and sew on the beading segment by segment.

12 Add the Beading and Roses

Sew through the double holes. Knot the thread inside the lid. Repeat for the other segments to form the swags. You may want to sew the ribbon roses at the same time as the beading with one stitch. Combining the two steps saves time. Stitch through the rose center.

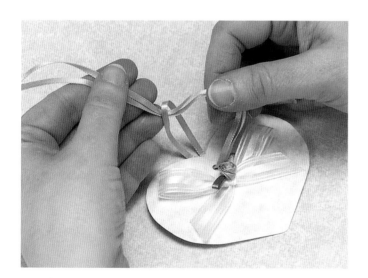

13 Make the Index Tags

The pattern for the tag is given on page 234. Cut a heart out of lilac cardstock and pierce a hole at the top. Glue on a bow made from 12" (30cm) of sheer stripe ⁵/₈" (15mm) wide ribbon. Glue on a ribbon rosebud, and loop a tie through the top hole. For each tie, you need 12" (30cm) of ¹/₈" (3mm) wide lilac satin ribbon. To attach the tag, tie it through a beaded swag.

14 Seam the Satin Ribbon

Cut 12" (30cm) lengths each of the 1" (25mm) sheer stripe and the 1" (25mm) white satin ribbon. Overlap and baste along one long edge. Machine-stitch close to the edge to make a double-width ribbon.

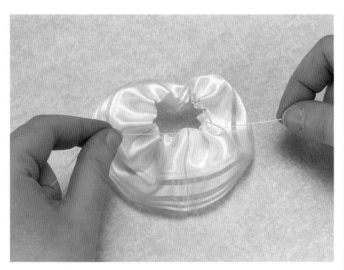

15 Gather the Satin Ribbon

Seam the short ends of the ribbon, then gather the top edge (see the Nosegay Towel project, pages 159-160, steps 8 and 9 for detailed instructions). Pull up the gathers, and knot on the wrong side.

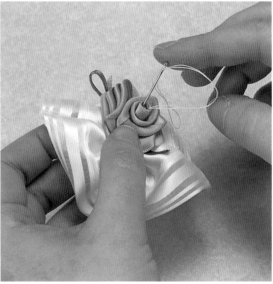

16 Sew on the Ribbon Rose

Make a lilac ribbon rose (see the Ring Bearer's Pillow on pages 244-245, steps 9-14). Sew the rose onto the satin ribbon center. Finally, glue the rose onto the lid of the smallest box, using craft glue.

variation **idea**

Custom-decorate the flower girl's footwear. Sew rosettes onto plain satin wedding shoes. Follow steps 14–16 to make the roses. The length of the ribbon pieces should be 10½" (26cm). Sew on rosebud-trimmed sheer ribbon bows at the heels. She'll look sweet going up the aisle.

Stack all four nested boxes on top of one another to create a tiered wedding cake centerpiece.

Ring Bearer's Pillow

A woven-ribbon heart, a romantic symbol of two lives

intertwined, is the motif for this exquisite ring pillow.

Designed with the occasion in mind, the pillow's bow

streamers will flutter gracefully as it is paraded up the

aisle. The woven heart is an ideal introduction to the

craft of ribbon weaving. The heart is constructed with

both satin and brocade ribbons in a variety of sizes and

outlined with a braided border of satin ribbons.

Ribbon

- $1/2$ yard (40cm) of $5/8$" (15mm) wide lilac double-face satin ribbon
- 1 yard (90cm) of $3/8$" (9mm) wide lilac double-face satin ribbon
- $2^3/8$ yards (2.2m) of $1/8$" (3mm) wide lilac double-face satin ribbon
- $1^1/2$ yards (1.3m) of $1/8$" (3mm) wide moss green double-face satin ribbon
- $2^1/2$ yards (2.3m) each of 1" (25mm), $5/8$" (15mm) and $3/8$" (9mm) wide bridal white double-face satin ribbon
- 2 yards (1.8m) of $1/8$" (3mm) wide white double-face satin ribbon
- $2^1/2$ yards (2.3m) each of 1" (25mm), $5/8$" (15mm), and $3/8$" (9mm) wide bridal white brocade ribbon
- $4^7/8$ yards (4.5m) of $3/4$" (20mm) wide bridal white sheer stripe ribbon

Supplies

- $3/8$ yard (30cm) off-white satin fabric
- $3/8$ yard (30cm) of 12 oz. (340g) polyester batting or one 10" (25cm) square pillow form
- 12" (30cm) of lightweight iron-on interfacing
- needle and thread
- straight pins
- fabric glue or liquid seam sealant
- tape measure
- press cloth
- toothpick

SEWING MACHINE REQUIRED

*Use this heart template for
the Ring Bearer Pillow.
Enlarge 143%.*

1 Begin the Ribbon Weave

For an easy method of ribbon weaving, pin the ribbons directly onto your ironing board. Cut a 9" (23cm) square of iron-on interfacing and place it adhesive side-up on the ironing board. Cut the plain and brocade ribbons into 10" (25cm) strips. To make up the vertical threads of the weaving, pin the ribbons side by side, alternating each one. Completely cover the interfacing using three or four strips of each ribbon type and width. Pin the ribbons at the top and bottom, angling the pins away from the ribbons.

2 Weave the Ribbon

Weave the horizontal ribbons through the vertical ribbons. Make sure the ribbons are flush with each other and at right angles to the vertical ribbons. Pin the ribbon ends. Press the ribbon weaving with a dry iron on a medium setting. Use a press cloth or a handkerchief to protect the ribbons.

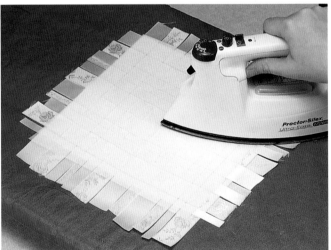

3 Press the Wrong Side

Remove all of the pins and flip the weaving onto the wrong side. Iron the interfacing according to the manufacturer's instructions to fuse the bond.

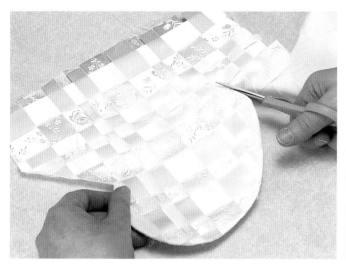

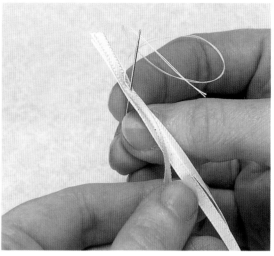

4 Cut Out the Heart Shape

Enlarge the heart template from page 116, so the length of the heart measures 6" (15cm) tall. Pin it onto the weaving and make an outline stitch around the shape in contrasting thread. With a sewing machine, zigzag around the outline. Next, cut out the woven heart, just outside the zigzag stitching. (If you do not have a zigzag sewing machine, a straight stitch or hand-sewn back stitch will do.)

5 Begin the Braid

Cut two 1-yard (90cm) pieces of $1/8$" (3mm) wide white ribbon, and one piece of lilac ribbon the same length. Stack the ends one on top of the other, sandwiching the lilac in between the white. Stitch through all the layers at the end to anchor the ribbons. This produces a flat, knot-free start to the braid.

tip *When making a three-strand braid, the length of each strand of ribbon must be about one and a half times the desired finished length of the braid.*

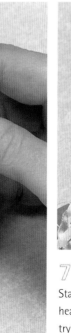
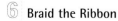

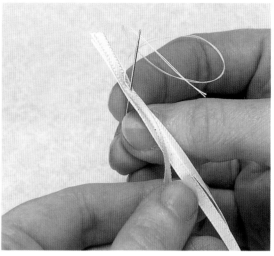

7 Sew the Braid Around the Heart

Starting and finishing at the heart "valley," hand stitch the braid around heart, concealing the machine zigzags. Use matching sewing thread, and try to hide your stitches.

6 Braid the Ribbon

Braid the three pieces of ribbon, keeping the ribbon flat at all times. Continue braiding until you have a braid 21" (52cm) long, then stitch the ribbon ends together, just as you did at the braid's beginning.

8 Sew on a Bow

Make a bow from 15" (38cm) of ³/₄" (20mm) wide sheer-stripe ribbon. Trim the ribbon ends, then seal them with fabric glue. Pin and then sew the bow onto the pillow.

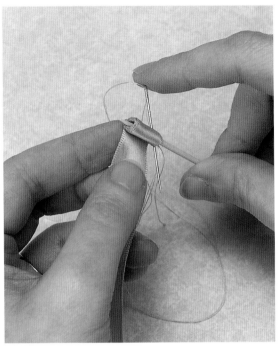

9 Start the Ribbon Rose

For the large ribbon rose at the top of the heart, cut 16" (40cm) of ⁵/₈" (15mm) wide lilac ribbon. Seal the ribbon ends. Start the rose by twirling the ribbon counterclockwise around a toothpick to make a tight coil—the rosebud. Add a few stitches at the base of the coil to secure it. Remove the toothpick after the coil is stitched.

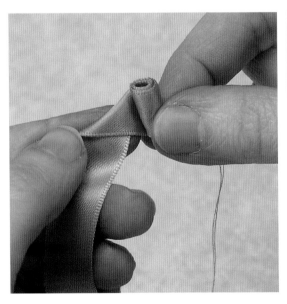

10 Form a Rose Petal

Fold the ribbon diagonally downward as you continue spiralling counterclockwise. This creates a rose petal.

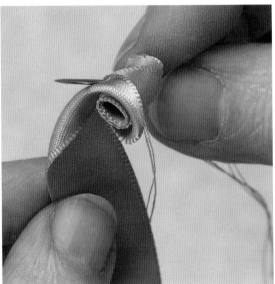

11 Secure Each Fold with a Stitch

As you roll the ribbon around the coil, stitch the ribbon to the coil at the bottom cross-point of each fold. The rosebud should not extend above the height of the petals.

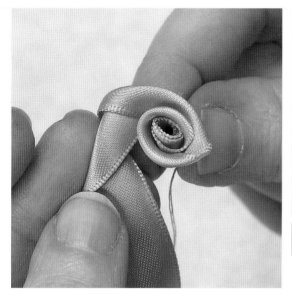

12 **Continue Spiralling and Stitching**

Fold, roll and stitch the ribbon to build up the rose. You can control the look of your rose by coiling loosely or tightly. This rose has a wide open appearance. For a more compact rose, coil with a tighter tension.

13 **Finish the Rose**

Continue spiralling until the ribbon ends, then fold the ribbon end under diagonally and stitch it down.

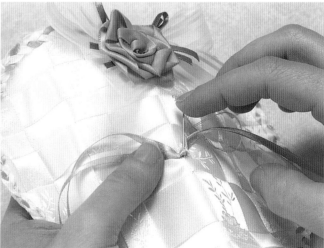

14 **Sew the Rose Onto the Heart**

Cut two 10" (25cm) pieces of moss green ribbon to make a double bow for the rose "leaves." Stack the ribbons and tie the bow, treating the two ribbons as one. Trim and seal the bow ends. Pin the bow, then the rose, onto the large white bow. Stitch through all of the layers at the heart "valley."

15 **Sew on the Ring Ties**

Cut two 25" (64cm) pieces of ¹/₈" (3mm) wide lilac ribbon. Place one piece on top of the other and knot at the center. Sew the knot onto the center of the woven heart.

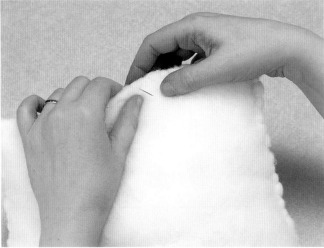

16 Stitch the Batting

Cut three 10" (25cm) squares from the batting. Stack them on top of each other and baste close to the edges. Stitch all around the edges to complete the pillow form. Remove the basting. You may also use a pre-made pillow form.

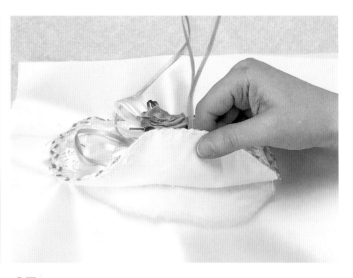

17 Hand-Stitch the Heart in Place

Cut out two pieces of lightweight interfacing 11¼" x 11¼" (28cm x 28cm). Bond each piece of interfacing onto the matte side of a piece of satin, following the manufacturer's instructions. Trim the satin to the exact size of the interfacing squares. Pin the heart onto the pillow front. Hand-sew the heart onto the pillow front using matching sewing thread.

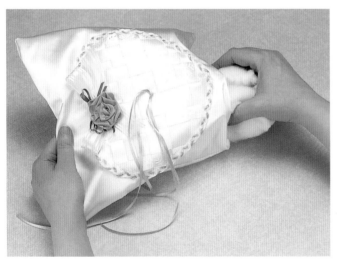

18 Sew and Stuff the Pillow

Pin the pillow front to the back, right sides together. Machine stitch around the pillow, using a ⅝" (1.5cm) seam allowance. Leave about 6½" (17cm) unstitched on one side. Turn the pillow right side out and insert the pillow form. Baste the opening shut, then slip stitch it into place. (To review Slip Stitch instructions, see page 147.)

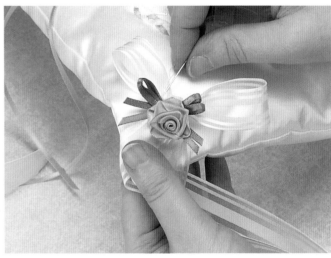

19 Sew on the Corner Bows

Cut four pieces of sheer-stripe ribbon, each 40" (1m) long. Tie each into a bow, trim the ribbon ends and seal them. Cut four pieces of ⅜" (9mm) wide lilac ribbon, each measuring 8" (20cm) long, and four pieces of ⅛" (3mm) moss green ribbon, each also 8" (20cm) long. Make four lilac ribbon roses and four leaf bows, repeating steps 9-14. Pin a white bow, a green bow and a rose onto each corner, ¾" (2cm) from the tip. Sew them onto the pillow through all the layers.

variation ideas

You can customize a purchased archival-quality scrapbook with the same rose trellis theme. Start with a moiré-covered album, about 12" (30cm) square. Make a woven heart appliqué (see above) and two lattice bands (see Wedding Cake Memory Boxes, page 233). Glue them onto the album cover. Cover the album with a piece of tracing paper, then weight the album with books as it dries.

Make a bridal purse by decorating an envelope of brocade fabric with a mini woven heart and a lattice band (see Wedding Cake Memory Boxes, page 233). For the shoulder strap, sew on pearl beading. To attach the beading, stitch it down at bag's side seams, catching the beading between beads. Add decorative bows to conceal the stitching. You can also use these techniques to dress up a storebought purse.

Use this precious Ring Bearer's Pillow as a keepsake to remember your special day.

Wedding Reception Papercrafts

After the ceremony, celebrate your marriage with a

personalized wedding reception. The Confetti Basket is a

beautiful alternative to throwing rice, and the Favor

Pillow Box is perfect for holding sweet treats. You can

also impress your guests with the Rose Trellis Menu Card.

Although elegant in appearance, this hand-made holder

for the menu doesn't take long to make. Inside the card,

glue a copy of the wedding dinner menu.

1 Confetti Basket • *page 250*

Ribbon

- 2$\frac{1}{4}$ yards (2.1m) of $\frac{1}{8}$" (3mm) wide lilac double-face satin ribbon
- 8 lilac ribbon rosebuds

Supplies

- $\frac{3}{8}$ yard (30cm) of white tulle
- lilac parchment-look cardstock
- $\frac{1}{16}$" (1.6mm) circle hand punch
- craft knife and cutting mat
- tapestry needle
- needle and thread
- craft glue
- confetti

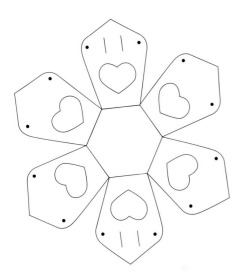

Use these templates for the Confetti Basket and Handle. Enlarge each 222%.

1 | Cut Out the Paper Basket

With the templates provided, cut out the basket and handle. Use a craft knife and ruler for straight lines, small scissors for the curves, and a hand punch to make the holes at the marked dots. If you don't own a hand punch, pierce the holes with a tapestry needle. Remember to cut slits for the basket handles.

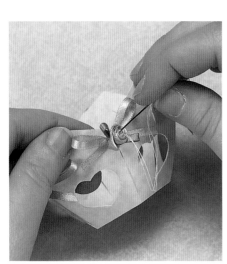

2 | Connect the Sides of the Basket

Cut six 8" (20cm) pieces of lilac ribbon for the ties. Thread a ribbon through the adjacent basket sides—a tapestry needle can help to get the ribbon through the holes. Tie a bow, trim the ribbon ends and seal with craft glue. Add a ribbon rosebud over the bow knot, sewing through all layers. Repeat for the remaining five sides.

3 | Make the Lattice Design

Cut a 20" (50cm) piece of ribbon. Knot one end and thread it through the hole at the end of the handle. Evenly wrap the ribbon around the handle, spiralling upward. Thread the ribbon through the hole at the opposite end of the handle. Make sure both knots lie on the same side of the handle. Attach the handle to the basket and set a tulle pouch filled with confetti inside.

Place these baskets at the reception tables filled with sweet treats, or tie nametags to the handles for placecards.

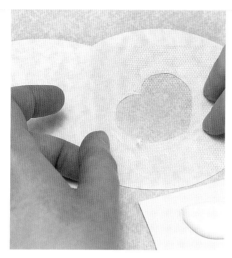

2 Favor Pillow Box

Ribbon

- ⁵/₈ yard (50cm) of ¹/₈" (3mm) wide lilac double-face satin ribbon
- 1 lilac ribbon rosebud

Supplies

- 4" (10cm) square of tulle
- lilac parchment-look cardstock
- deep lilac pearlescent paper
- ¹/₂" (12mm) heart-shaped paper punch
- craft knife and cutting mat
- needle and thread
- craft glue

1 Cut Out the Box and Glue the Tulle

Use the template below to cut out a pillow box form. On the right side of the box, lightly score the curved flaps and the long straight folds. Cut a square of tulle measuring 2¹/₄" (6cm). On the wrong side, apply glue around the edge of the heart-shaped window. Glue the tulle behind the window, smoothing it into place.

2 Glue the Box Together

Crease the box along the straight scored lines. Apply glue to the long flap, then glue down the back of the box.

Fill this box with sugared almonds or other sweets for your guests at the reception.

3 Embellish the Box

Punch out two hearts from pearlescent paper. Glue them onto the box front, as shown. On one side, fold under the back flap, then the front flap. Fill the box with candy, then close the remaining two flaps in the same order. Cut a 20" (50cm) piece of ribbon and wrap it around the box. Tie a bow at the top left corner and sew on a ribbon rosebud.

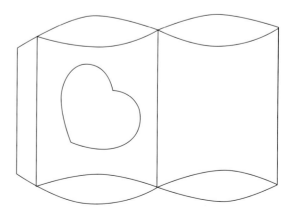

Use this template for the Favor Pillow Box. Enlarge 182%.

3 Menu Card

Ribbon

- ½ yard (40cm) of ⅜" (3mm) wide lilac double-face satin ribbon
- 1¼ yards (1.1m) of ⅛" (3mm) wide lilac double-face satin ribbon
- 1 yard (80cm) of ⅛" (3mm) wide moss green double-face satin ribbon

Supplies

- lilac parchment-look cardstock
- white parchment-look paper
- 26 white pearl beads
- 1/16" (1.6mm) circle hand punch
- craft knife and cutting mat
- tapestry needle
- needle and thread
- craft glue
- glue stick
- metal ruler

1 Cut Out the Menu Card

Fold each side of the lilac cardstock in toward the center of the paper, so that the edges are touching one another. Your paper should now have a left and a right flap, resembling double doors. Using the template below, match the center line of the cardstock with the center line of the template. Cut out the menu card, score the folds and punch holes at the marked dots.

NOTE: *For multiple cards, make a template out of heavy cardstock or cardboard.*

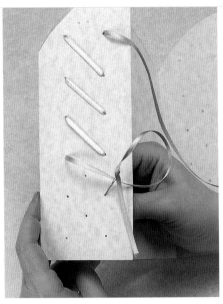

2 Begin to Lace the Lattice

Cut two pieces of ⅛" wide lilac ribbon, each measuring 21" (52cm) long. Thread the ribbon with a tapestry needle and lace through the two top trellis holes with roughly half the ribbon on each side. The closely spaced holes at the very top of the card are for attaching the roses; the trellis holes are below them. Stitch the first left-to-right diagonal. Progress from top to bottom, lacing all the lefthand diagonal stitches.

3 Complete the Lattice Crosses

To complete the lattice, re-thread the needle with the remaining ribbon on the righthand side. Lace all the right-to-left diagonals, completing the crosses.

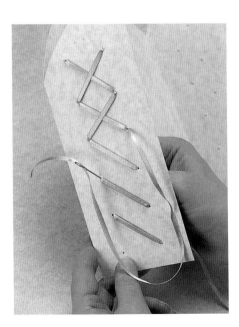

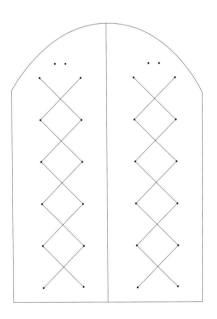

Use this template for the Menu Card.
Enlarge 200%, then 143%.

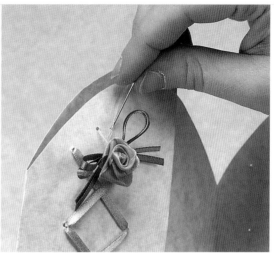

4 Tie Off the Ribbon

Tie a knot at the bottom of the card. Trim the ribbon tails close to the knot. Lace the other side of the card in the same way.

5 Add a Ribbon Rose

For each ribbon rose, you need 8" (20cm) of $^3/_8$" (9mm) lilac ribbon, and two 8" (20cm) pieces of moss green ribbon. Make two ribbon roses, following steps 9–14 for the Ring Bearer's Pillow on pages 244 and 245. Sew each ribbon rose onto the front of the card, using the lacing holes provided.

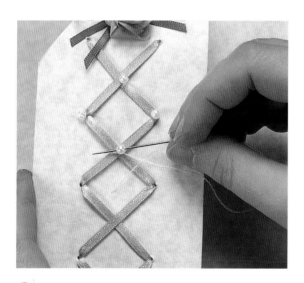

6 Add the Final Touches

Using doubled white thread, sew on a pearl bead at the diamond corners. Ad beads at the bottom end of the lattice if you wish. Knot the thread on the card back. Conceal the ribbon work on the back of each flap with a piece of white paper, cut to fit. You only need to glue it around the edges. Last but not least, glue a menu onto the card interior center panel of the card.

Write out the wedding menu in calligraphy. Or, hand-letter the original photocopying the rest.

Nursery Carousel

✦

This fantasy confection of pastel ribbons and bows

makes a delightful addition to any child's room.

It is also very economical to make—this mobile

consists of a wooden embroidery hoop, ribbon and

paper. It makes a great baby shower gift for a boy or

girl. The new baby will be mesmerized watching the

chicks on the carousel go 'round and 'round.

Ribbon

- $2^7/_8$ yards (2.6m) of $^1/_4$" (7mm) wide blue satin ribbon
- $^7/_8$ yard (80cm) of $^1/_4$" (7mm) wide pink satin ribbon
- $^7/_8$ yard (80cm) of 1" (25mm) wide blue sheer ribbon (such as polyester organdy)
- $^7/_8$ yard (80cm) of $1^1/_2$" (39mm) wide yellow sheer ribbon (such as polyester organdy)
- $1^3/_4$ yards (1.6m) each of $^1/_8$" (3mm) wide double-face satin ribbon in yellow, lilac, pink and blue satin

Supplies

- yellow, lilac, pink and blue pearlescent cardstock
- yellow, purple, pink and blue paper
- 12" (30cm) diameter wooden embroidery hoop
- 1" (2.5cm) diameter plastic curtain ring
- 1 large-holed frosted plastic bead, about 1" (2.5cm) in diameter
- pastel yellow acrylic craft paint and paintbrush
- $^1/_4$" (7mm) and $^1/_{16}$" (1.6mm) circle hand punches
- craft knife and cutting mat
- tapestry needle
- needle and thread
- straight pins
- craft glue
- glue stick
- tape measure

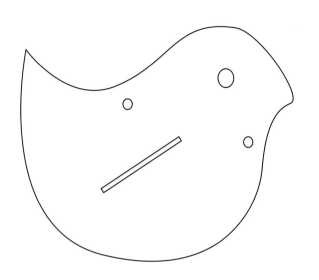

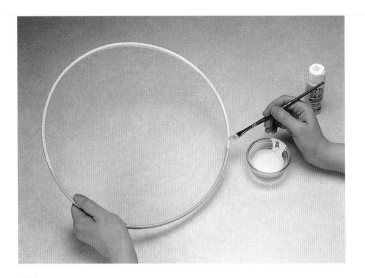

Use this template for the Nursery Carousel. Enlarge 125%.

1 Paint the Hoop

For the mobile, you only need the inner ring of the embroidery hoop. Brush on the yellow acrylic paint, completely covering all of the surfaces. You may need to add a second coat.

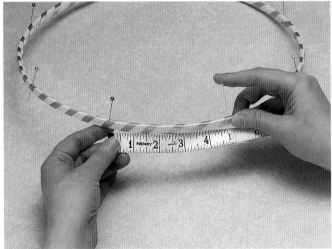

2 Spiral Ribbon Around the Hoop

Use masking tape to secure the ribbon end onto the hoop, and then wrap the ribbon counterclockwise around the hoop. Join the ribbon ends on the inside of the hoop, overlapping them to make a continuous ribbon spiral. Use craft glue to hold the ribbon in place. Remove the masking tape after the glue has dried on the joined ribbons.

3 Pin the Hoop at Equal Segments

Measure the hoop circumference and divide by eight. For a 12" (30cm) hoop, each segment equals about 4⁷/₈" (12cm). Mark each segment by pinning vertically through the ribbon.

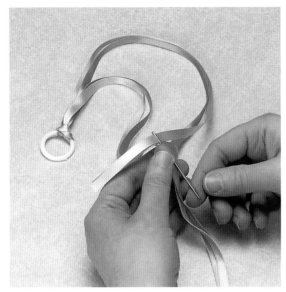

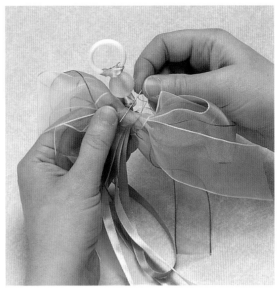

4 Loop the Ribbon and Thread the Bead

To make the harness for the mobile, cut two 14" (35cm) pieces of ¹/₄" (7mm) wide ribbon—one pink and one blue. Place one ribbon directly on top of the other and fold them in half. Pass the fold through a plastic curtain ring, and then thread the ribbon tails through the loop. Pull it tightly. Thread the ribbon tails, two at a time, through the eye of a tapestry needle. Then pull them through the bead. Push the bead to the top of the harness. Knot all four ribbon strands together below the bead.

5 Add a Sheer Ribbon Bow

Lay the sheer blue ribbon on top of the sheer yellow ribbon. Treat them as one length of ribbon and tie them in a bow. Cut the ribbon tails at an angle, and seal them with glue to prevent unraveling. Sew the bow onto the ribbon harness, below the bead knot.

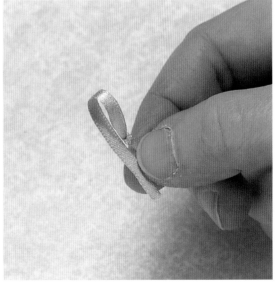

6 Attach the Harness

The carousel harness consists of four "arms" of ribbon. Sew the arms onto the hoop, spacing them equally apart (an arm at every other pin position). Alternate the ribbon colors, and make sure the ribbon doesn't twist. Wrap each ribbon end around the hoop as shown, then sew it in place at the corners with matching thread.

7 Add the Top Knot

Each paper bird is suspended from the mobile on a hanging strand of narrow ribbon. Cut two 10" (25cm) pieces each of pink, blue, lilac and yellow ¹/₈" (3mm) wide ribbon. Knot each piece of ribbon 2" (5cm) from an end. Loop the short section of ribbon down, behind the knot.

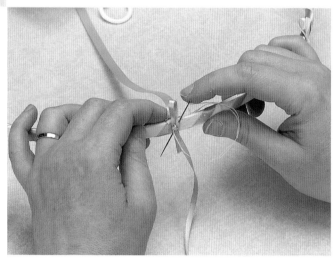

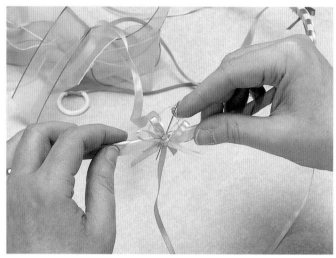

8 Sew Hanging Strands

Stitch the hanging strands onto the ribbon-wrapped hoop at the eight pinned positions. Sew through the knot, the loop of the hanging strand, and the spiralled ribbon, catching all layers. Use matching sewing thread. Alternate the ribbon colors—lilac, yellow, pink, blue—then repeat.

9 Tie a Mini-Bow

Sew a same-color bow, made from 8" (20cm) of ⅛" (3mm) wide ribbon, onto each hanging strand, below the knot at the top. Seal the ends of each bow with glue to prevent unraveling.

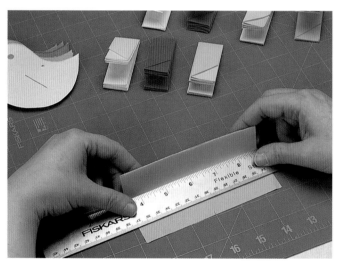

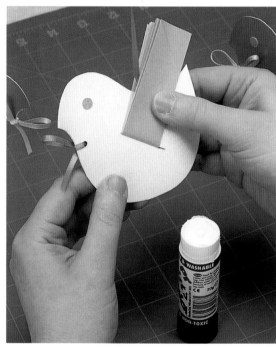

10 Begin Making the Chicks

Use the template provided to make eight chicks to hang from the carousel. For each chick, you need to glue two pieces of pearlescent paper back-to-back with a glue stick to make double-sided pieces of paper. Cut the wing slot and punch the small ribbon holes. Punch contrasting-colored dots, using the ¼" (7mm) circle punch, for the eyes. Glue the eyes in place using craft glue applied with a toothpick. For each pair of wings, cut a paper rectangle in a contrasting color measuring 8" x 5½" (20cm x 14cm). Make two pairs of wings in each paper color. Fold eight 1" (2.5cm) wide pleats across the width of each piece of paper, then fold the wings in half, creasing at the center.

11 Complete the Chicks

Make an angled cut at each wing end. Cut from the outer to the inner edge of the outside pleat. Slide the wings through the slot in each bird. Use a glue stick to fasten the wings onto each side. Tie a matching bow through the hole below the beak. Use 10" (25cm) of ⅛" (3mm) wide ribbon for each bow. Stitch through the bow knot with matching thread to secure. To attach the chick knot the ribbon through the small punched hole at the top of each chick.

Many different versions of the carousel mobile are possible. Let your imagination take flight! Instead of paper chicks, substitute with origami animals, paper dolls, clip art cut-outs or miniature stuffed toys, to suggest a few.

Love and Kisses Baby Blanket

What could be more cuddly than a baby wrapped

in a soft blanket? This project allows you to transform

a store-bought fleece blanket into a treasured baby

shower gift. And it doesn't take a long time to make!

To create the border design, strips of ribbon are

slipped into slits cut in the background fabric.

The precious baby will stay warm at night and feel

loved under this special keepsake.

Ribbon

- 1¹/₂ yards (1.3m) of ⁵/₈" (15mm) wide dusty pink single-face satin ribbon
- 1 yard (80cm) of ⁵/₈" (15mm) wide mint green single-face satin ribbon
- 4¹/₂ yards (4.1m) of ¹/₈" (3mm) wide pink double-face satin ribbon

Supplies

- 28" (71cm) wide lilac acrylic fleece blanket
- ¹/₂ yard (50cm) of white machine-washable felt
- ¹/₂ yard (50cm) of fusible web
- ³/₈ yard (30cm) of fusible interfacing
- 1 skein each of mint green and dusty pink six-strand embroidery floss
- 1 skein of blue matte embroidery cotton
- craft knife and cutting mat
- embroidery, chenille and tapestry needles
- needle and thread
- straight pins
- fine-point pen or embroidery marker
- tape measure

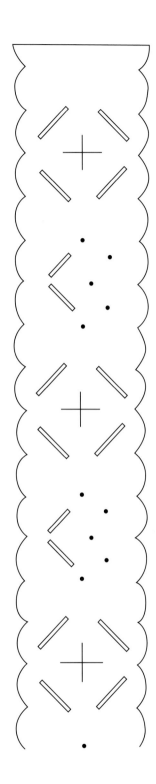

Use this template for the Love and Kisses Baby Blanket. Enlarge 143%.

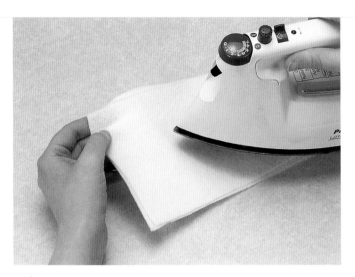

1 Fuse a Double Layer of Felt

Because you will be able to see the ribbon through the white felt, you need to double up the felt. For each of the two blanket borders, cut two strips, each measuring 4" (10cm) wide by the width of your baby blanket. Cut one strip of fusible web to the same dimensions for each of the two borders. Following the manufacturer's instructions, bond the two layers of each strip together. Prepare two borders in this way.

2 Stencil the Pattern Onto the Felt

Make a blanket border pattern in heavyweight paper using the template to the left. Cut out the slits with a craft knife. Pierce the dots with a tapestry needle. Pin the stencil onto the felt and mark the pattern through the slits and holes. (If you prefer not to use pen ink, use a special embroidery marker.) Cut the felt on the marked lines, using a craft knife pressed against a metal ruler. A good method is to make the initial cut with a craft knife, then use embroidery scissors to finish the job precisely. The pattern markings are on the wrong side of the border.

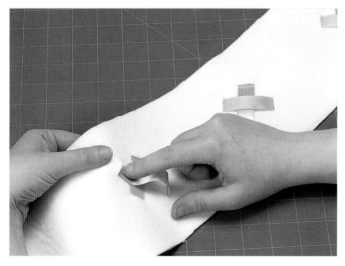

3 Insert the Ribbon "Kisses"

For each X-shaped "kiss," cut two 3¹/₄" (8cm) strips of ribbon. Insert the righthand side of the X into the slits first. Next, complete each X with the lefthand strip of ribbon.

4 Sew Down the Xs

To prevent little fingers from getting caught in the ribbon layers, sew down the corners. Thread a needle with two strands of embroidery floss, and take a few stitches at each ribbon corner.

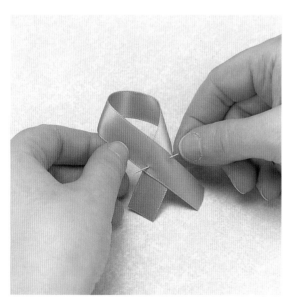

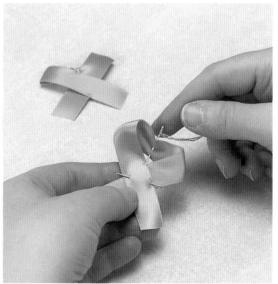

5 Make a Loop for the Heart

Pin a 6" (15cm) strip of ⁵/₈" (15mm) wide ribbon into a fish loop (see page 145), left ribbon over right, as shown. The tails extend ³/₄" (2cm) from the end.

6 Gather the Loop to Form the Heart

Thread a needle with a doubled strand of embroidery floss. Take three small stitches across the center top of the loop, then pull the gathers. With a stitch, connect the top of the loop to the intersection to form an X. Reinforce the shape with another stitch at the bottom of the intersecting ribbons. These shapes will become the hearts in the blanket.

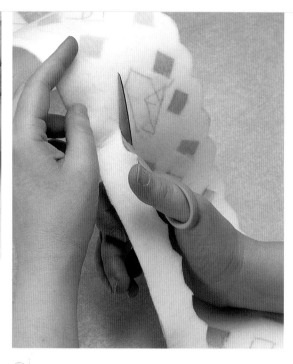

7 Sew Hearts Onto the Border

Insert the tails into the slots, forming a heart. Pin the heart onto the felt (use the dots on the wrong side of the border as positioning guides for the top corners of the heart). Sew the heart onto the felt, making stitches at the corners and points where the ribbons cross.

8 Iron Interfacing and Cut Scalloped Borders

Cut a piece of iron-on interfacing to the border dimensions. Iron it onto the wrong side of the border, following the manufacturer's instructions. This seals down all the ribbon ends. With embroidery scissors, cut scallops as marked along the top and bottom edges of the border.

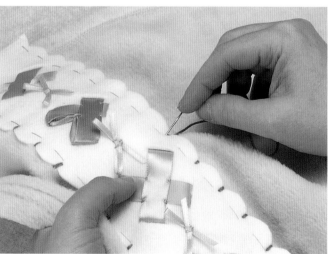

9 Sew on the Accent Bows

For each bow, cut 8" (20cm) of narrow ribbon. Tie the bows and seal the ends of each bow. Sew a bow in between each heart and kiss. Stitch through the knot, so the bow cannot untie.

10 Sew the Borders Onto the Blanket

Pin the borders onto the blanket, 3" (8cm) from the blanket edges. Baste the borders onto the blanket and remove any pins. Thread an embroidery needle with blue matte embroidery cotton, and sew the borders onto the blanket by stitching between the scallops.

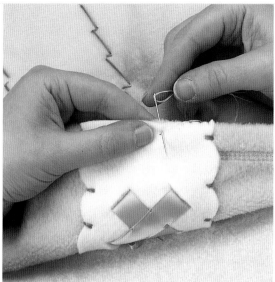

11 | Sew the Sides

For the baby's safety, stitch down the gaps at both sides of the borders. Thread a needle with white sewing thread and stitch the felt to the blanket.

variation idea

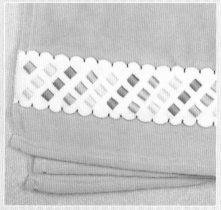

Ready for a more advanced slotted ribbon project? To make this multi-colored diamond-lattice border, insert diagonal bands of ribbon (⁵⁄₈" [15mm] wide ribbon, each strip 4" [10cm] long, in three alternating colors) into the slotted felt background. The border is not difficult to make, but it does require patience.

Your little one will sleep blissfully, wrapped in this Love and Kisses Blanket that you lovingly created.

✳ RIBBONS

BERISFORDS
P.O. Box 2
Thomas St.
Congelton
Cheshire CW12 1EF
United Kingdom
+44 (0) 1260 274011
www.berisfords-ribbons.co.ukl

• *Carrier of a variety of sheer and bridal ribbons*

C.M. OFFRAY & SONS, INC.
360 State Route 24
Chester, NJ 07930
(800) 344-5533
www.offray.com

• *Supplier of woven-edge satin, grosgrain and fancy ribbons*

CONSO PRODUCTS COMPANY
P.O. Box 326
513 N. Duncan By-pass
Union, SC 29379
(800) 845-2431
www.conso.com

• *Distributor of decorative trims, cording, roping, tassels and fringes*

ELEGANT LACE
2960 Campbell Dr.
Auburn, CA 95602
(800) 623-6644
www.elegantlace.com

• *Carrier of hand dyed doilies for home décor, weddings, crafts, office and parties*

PRYM–DRITZ CORPORATION
P.O. Box 5028
Spartanburg, SC 29304
www.dritz.com

• *Supplier of decorative braids, cords, fringes and tassels for fashion and home furniture*

HYMAN HENDLER AND SONS
67 W. 38th St.
New York, NY 10018
(212) 840-8393
www.hymanhendler.com

• *Distributor of a fabulous selection of ribbons*

LACIS
3163 Adeline St.
Berkeley, CA 94703
(510) 843-7178
www.lacis.com

• *Supplier of lace and lace supplies, ribbons, tassels, stamens and beads*

M&J TRIMMINGS
1008 Sixth Ave.
New York, NY 10018
(800) 9-MJTRIM
www.mjtrim.com

• *Supplier of satin, grosgrain and taffeta ribbons*

RIBBON DESIGNS
P.O. Box 382
Edgware
Middlesex HA8 7XQ
United Kingdom
+44 (0) 20 8958
www.wilkribbon.co.uk

• *International mail order supplier of ribbon, including satin, organdy and rat-tail cording*

THE RIBBON FACTORY
602 N. Brown St.
P.O. Box 405, Dept. 2
Titusville, PA 16354
(866) 827-6431
www.ribbonfactory.com

• *Carrier of wired edge, grosgrain, lamé, satin, and decorative florals*

THE RIBBONERIE INC.

191 Potrero Ave.
San Francisco, CA 94103
(415) 626-6184
www.theribbonerie.com

• *Carrier of domestic and imported ribbons*

SELECTUS LTD

Panda Ribbons
The Uplands, Biddulph
Stoke-on-Trent, Staffs, England
ST8 7RH
United Kingdom
+44 (0) 1782 522316
www.selectus.co.uk

• *Seller of satins, taffeta, woven and printed fancies, tartens, metallics, velvets, bindings and galloons*

TINSEL TRADING COMPANY

47 W. 38th St.
New York, NY 10018
(212) 730-1030
www.tinseltrading.com

• *Distributor of antique trims, braids and ribbons*

YLI CORPORATION

161 W. Main St.
Rock Hill, SC 29730
(803) 985-3100
www.ylicorp.com

• *Provider of pure silk ribbons, thread and yarn*

✻ CRAFTS

BROOKLACE, INC.

300 Callegari Dr.
West Haven, CT 06516
(203) 937-4555
www.brooklace.com

• *Manufacturer of lace and linen doilies in a variety of shapes and sizes*

DALEE BOOK COMPANY

129 Clinton Pl.
Yonkers, NY 10701
(800) 852-2665
www.daleebook.com

• *Manufacturer of archival-quality, acid-free bridal albums and scrapbooks*

FISKARS BRANDS, INC.

7811 W. Stewart Ave.
Wausau, WI 54401
(800) 500-4849
www.fiskars.com

• *Manufacturer of scissors, paper edgers and hand punches*

FRED ALDOUS LTD.

37 Lever St.
Manchester M1 1LW
United Kingdom
08707 517 300
www.fredaldous.co.uk

• *Mail-order craft supplier of crafts, including papier maché boxes*

KUNIN FELT

Foss Manufacturing Company, Inc.
380 Lafayette Rd.
P.O. Box 5000
Hampton, NH 03843-5000
(603) 929-6100
www.kuninfelt.com

• *Manufacturer of machine-washable Rainbow Classic felt*

PHRAZZLE CARD LTD

29 Hest View Rd.
Ulverston
Cumbria LA12 9PH
United Kingdom
+44 (0) 1229 588880
www.phrazzlecard.co.uk

• *Mail order supplier of corrugated cardboard and pearlescent paper*

The art featured above is from the book *Making Greeting Cards with Creative Materials* by MaryJo McGraw.

making Greeting cards *with* creative materials

making
Greeting
cards *with*
creative materials

✳ MaryJo McGraw

NORTH
LIGHT
BOOKS

www.artistnetwork.com

TABLE *of* CONTENTS

INTRODUCTION

So many ideas, so little time. With the abundance of new materials and products to use on your greeting cards, how can anyone find time to experiment with them all? Expanding upon the traditional greeting card format, I will be using some everyday materials in new and different ways—items that might be familiar from other craft projects, such as fabric bond, decorative threads and yarns, plastic and foil wrap, shipping tags, office supply items, facial tissue, newsprint, paper towels and handmade papers from around the world. The more unusual items such as mica tiles, ROXS, copper sheeting, watch crystals and picture pebbles, although more difficult to find, give your personal greeting a unique look.

TOOLS *and* MATERIALS

❈ RUBBER STAMPS

There are generally three parts to a rubber stamp: the mount, the cushion and the die. Quality mounts are made from hardwood. The cushion is made of foam from ⅛" to ¼" (3mm to 6mm) thick. The die, the most important part of the stamp because it transfers the design, should be closely trimmed. In some projects, I use metal stamps, which are available at most hardware and some stamp stores. They are simple to use with most metals, especially thin copper.

❈ PAPER

I could write a whole book on paper! There are so many exciting papers available I can't even begin to explain the different types. So I will give a very basic way to decide what you need for a project. The thicker the paper or cardstock (card), the more adhesive you need to adhere it! Most heavy porous papers may need extra time for a glue or adhesive to sink in and set up. The more textured the paper, the more you must work it in to the surface. Most of the papers and cardstocks I have used in the book are not extremely textured, so I can use fabric bond or double-sided tape effectively.

❈ CHIPBOARD

Chipboard is a cheap, useful material (used to make cereal boxes and the backs of paper tablets). I use it in this book for a variety of card additions, such as the heart in the Dye Card. You can substitute mat board or any recycled cardboard for chipboard.

❈ INKS

There are three basic ink types: dye, pigment and solvent. Dye-based pads are the type you see lying around the house or office. Dye-based ink is water soluble. Pigment inks are now widely available through stamp and gift stores and are a good choice when using uncoated papers. They are also used for embossing and for archival applications, such as scrapbooking. Solvent-based inks are used mainly for stamping on unusual surfaces such as wood, plastic and ceramic. I use them for a nice, crisp, black outline that won't smear like dye inks do.

❈ DYE REINKERS

Dye reinkers are the small bottles of ink you normally use to refill your dye-based ink pads. Be careful when using inks straight from the bottle; they are very concentrated and will easily stain clothing. Be sure to use the smallest amount possible; you can always add more. You can also use dye ink to alter the color of water-based paints or PearlEx powdered pigments mixed with binder.

❈ DOUBLE-SIDED TAPES

Double-sided tapes come in a variety of forms. When working with most paper projects I prefer paper-lined doublestick tape, although when the surface is sheer or clear (vellum or acetate) a clear tape would be preferred. Most art supply and stamp stores carry a variety of both.

❈ DIAMOND GLAZE

I often use this dimensional adhesive because it dries to a clear, glasslike finish and securely holds many mediums. You can also brush it on thin for a laminated look. It can be used as a medium to mix with many other paint products.

❈ ACCESSORIES

Accessories such as threads, beads, paper cord, tassels, gift tags, charms and buttons can be found at most stamp stores. I also find these items in specialty stores for beads and needlecrafts. Office supply stores are great for unusual items too.

❈ BEADS

I use many types of beads and beadlike accessories in this book. The glass beads I use are tiny and have no holes. They also have a metallic finish. I also use ROXS, which is a cross between glitter and beads and makes for an eye-catching embellishment. ROXS can be embedded under Diamond Glaze or layered between embossings.

❈ PICTURE PEBBLES

Some projects use picture pebbles, which are glass marbles with one flat surface. They come in a wide variety of sizes and colors and are available in many stamp or craft stores. When placed over an image, it magnifies the design, which is perfect for small photos. When using colored pebbles, keep the colors on the image light. The clear ones are perfect for darker pieces. The pebbles are also great for quick jewelry projects.

❈ WATCH CRYSTALS

These discs can be used to enliven your artwork in a variety of ways. The crystals I have used in this book are plastic and inexpensive. I like them for a clear dimensional look. The crystals can also be filled with beads, seeds, sand, small toys and pictures. You can find these in paper specialty and stamp stores. For glass crystals and other watch parts check out the online auction sites.

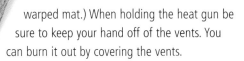

❋ BONE FOLDER

The bone folder is a great tool for scoring paper and smoothing down creases. Bookbinders use it for turning corners and scoring. Some are made from bone, while others are made from resin or wood. They come in several lengths and are very helpful in several crafts.

❋ CRAFT KNIVES

A craft knife is an invaluable tool when creating greeting cards. The blade should be pointed and very sharp. Change your blades often to ensure clean cuts.

❋ PUNCHES AND CUTTERS

Many projects use a variety of paper punches, including circle punches, square punches, spiral punches and leaf punches. These are widely available at craft stores. You might consider investing in a circle cutter, which can be adjusted to cut circles in a range of diameters. In this book I also use ¼", ⅛" and ¹⁄₁₆" (6mm, 3mm, and 2mm) hole punches. Sometimes an awl will work just as well as a hole punch.

❋ HEAT GUN

Look for a heat gun that is specially made for stamping: They are usually geared at a safe temperature for paper projects. Keep your heat gun away from your cutting mat, as it can distort the surface. (It's hard to cut on a warped mat.) When holding the heat gun be sure to keep your hand off of the vents. You can burn it out by covering the vents.

❋ PEARLEX POWDERED PIGMENTS

PearlEx powdered pigments are raw pigments used for a variety of purposes, including making your own paints. You can also use PearlEx as a surface coating on paper or collage projects. Powdered pigments do need what is known as a "binder" to keep them adhered to your project. In this book we will be using Diamond Glaze as a binder. Other options include white glue, paint mediums, gum arabic or spray fixative. Mixing any of these with PearlEx will create a colored medium you can apply to surfaces as you wish.

❋ TASSELS AND CORDS

Tassels make a great addition to a beautiful card. The ones used in this book are available at most stamp stores. Paper cord is also available. As you will see in this book, paper cord is an extremely versatile decorative item. Both tassels and cords are usually sold in assortments of colors.

❋ TEMPLATES

Plastic and brass templates are a great investment. They last forever, are inexpensive, and there are many types available. Look for envelope, box and card templates at stamp stores.

Embossing Powders
To use embossing powder, stamp an image with pigment or embossing ink. Sprinkle the powder over the wet ink and shake off the excess. Use a heat gun to melt the powder and create a raised design. Be sure to have a variety of colors; embossing looks great in almost any color. Embossing powder comes in solid-color and multicolor forms.

Acetate
The acetate used in this book can be found in stamp stores. You want to be sure to get embossable acetate (also known as "window plastic") in case you want to heat the piece. The same is true of heavy cold laminate used here; it should be embossable. The thicker the laminate is, the better for the projects in this book because of the beating the pieces will take.

Mica Tiles
Mica tiles are compressed layers of mica that can be cut and layered. I use them in many projects as a decorative and protective covering over photos. They are heat-resistant, acid-free and lightweight.

Metal Accessories
Some projects include copper wire, thin copper sheets or fun metal shapes as embellishments. These items can be found at craft, stamp and hardware stores.

Eyelets
In this book I have several projects with eyelets. Eyelets are similar to grommets but are a single unit. Using the setting tool will roll down the backside of the eyelet. This tool and many colored eyelets are available at stamp and paper stores.

Gesso
Gesso is a wonderful primer paint that can be used in many projects. In this book I have used it as a primer and as a mixing agent with dyes and paints. It is the best primer I know for canvas, Styrofoam and especially papier maché. It comes in black and white and can be found at most good art supply stores.

Fabric Bond
Found at fabric stores by the yard, fabric bond is an excellent way to adhere fibrous materials together, especially handmade papers.

Vellum
What is commonly called "vellum" is really translucent vellum. It's a sheer paper that can be found in all stamp, paper and scrapbooking stores and is a perfect paper for overlay work. Many types come with designs already printed on one side. Its color can be altered with dye ink.

Paint Pens
There are many types of paint pens. Many simply use the same type of paint you can apply with a brush in pen form and work effectively only on paper. For all nonporous surfaces (clays, plastics, wood, papier maché, chipboard and metal), you will need a permanent type. The only pens that I find hold true metallic color on most surfaces are the Krylon Gold, Silver and Copper Leafing pens.

Cold Laminate
Some laminates need heat setting to make them adhere, but cold laminate is an extremely clear, heavy acetate that is sticky on one side. This makes it much easier to use and no other equipment is necessary to get it to work. It gives any paper surface a high-gloss finish, and it can also be embossed.

Acrylic Inks
These inks can usually be found near calligraphy or airbrush supplies. Pearlescent Liquid Acrylic inks are very thin, making them perfect for washes and drip applications. Most can be mixed with a variety of mediums, including Diamond Glaze, gesso and many kinds of paint.

chapter one

These faux handmade papers can be made with any house-

hold paper—such as paper towels, kitchen parchment, facial tissue or

newsprint—and yet look like lovely handmade papers. You can use

these papers to decorate paper boxes, ceramic, glass or wood items.

faux
paper

dyed paper

This is probably the easiest method I know to create a great looking paper. All you need are some paper towels and dye, and you're ready to go! The two card projects that follow this technique will put your efforts to good use—you'll wrap the dyed paper over pieces of chipboard that will create lovely accents for any card.

what you'll need

two-ply paper towels • several colors of dye ink • metallic ink or paint • small cups or bowls • water

one: Dyed papers begin with two-ply paper towels. Prepare several bowls of dye or stain.

TWO: Add five drops of dye or ink to two tablespoons (30ml) of water. The dye should appear darker in the bowl than the desired color.

TIP

If you would like a more metallic cast to your papers, add a few drops of acrylic metallic inks (the type calligraphers use).

THREE: Fold the towel down to a small square, then dip the corners into the different-colored dyes. Fan folding the towel will give you a different pattern.

FOUR: Once the colors have bled together, allow the piece to dry completely.

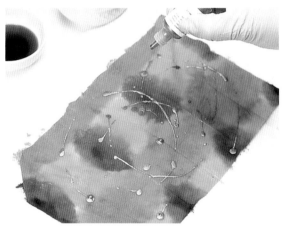

FIVE: Sprinkle metallic ink or paint over the paper surface for a splatter effect. Create several different-colored sheets using this technique. Let the paper dry overnight.

(✺✺✺) **TIP** (✺✺✺)

If you have a very light-colored piece, stamp it with a large background stamp.

DYE
card

Once you've created a nice dyed paper from the previous technique,

experiment with this simple yet elegant card.

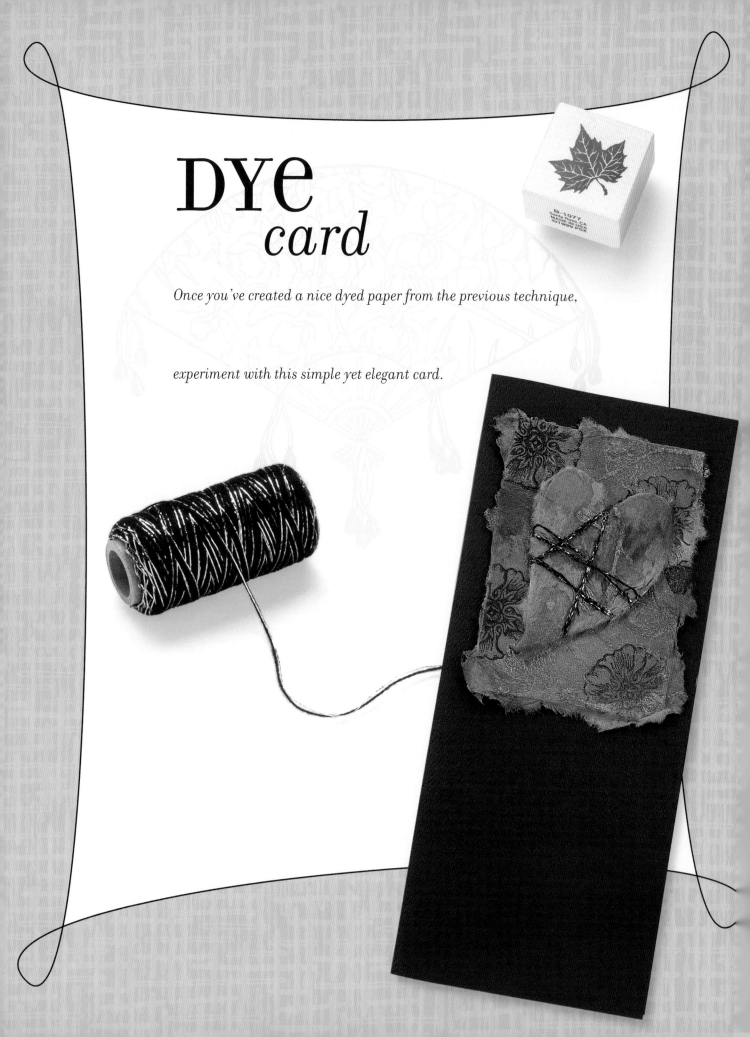

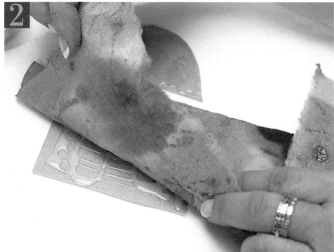

one: Cut a 3" x 2" (8cm x 5cm) piece of chipboard and a smaller piece in the shape of a heart. Cover the pieces of board with a coat of clear glue.

TWO: Quickly apply the dyed paper to the board, allowing the paper to retain any creases or wrinkles. Repeat the steps on the heart-shaped part.

THree: Tear away the excess paper.

FOUR: Stamp a few images on it.

FIVE: Crisscross yarn or thread over the heart. Tie the thread together on the back side of the heart and secure with doublestick tape.

SIX: Apply a dab of glue to the board, then layer the heart on board.

SEVEN: Add doublestick tape to the back of the square and apply to cardstock.

(◦◦◦ TIP ◦◦◦)

Try colored wire strung with beads instead of thread.

paper
& bead *card*

This card adds a few elegant touches to the first basic card. Cut a

1½" x 3" (4cm x 8cm) rectangle and 1½" (4cm) square piece of

chipboard to start.

WHAT YOU'LL NEED
··•··

dyed paper *(from basic technique demo)* • cardstock

¼" (6mm) hole punch or awl • doublestick tape

craft knife • eyelet • eyelet tool

small hammer • metallic thread • clear glue

chipboard *(cardboard)* • beads

··•··

⟨⟨∿ TIP ∿⟩⟩

The punch I used here is a Japanese screw punch, generally a bookbinding tool. You can use a regular ¼" (6mm) hole punch or even an awl.

ONE: Punch a hole in the center of a 1½" (4cm) square piece of chipboard using a ¼" (6mm) hole punch.

TWO: Layer the dyed paper over the square chipboard using clear glue. Do the same for the 1½" x 3" (4cm x 8cm) piece of chipboard.

THREE: On both pieces, trim the excess leaving about ½" (1cm) remaining. Trim the corners at an angle, leaving just an ⅛" (3mm) edge at each corner.

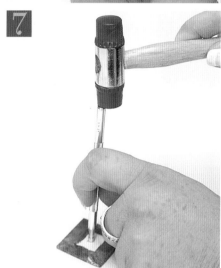

FOUR: Fold in the sides of both pieces; on the square piece, poke through the hole with an awl or needle.

FIVE: Insert a colored eyelet.

SIX: Insert the eyelet setting tool.

seven: Using a small hammer, set the eyelet on the back.

eIGHT: Lightly tap the back of the eyelet to finish. (*Try using an eyelet in a contrasting color.*)

nine: Thread each bead on a loop of thread.

TEN: Draw the loops through the eyelet.

ELEVEN: Attach a square of double-stick tape to the back of the piece.

TWELVE: Layer all the parts onto the cardstock with the doublestick tape.

chapter two

Use napkins, paper towels, newsprint or tissues on kitchen foil to

create a very moldable paper. With this approach, you can create

some interesting shapes to give your greeting a sculptural quality.

Since the paper can be wrinkled and remolded several times, it's

great for wrapping cardboard, boxes and more. When layered back to

back, the same technique can be used to create small bowls or boxes.

SCULPTURE paper

sculpture paper

Any scrap paper, thin junk mail, newspaper, newsprint, paper towel, napkins, bath tissue, wrapping tissue or bond paper can be used. Start with a 12" (30cm) length of heavy foil. In this case for the paper I am using a plain paper towel.

For this particular technique, gesso is used, which can be found at most good art supply stores. Gesso is a wonderful primer because it covers many items completely with only one coat.

WHAT YOU'LL NEED

kitchen foil · white gesso · paper towel · foam brush

any art medium—watercolor, acrylics or inks *(I'm using Diamond Glaze and PearlEx)*

black acrylic paint · hair dryer

one: Place the paper towel in the center of the foil. Pour a 1"-wide dollop (3cm) of white gesso in the center of the paper towel.

TWO: Using a foam brush, spread the gesso out. Moving any liquid paint, gesso or medium is always more effective if spread from the center of the project paper.

THREE: Go over the edges of the towel. Let it dry.

FOUR: To this base paper you can apply almost any art medium including acrylic paints, inks and watercolor paints. I am using a combination of Diamond Glaze and PearlEx. The ratio of PearlEx to Diamond Glaze can vary. I usually start at four parts Diamond Glaze to one part PearlEx, then gradually add more powder for a more opaque paint.

FIVE: Apply the first color thoroughly over the gesso. Let it dry.

SIX: Crumple the base paper then lay it out flat. Using a foam brush, mix a teaspoon (5ml) of Diamond Glaze with ¼ teaspoon (1ml) of black acrylic paint. Brush this mixture lightly over the cracks of the paper.

seven: To speed the drying time, try a hair dryer. Do not use a heat gun for this process—it could make the paint bubble!

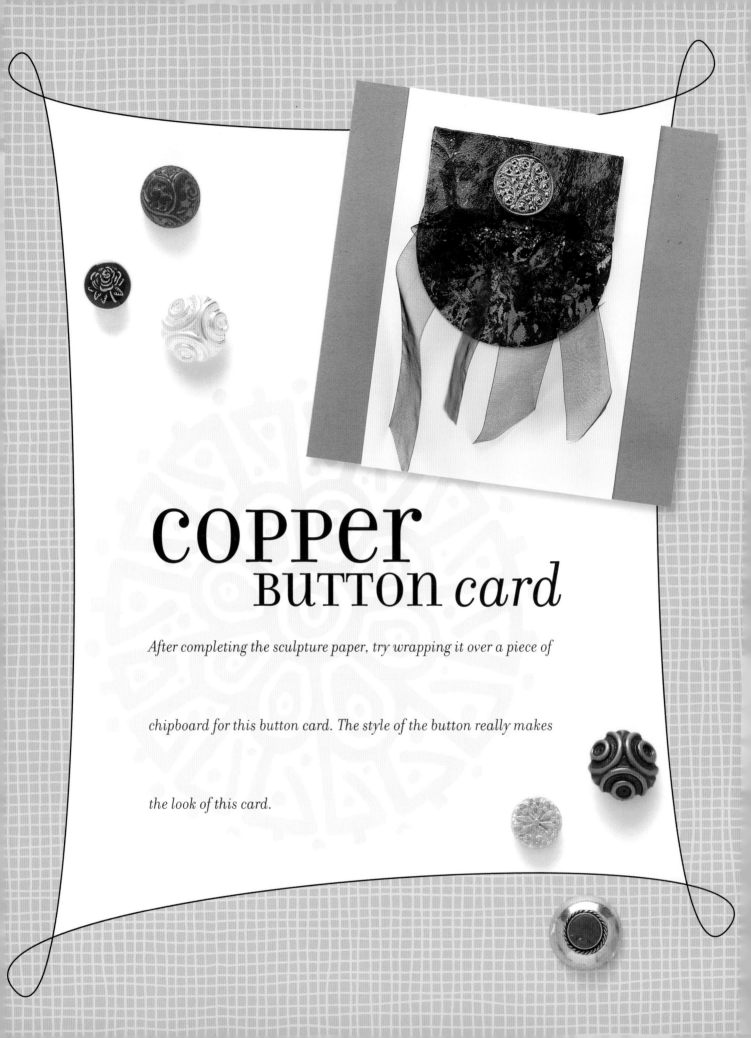

copper
button *card*

After completing the sculpture paper, try wrapping it over a piece of

chipboard for this button card. The style of the button really makes

the look of this card.

ONE: Once the sculpture paper is completely dry, trim it to the desired size.

TWO: For this card I am using a small piece of chipboard about 3" x 1" (8cm x 3cm). Wrap this board with the sculpture paper. No glue necessary!

THREE: Punch a hole large enough for the shank of a button to fit through.

FOUR: You might need to enlarge the hole to a more oval shape depending on the size of the shank. This is easy to do by twisting a craft knife through the existing hole.

FIVE: Insert the button. It should be a snug fit.

SIX: Apply a small amount of glue to the back of the button. Set this piece aside to dry.

SEVEN: From black cardstock, cut out a 3" (8cm) circle. Apply gold leafing pen to a crumpled paper towel then stamp on the cardstock.

EIGHT: Repeat the process until the circle has been covered evenly.

NINE: Add doublestick tape to the back of the sculpture piece, then adhere to the circle.

TEN: Apply a bead of glue to the front seam.

ELEVEN: Shake ROXS over the glue. Allow the ROXS to set for one minute before removing the excess.

TWELVE: Once the piece has dried, adhere to a card with doublestick tape.

THIRTEEN: For a finishing touch, wrap a tassel around the button.

PHOTO
nugget *card*

Here's a variation on the sculpture paper using black gesso. This project

also uses picture pebbles, which are glass marbles with one flat surface.

When placed over an image, it magnifies the design, which is perfect for

small photos.

HOW TO **PREPARE** THE SCULPTURE PAPER

Begin by tearing off a 10" x 10" (25cm x 25cm) piece of foil, then lay your choice of paper on it. Plain newsprint gives a smooth appearance, paper towels a more fuzzy texture. For this piece I have chosen a plain paper table napkin which tends to look like canvas when finished.

Pour a 1" (3cm) dollop of black gesso in the center of the unfolded napkin and, with a foam brush, spread it out to the edges onto the excess foil. Allow this to dry thoroughly. (In some climates, this may be overnight.) The gesso that seeps though the table napkin will adhere the foil to the paper. Crumple the piece for added texture.

ONE: Mix Diamond Glaze with a small amount of PearlEx or acrylic metallic ink.

TWO: Brush over the wrinkles with a foam brush. On this paper I painted half green and the other half gold. Now I can get the contrasting colors I need in one piece of paper.

⟨⟨⟨ TIP ⟩⟩⟩

Try rubber stamping the surface with acrylic inks for a more definite pattern. Some acrylic inks now come in pads, which makes them easier to apply to a stamp.

THREE: Drizzle on inks or paints for more interest. Dry with the hair dryer to speed things up.

FOUR: Choose two contrasting pieces of the sculpture paper. Cut a circle out of each color about 1½" (4cm) in diameter. Place them together foil to foil.

FIVE: Begin rolling the edges together so that the lighter-color paper is on the inside. Mold the paper to form a small bowl.

SIX: Use a ½" (1cm) circle punch to cut a circle from a copy of an old photo.

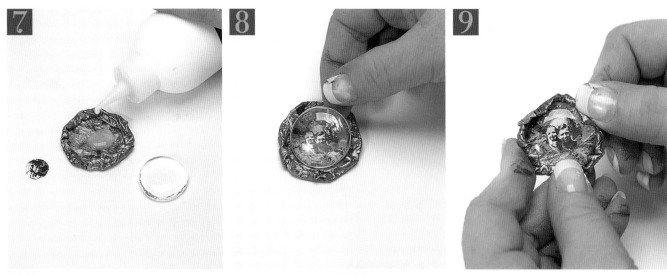

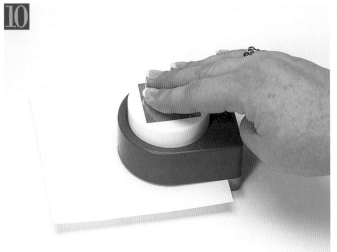

seven: Pour into the bowl a pea-size dollop of Diamond Glaze. Place the photo in the bowl.

eight: Lay a picture pebble into the bowl.

nine: Crimp the edges of the paper around the pebble. Allow the piece to dry.

ten: Punch out a 1½" (4cm) square on white cardstock. Ideally you want a ¾" (2cm) edge.

eleven: Use a transparent ruler to cut off excess from the other side.

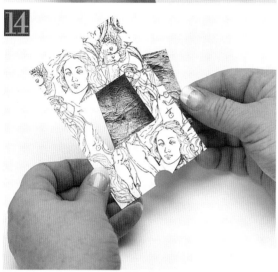

(◦◦◦ TIP ◦◦◦)

Using just a portion of a decorative punch along the edge of cardstock is a great way to add excitement to layers, envelopes or pockets.

TWELVE: To accent the two edges, use the same circle punch used on the photo to cut a half-circle embellishment.

THIRTEEN: Using black dye ink, stamp several images or one large background stamp onto the cardstock.

FOURTEEN: Add a small piece of sculpture paper behind the cutout.

FIFTEEN: Assemble card with double-stick tape; glue on the picture pebble.

chapter three

Duo papers are great for many projects including journals, portfo-

lios, origami boxes and of course greeting cards—especially trifolds

and accordion folds. Any project that shows two sides of a single

paper is perfect. The dyed papers you created in Chapter One are

perfect for the next projects because they are extremely porous and

provide a perfect base for a plastic liner to adhere.

duo paper

duo paper

Plastic wrap laminating is certainly not a new technique. Quite often I run into people who have made plenty of this type of paper but have never used it! Duo papers can be tricky in putting cards together because of the different-colored sides. One card that uses this paper to its full advantage is the triptych card. First let's look at one of the basic laminating methods.

what you'll need

plastic wrap • iron • lightweight handmade papers

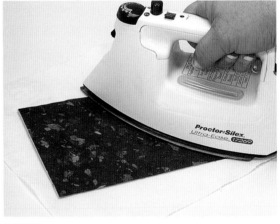

one: Take two very distinct lightweight papers. Good choices are inexpensive tissue papers, lightweight handmade papers or any uncoated text-weight papers. Lay the plastic wrap to the back side of the first paper. Layer the second paper (good side up) over the plastic wrap.

two: Using a warm iron, press the two pieces together. This may require a few test runs because irons and wrap will vary.

three: My preference is to fold the paper in half as soon as possible. This makes the crease very crisp.

TIP

The less expensive the wrap is the better it seems to work. Also, if the papers you choose are very thin, you can layer smaller die-cut paper pieces in between the two layers.

natural
leather *card*

Bags of scrap leather are available at most craft stores. Most bags have a

good variety of colors and sizes that are perfect for stamping.

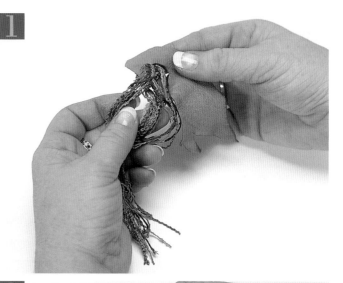

one: I've chosen a piece of leather with a small hole in it—the perfect size for a picture pebble to fit in snugly. Fibers and yarns will give a unique look to your greeting. Here I have attached a selection of them through the hole in the leather.

TWO: To check composition, lay the leather on the duo paper then trim the fibers.

THREE: Select a stamped image or small photo to go under the pebble. In this case I have chosen a small Asian image simply stamped in black ink.

FOUR: Once the image has dried, apply a small amount of clear glue then lay the pebble over the image. Allow this to dry thoroughly.

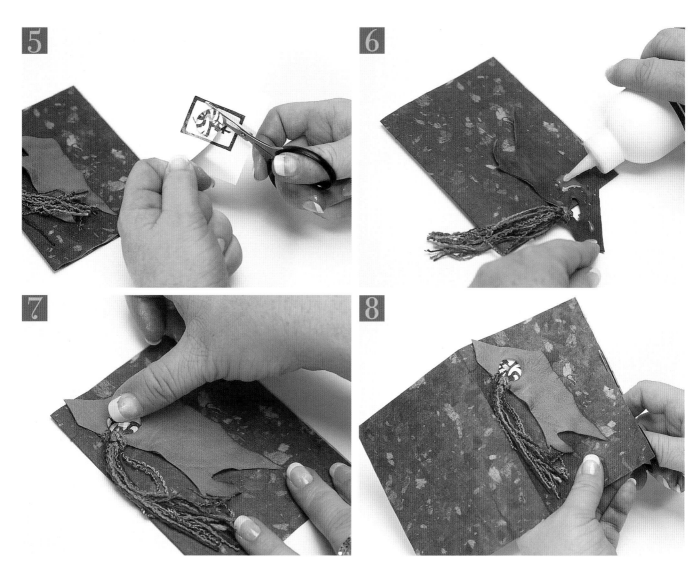

FIVE: Trim tightly around the pebble with scissors.

SIX: Add a small amount of clear glue to the back of the leather. Layer onto the duo paper card.

SEVEN: Adhere the picture pebble with a drop of the clear glue. Apply pressure for a minute.

EIGHT: Trim off ¼" (6mm) of the front of the card to reveal the lighter paper on the inside.

TRIPTYCH
card

This style of card can be made into an arch form or an easy double door

style. For this duo paper project, heavier papers should be used to accom-

modate the weight of decorations. Keep this in mind when creating your

duo papers.

HOW TO PREPARE THE DUO PAPER

Trace the template on page 378 onto cardstock and cut out. Score the panels. Place a sheet of plastic wrap between the cutout triptych and your choice of handmade paper. Trim away as much of the plastic wrap as possible. Continue on to step one.

ONE: Press your triptych shape with a warm iron (silk setting). Trim away the excess plastic and paper.

TWO: Using a circle cutter, remove a circle about 3½" (9cm) from the center panel.

THREE: Mix about ½ teaspoon (2ml) of PearlEx with a tablespoon (15ml) of Diamond Glaze.

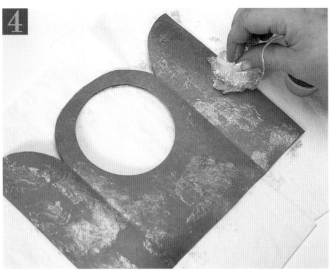

(◦◦◦ TIP ◦◦◦)

Decorating the cardstock after it has been trimmed allows more

precise placement of the images.

(◦◦◦ TIP ◦◦◦)

You can find round or wooden paper clips at specialty office

supply stores and bookstores.

FOUR: Scrunch a piece of plastic wrap to use as a texture tool. Dip into the paint mixture and apply to the cardstock. Let it dry.

FIVE: Many rubber stamp companies sell unmounted rubber only. Quite often I don't have time to mount them on wood, so I use a piece of doublestick tape to temporarily mount the rubber to a stamp pad or small tin.

SIX: Stamp and decorate the plain cardstock.

seven: Bring on the embellishments! Here I have used a round paper clip to hang a large stone bead with metallic thread.

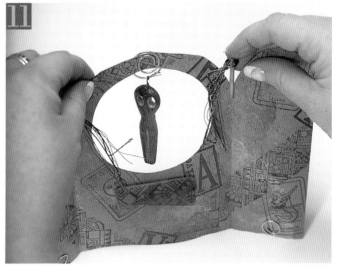

EIGHT: This charm is quite heavy, so I need an embellishment of equal weight to counterbalance the card when it is standing. Here I have used a small piece of stained glass that has been sanded to give soft edges and an opaque finish. Any glass can be stamped with permanent black ink. To stamp an image on the glass, it is easier to lay the glass onto the stamp.

NINE: A small amount of Diamond Glaze added to the back of the glass will keep it adhered to the paper.

TEN: Press firmly for a minute or weigh the piece down with a heavy book.

ELEVEN: Once the glue has set, finish off the embellishments by adding wooden paper clips tied with threads or fibers.

chapter four

Use fabric bond to artfully adhere fabric, beads or ROXS and

handmade papers to cards. It will add an unusual dimensional look

to a greeting. Since thick handmade papers can be difficult to layer

together with plastic wrap because of the bumpy quality of the fibers,

fabric bond easily solves the problem.

Fabric
Bond

GOLD LeaF
cIRcLe card

This project introduces you to the interesting modern-art effect you can

achieve when using fabric bonding material.

ONE: Take a few small pieces of the fabric bond. Several small leftover pieces will work. Arrange the fabric bond on a circle of cardstock or art board. Melt the material with a heat gun.

TWO: Lightly sprinkle embossing powder over the entire surface. Or, instead of embossing powder, try extra fine glitter or an assortment of tiny beads on the fabric bond.

THREE: Layer a few more pieces of the fabric bond then add another color of powder. Heat.

FOUR: While the piece is warm, lay gold leaf over the edge area. Press firmly. Allow the piece to cool then remove the excess leaf.

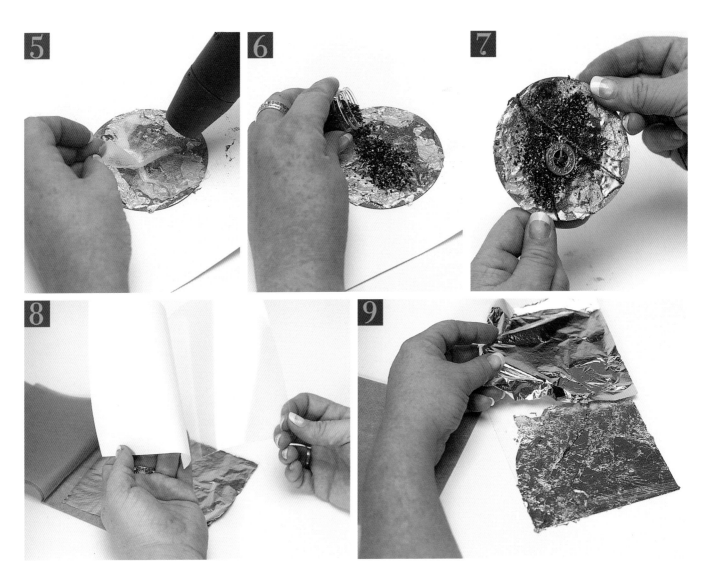

FIVE: Place a few more small pieces of the bonding material on the center of the circle. Heat until melted.

SIX: Pour on ROXS.

seven: Place a charm and/or beads on metallic thread. Wrap the thread around the piece and secure with doublestick tape.

eIGHT: Create the background layer with laminating sheets and gold leaf. Peel the backing from a clear laminating sheet.

nine: Lay the sheet sticky side up. Carefully lay the sheet of gold leaf on the laminate.

TEN: When using sheets of foil, your fingers can gently brush away the excess. Some foil comes in small pieces contained in a box or bag. For this type of foil it is best to use a stencil or stippling brush to gently brush away the excess.

ELEVEN: This technique of applying the foil to the laminate is much easier than using foil glues. Also you can use either side of the foiled laminate. If you like a matte gold finish, use the piece foil side up; if you like the surface to be extremely shiny, use the laminate side up. Either side can be placed on your card with doublestick tape.

TWELVE: Layer all the elements onto cardstock with doublestick tape.

(◌◌ TIP ◌◌)

Using a box lid or plastic tray will catch the excess foil, which you can use again. Even the tiniest piece can be used on another project. Also do not worry if the foil folds over itself, since the excess can be retrieved by softly brushing the surface.

chinese
charm *card*

Introducing interesting fabric scraps and charms to your cards can add

an elegant look for a variety of occasions.

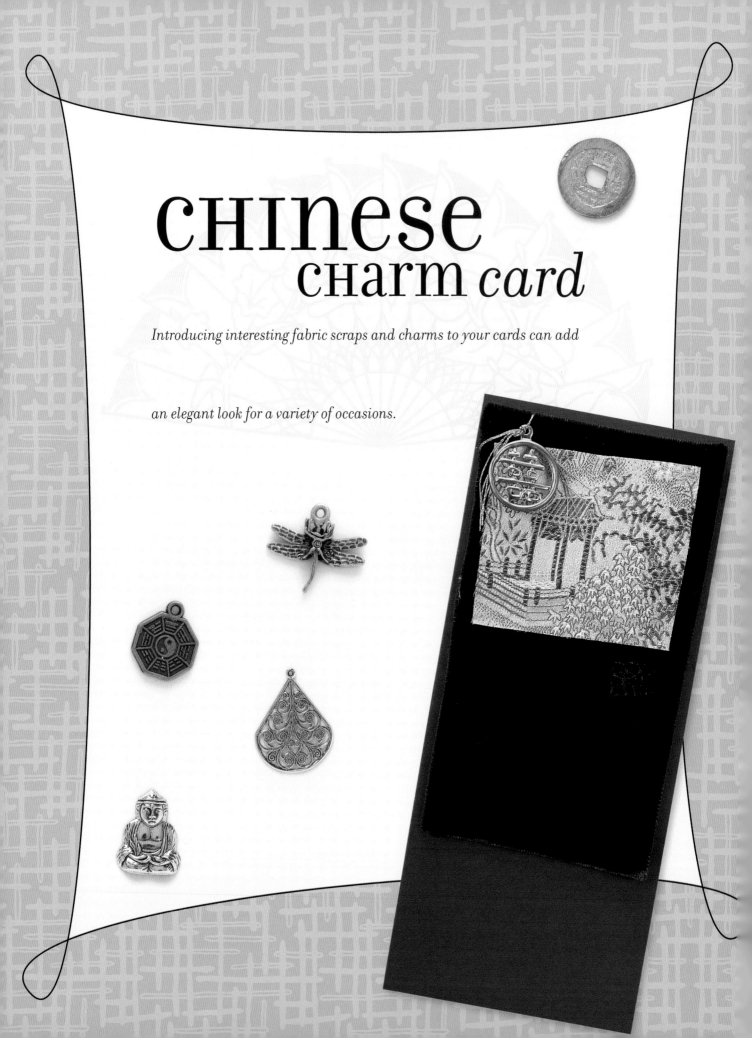

WHAT YOU'LL NEED

...

cardstock • velvet • satin or silk fabric • charm

metallic thread • rubber stamp • scissors

fabric bond • doublestick tape

...

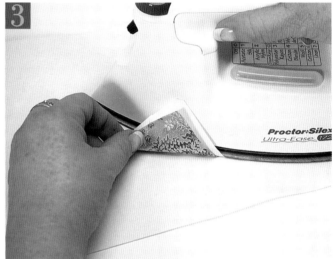

one: Begin with a small rectangle of good velvet. About 3" x 6" (8cm x 15cm) of rayon or acetate works best. Set your iron to the wool or cotton setting. Choose a stamp with a thick-lined pattern to it. Many people use only bold stamps. Even though this stamp is small, the line is heavy.

TWO: Flip the stamp and velvet over so that the back side of the fabric is facing you. Mist the back of the velvet lightly; iron directly on the stamp for 10–15 seconds.

THREE: Choose another piece of fabric. I'm using a piece I picked up at a fabric show. I am only using a 2" x 3" (5cm x 8cm) piece. Iron the bonding material to the fabric following the package directions.

TIP

Choosing the second piece of fabric is what really makes the card. You can use a very small piece of heavy patterned silk, satin or even a remnant of upholstery material. For most heavy fabrics on cards, Leave the fabric with a raw edge. Velvet is the exception because it frays.

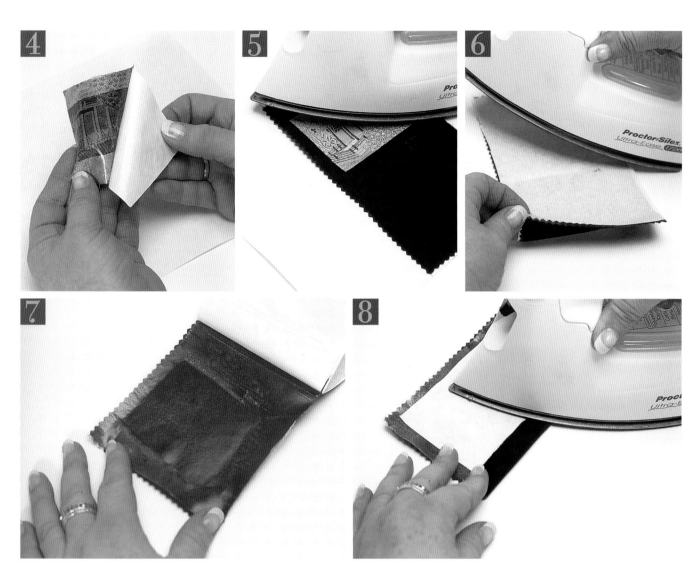

(((◦ TIP ◦)))

To eliminate bulky corners, trim the excess from the corners

before folding in, as we did with the papers in Chapter 1.

FOUR: Remove the backing from the bonding material.

FIVE: Position this fabric on the front of your velvet. Carefully iron it to the velvet using the tip of the iron.

SIX: Iron the bonding material to the back of the velvet. Do not overheat or you could lose the image pressed into the velvet.

SEVEN: Remove the backing then place on a piece of cardstock cut to the desired size. In this case, it is about 5" x 3" (13cm x 8cm).

EIGHT: Fold over the raw edge. Iron down.

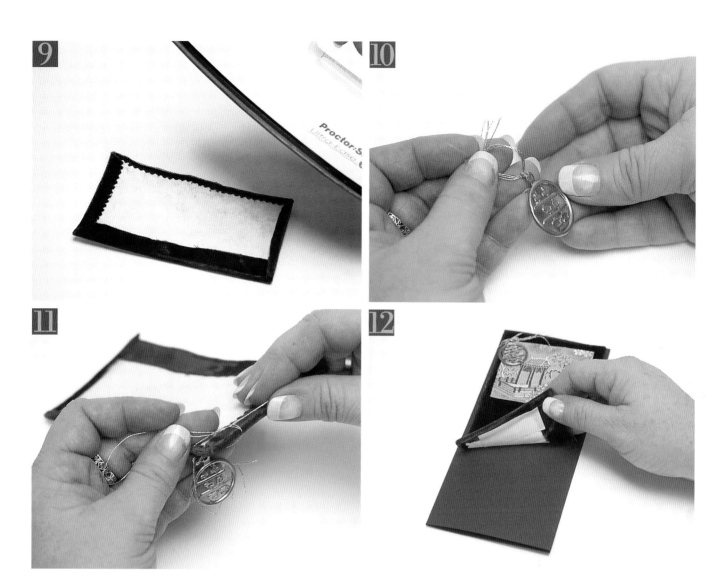

nine: Press the completed piece once more, especially at the corners.

Ten: Create a loop with metallic thread and tie on the brass charm.

eleven: Attach the charm to the top left corner.

Twelve: Add doublestick tape to the back of the piece and layer onto cardstock.

| chapter five |

I have taught window illusion cards for many years, and it is still

one of my favorite classes. This technique uses two layers of vellum

or acetate to create the illusion of floating elements. The second card

is an updated version of the original card using mica tiles.

m1 amou

WINDOW ILLUSIONS

BeaTNIK *card*

Select two pieces of cardstock of the same size and color. Square cards

are great for this project since the measurements will be the same all

the way around the card. This project will use removable tape, which

is available at stamp stores and office supply stores. If you cannot find

removable tape, here is a trick

that works in a pinch.

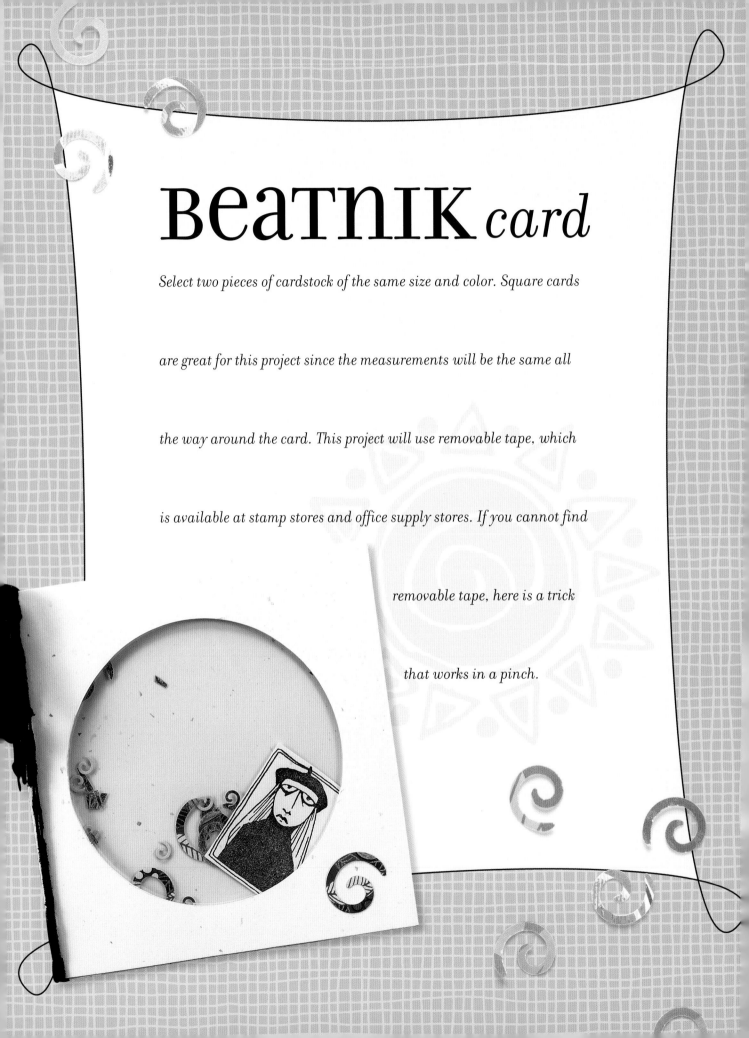

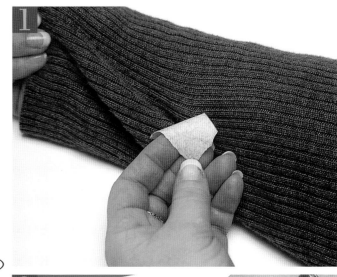

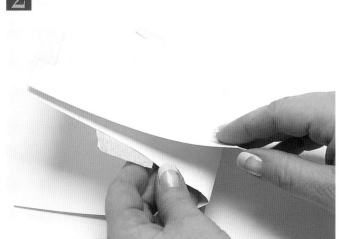

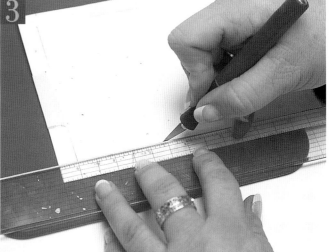

ONE: Take any kind of tape—here I am using the same doublestick tape I use for most projects—and place it several times on any fabric. This will create a surface on the tape that is not as sticky and presto—removable tape!

TWO: Begin by taping the two identical cards back to front.

THREE: Using your craft knife and a transparent ruler, cut a ½" (1cm) frame out of the taped section. You will be cutting through two pieces of cardstock, so be sure to have a fresh blade in the knife.

(((∞ TIP ∞)))

With any type of tape try not to stretch it taut, as it will pull

back to its original size causing a bubble in the tape and paper.

FOUR: Now the frame will match up perfectly when you put the finished card together.

FIVE: Apply clear doublestick tape around one of the frames.

SIX: Cut two pieces of acetate (about 5" [13cm] square and 4¾" [12cm] square) to use inside the frame. The smaller piece creates a pocket of acetate so that you will not need as much tape. Place the larger piece of acetate on the frame that has been taped.

SEVEN: Stamp two identical images. Using doublestick tape, adhere the images back-to-back. Lay these images and other elements on the acetate.

EIGHT: Here I have used punches to create my own confetti from leftover paper scraps. Make sure the paper you are punching looks good on both sides, and try to keep all of the materials in the center of the acetate as they tend to gravitate toward the exposed tape.

NINE: Sandwich your smaller piece of acetate over the tape; there should be a small strip of tape still exposed.

TEN: Line up the inside edges of the second frame, then lay the top frame onto the tape.

(◎◎ **TIP** ◎◎)

For the inside of the acetate pocket, you can also use confetti, tiny beads, colored mica chips, glitter and back-to-back stickers.

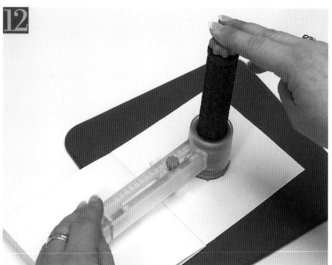

eLeven: Trim any excess tape, acetate or cardstock from the outside edges of the card with a craft knife.

TWeLVe: On the front panel of the card (which can be left solid) I have created a large circle frame with my cutter.

THIRTeeN: To add a bit of color, tie on a bit of chenille yarn.

(TIP)

Keeping white cardstock clean is tough. Keep a white rubber eraser and craft knife nearby for quick cleanups. Lightly scrape smudges with the knife, then even out the paper surface with the eraser.

mica
HEIRLOOM *card*

I like the natural look of these mica tiles, particularly with old photos.

The crinkled texture of the mica is much more interesting than simple

acetate, especially when creating a graphically simple card. Begin with

two square cards and one dark green standard note card.

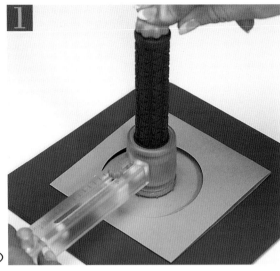

one: Using a circle cutter, punch or craft knife, cut a 3" (8cm) circle out of the center of a square card.

TWO: This circle should go through both sides of the card.

THREE: Carefully separate a mica tile into two thin pieces of equal size larger than the circle.

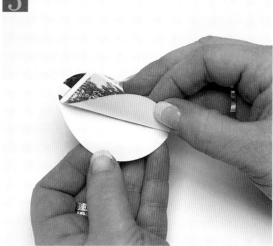

FOUR: Cut two smaller circles (about 2"
[5cm]) out of identical color copies of an
heirloom photo.

FIVE: Attach the photos back-to-back
with a small piece of doublestick tape.

SIX: Insert the photos between the mica
tiles. Apply a drop of clear glue to an incon-
spicuous spot on the photo to keep the
photo in place. Attach the entire element to
the inside of the card using doublestick tape.

SEVEN: Seal the card up.

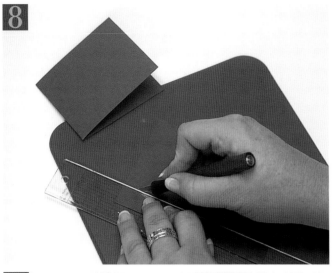

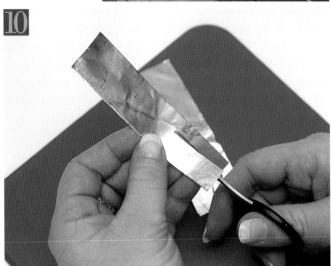

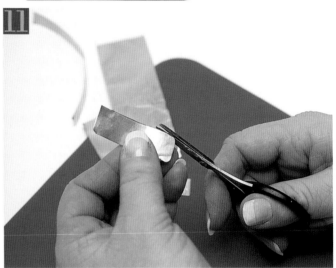

(◊◊◊ TIP ◊◊◊)

On some of the other samples, I have simply used two cards of different colors then trimmed the front of one card to achieve the ¾" (2cm) border fold.

EIGHT: From the folded dark green note card, trim a ¾" (2cm) width of the scored fold.

NINE: Cut your second square card in half; you will use one of these halves to create the heirloom card's back panel. Place a section of doublestick tape on the inside of the dark green fold. Position the fold onto the framed photo and the back panel. Press well.

TEN: Metal alphabet stamps are available at most hardware and some stamp stores. They are simple to use with most metals, especially this thin copper. With scissors, cut out a small strip of copper.

ELEVEN: Round off the corners.

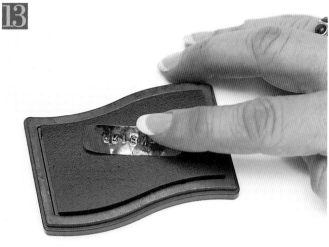

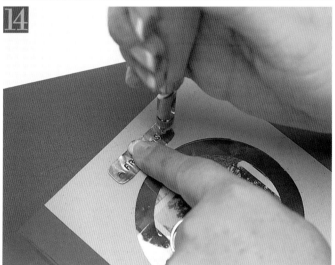

(ᴅᴅ TIP ᴅᴅ)

When stamping a word with an alphabet set, write out the word on a piece of paper the same size as the area to be stamped, then set the paper above the area. Begin with the center letter and work your way out to each side.

TWELVE: Holding each metal stamp straight up on the copper strip, tap the top of the stamp several times with a small hammer.

THIRTEEN: After completing the stamping rub a bit of black ink over the stamped letters; wipe any excess off of the copper.

FOURTEEN: Punch a hole on either end of the copper strip with a ⅛" (3mm) hole punch. Lay the strip on the front of the card for placement. Mark the holes with a pencil, then punch corresponding holes in the cardstock.

FIFTEEN: Use tiny brads to hold the strip in place.

| chapter six |

Give a new look to your greeting cards by using shipping tags.

Tags are available at discount, hardware, craft, stamp and office sup-

ply stores and come in a variety of papers as well as metal. In both

projects punches are used to add pattern and depth.

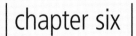

SHIPPING Tags

LEaF
TaG *card*

Gold leaf and cold laminate are generally found at craft and stamp

stores. Quite often gold leaf can be messy and

difficult to use since it tends to fly away. Cold

laminate can make the process much quick-

er and neater than glues.

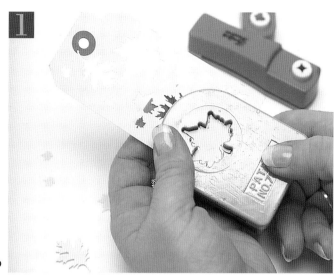

 TIP

Turning a punch upside down will make positioning shapes

much easier.

ONE: Start with a large shipping tag. Remove the string. Punch out most of the surface of the tag with a variety of leaf craft punches. These punches are widely available from craft, stamp and scrapbooking stores.

TWO: Once you have completed the punching, apply a piece of laminating sheet to the back of the tag. Trim away the excess laminate.

THREE: Lay gold leaf on the sticky side of the tag.

(((⌒ TIP ⌒)))

Pigment ink works well for this project since the paper on most

tags is uncoated. It also wipes off the foil effortlessly.

(((⌒ TIP ⌒)))

Simple geometric punches and vivid colors work well on a

birthday card.

FOUR: Press the gold leaf well into the crevices. Gently use a stiff brush to remove the excess foil.

FIVE: Color the tag with a brown pigment ink pad. The coverage on the tags is better if you apply the ink after every image has been punched; it covers the cut edges of each image.

SIX: Remove the excess ink from the gold leaf with a tissue.

SEVEN: Cover the brown reinforcement and edge the tag with a gold leafing pen.

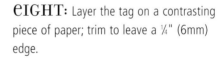

eight: Layer the tag on a contrasting piece of paper; trim to leave a ¼" (6mm) edge.

nine: Add a coordinating ribbon and layer the tag element on a tall card.

ten: For an extra touch, add a strip of the contrasting paper to the inside bottom of the card.

eleven: Finish by punching a few tiny leaves along the front bottom edge of the card.

corset *card*

These corset (or banded) cards are great fun to unwrap when you use

fancy ribbons, wild fibers and charms. Punches are again the key to

achieving a lacy look. The more you punch, the

fancier it looks!

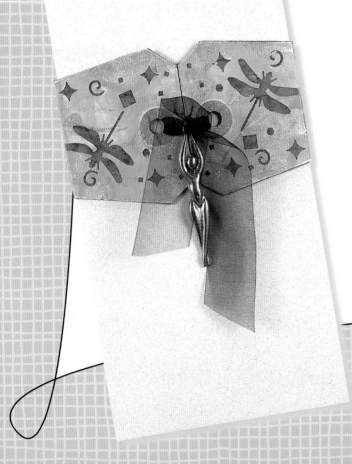

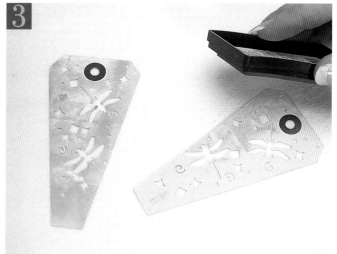

ONE: Cut two large shipping tags into a triangular shape.

TWO: Punch out a variety of shapes, creating a lacy-type effect on the tags.

THREE: Rub green metallic pigment ink over the tags.

TIP

Punch the larger shapes first, then fill in with punches of decreasing size.

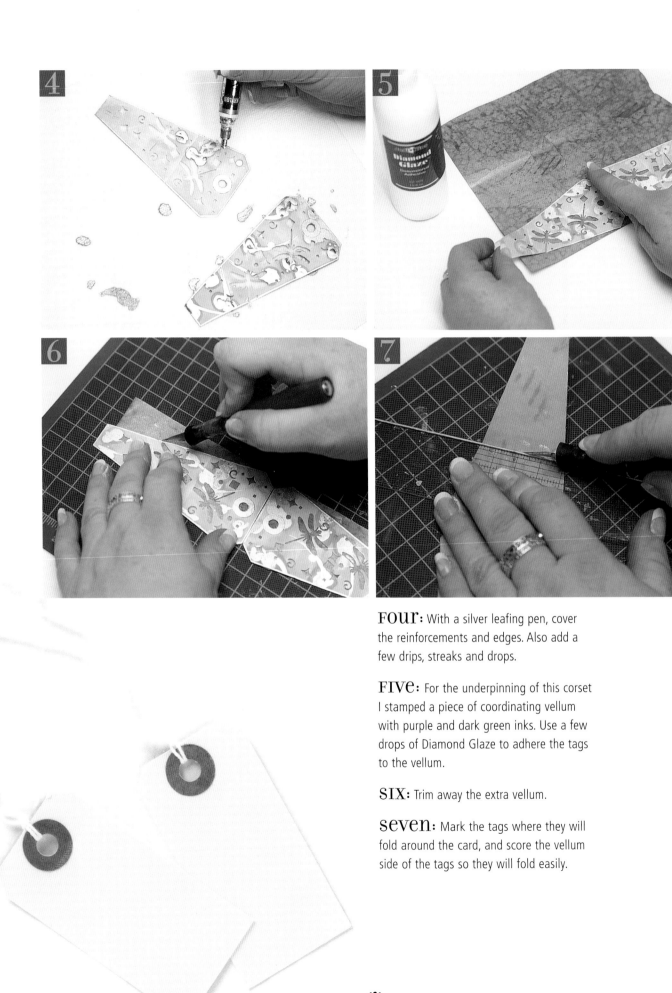

FOUR: With a silver leafing pen, cover the reinforcements and edges. Also add a few drips, streaks and drops.

FIVE: For the underpinning of this corset I stamped a piece of coordinating vellum with purple and dark green inks. Use a few drops of Diamond Glaze to adhere the tags to the vellum.

SIX: Trim away the extra vellum.

SEVEN: Mark the tags where they will fold around the card, and score the vellum side of the tags so they will fold easily.

(((⟅ TIP ⟆)))

I have scored the tags with the back side of my craft knife. This creates a very sharp crease.

(((⟅ TIP ⟆)))

A corset band can be made to open in the front by cutting the front seam open with a craft knife.

EIGHT: Trim out the holes of the tags.

NINE: Thread a piece of sheer ribbon through the holes.

TEN: Wrap the corset around the card and secure with doublestick tape.

ELEVEN: Add a large silver charm or bead. The card should be opened by sliding the whole corset up over the top of the card.

chapter seven

I cannot resist cool fibers, ribbons or thread, and since I do not

sew, it is hard to justify buying them. Then I tried this technique

with the same fabric bond we have used in a previous chapter—what

fun! These fiber cards are a joy to make, and they're so simple and

quick! I try to choose natural fibers when possible. Nylon is not a

good thing near a hot iron!

FIBERS

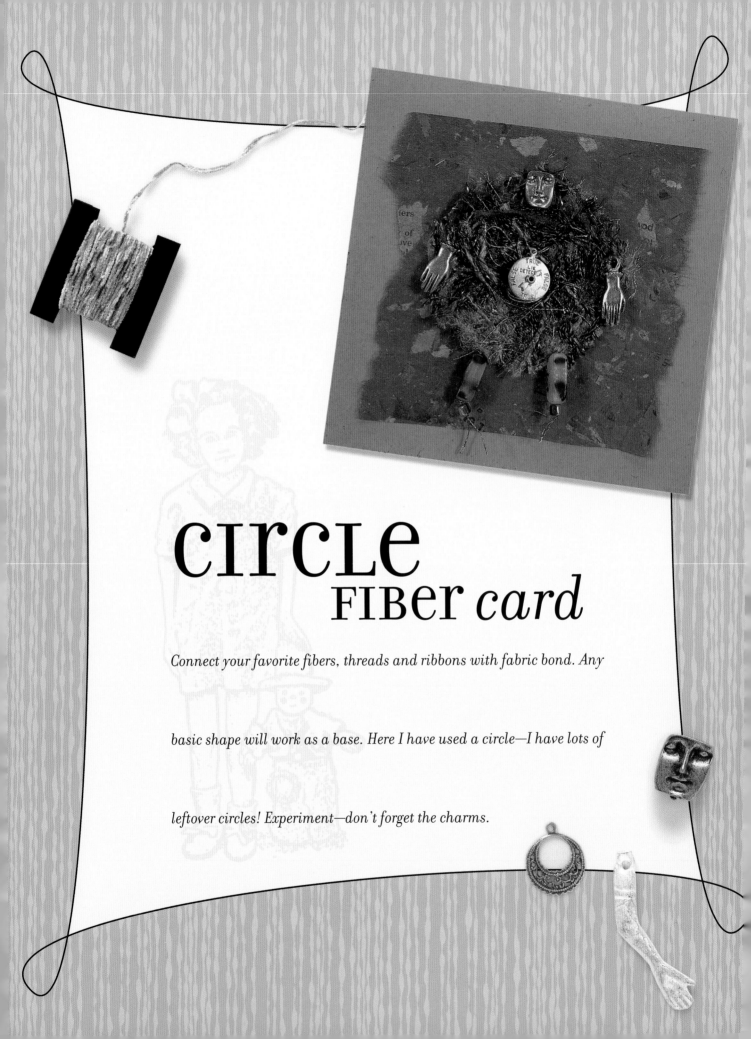

circle
FIBER *card*

Connect your favorite fibers, threads and ribbons with fabric bond. Any

basic shape will work as a base. Here I have used a circle—I have lots of

leftover circles! Experiment—don't forget the charms.

one: Using a round piece of cardstock or chipboard as a base, iron on a piece of bonding material. Remove the backing.

TWO: Cut the fibers into smaller bits of varying lengths; lay an assortment on the bonded side of the cardstock.

THREE: Press with a hot iron. Check the fabric bond package direction for the right temperature.

(⟅⟅⟅ TIP ⟅⟅⟅)

You will find the fibers may not cover your cardstock complete-
ly, so add small pieces of the bond to cover those areas. Then
repeat the process.

FOUR: Turn the piece over and then iron the cardstock side.

FIVE: Leave a little edge when trimming. Simply even up the fibers. The edge of the cardstock should not be showing.

SIX: The background layer on this card uses a coordinating handmade paper. Tear some of the edges to correspond with the ragged fiber element.

(⟅⟅⟅ TIP ⟅⟅⟅)

Instead of trimming the fibers to the exact size of the cardstock,
allow a bit of overhang for a rag rug appearance.

SEVEN: Add a few pieces of the bonding to the back.

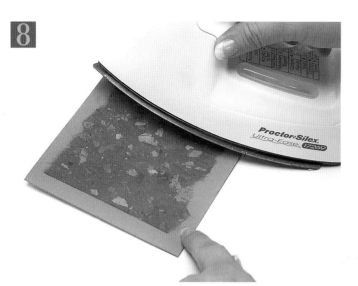

eIGHT: Iron directly onto a piece of cardstock.

nIne: Sew on head, hands and feet charms for the character.

Ten: Adhere the fiber element to the card with doublestick tape.

(◊◊◊ TIP ◊◊◊)

The charms do not have to be in the shapes of hands and feet. You can use charms that represent those features. Small bells or beads can be substituted.

(◊◊◊ TIP ◊◊◊)

This card makes an excellent card/gift. Instead of permanently fixing the fiber element to the card, add a pin back or a cord for a necklace. When creating jewelry, I recommend using colored mat board as the base.

FIBER
KEY *card*

Start this project by cutting a rectangle of cardstock or chipboard and a

piece of bonding material 3" x 4" (8cm x 10cm). Place the bonding piece

on the front of the cardstock. Iron the two pieces together. When cool,

remove the backing from the bond.

WHAT YOU'LL NEED

•••

sculpture paper • scissors • assorted fibers • key

fabric bond • assorted-color cardstock • doublestick tape

chipboard *(cardboard)* • iron

•••

One: Cut an array of beautifully colored threads, narrow silk ribbons and fancy yarns to lay on the cardstock. Leave at least ⅛" (3mm) overhang on all sides. Cover the piece generously. Add more bonding pieces as needed over the fibers, then iron over the entire piece.

TWO: Tie a piece of chenille or ribbon to an old key or charm.

((((TIP))))

Metallic threads add dramatic flair to natural fibers and silk ribbons.

THREE: Tie the key to the fiber piece, and wrap extra chenille around the base.

FOUR: A piece of sculpture paper is a great background to this fiber art. Fold the edges back to the desired size.

 TIP

Try old skate, luggage or drum keys instead of door keys. Seek out antique stores, army surplus stores and flea markets for old, flat metal objects that can be used on greeting cards.

FIVE: Add a light-colored layer of cardstock.

SIX: Trim away the excess fibers.

seven: Add doublestick tape to the back of the fiber piece. Layer onto the card.

(◌ TIP ◌)

Try not to trim the fibers too evenly—retain the ragged appearance.

| chapter eight |

I am always on the look out for unusual materials to use on my

latest greetings. I love experimenting with new looks and little sur-

prises. Since most cards are sent in simple envelopes, the size of an

embellishment is very important. Look for items no thicker than $\frac{1}{4}$".

Otherwise you will need a box for mailing.

COOL TRINKETS

cute
crystal *card*

Watch crystals are not always easy to find but are well worth the hunt.

You'll find specific resources in the back of the book. I am using watch

crystals that are new and plastic. Check out

antique stores or Internet auctions for old crystals

or timepiece dealers for new glass ones.

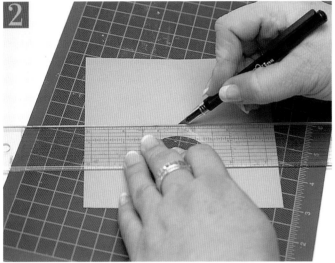

one: Punch a circle from a piece of cardstock. Push the punch in as far as possible.

TWO: Trim away the excess of the cardstock leaving ½" (1cm) on either side.

THRee: Punch three small circles (1/16" [2mm]) along the top of the large circle.

(◌◌ TIP ◌◌)

Try punching wax paper to help paper punches work more smoothly.

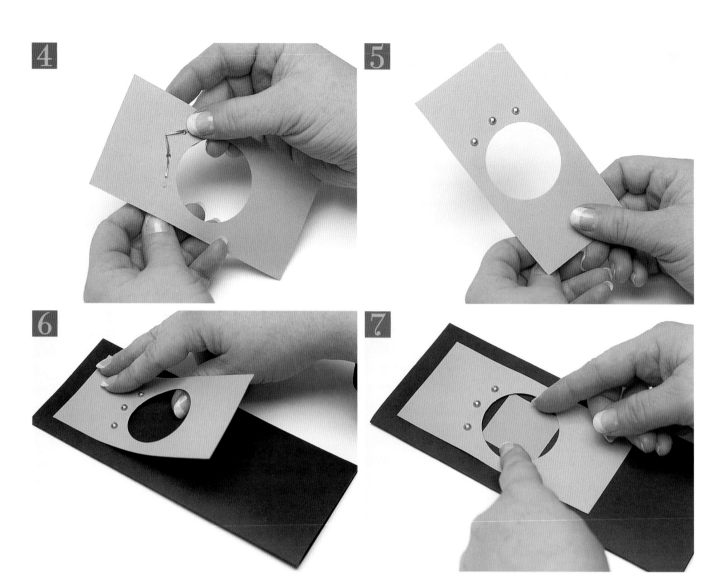

FOUR: Insert small brads into the tiny circles. Bend the prongs back tightly.

FIVE: Check the front of the frame to be certain the prongs are hidden.

SIX: Using doublestick tape at the top and bottom of the frame only, apply the piece to the front of a tall card.

seven: For added contrast, punch a 1" (3cm) square from pale green card-stock. Apply doublestick tape to the back, then insert the square into the circle frame. Set aside.

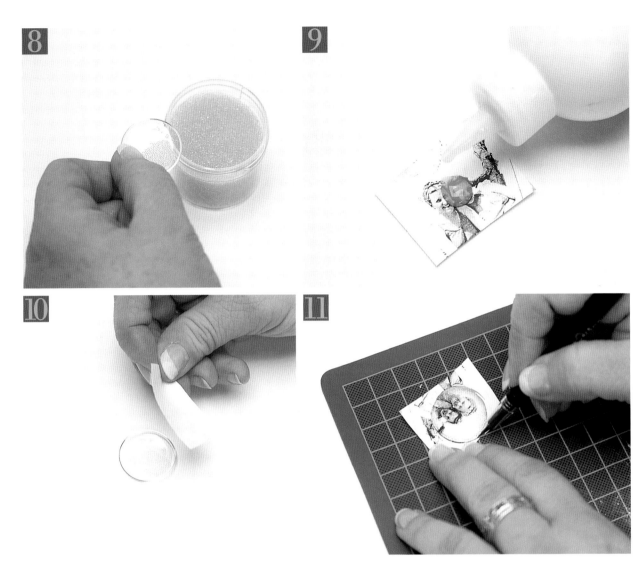

TIP

While the Diamond Glaze is damp, pull the copy gently to flatten the surface before applying it to the rim of the crystal.

EIGHT: Dip the plastic watch crystal into the tiny holeless beads. Leave the crystal open side up on the table while you prepare the paper backing.

nine: Use a color copy of an old photo as the backing to the crystal. Apply a small amount of Diamond Glaze evenly over the surface of the copy.

Ten: Allow the copy to dry for 30 seconds, then apply carefully to the rim of the crystal. Allow this piece to dry in this position for 20 minutes.

eLeven: Trim the excess paper from the watch crystal edge.

TWELVE: Apply doublestick tape to the back of the finished crystal. Attach the crystal to the card.

THIRTEEN: Using black dye ink and a small alphabet stamp, stamp a word along the bottom of the circle frame.

fancy
aunt *card*

This is one of my favorite photos of my Aunt Caroline. I have color-copied

it many times to use on cards, journals, boxes and jewelry. I think she

would have liked it too since she looks so svelte! The mica tiles add to the

heirloom look of the photo, and this

technique is a great way to use the

smaller tile pieces.

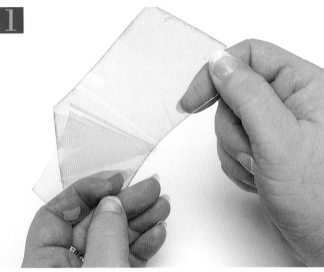

ONE: Tear the mica tiles into smaller, thinner pieces.

TWO: Tear away the edges of the photocopy. Apply a thin layer of clear glue with a paintbrush to the surface of the tile.

THREE: Layer the copy on the tile, then cover the photo with clear glue.

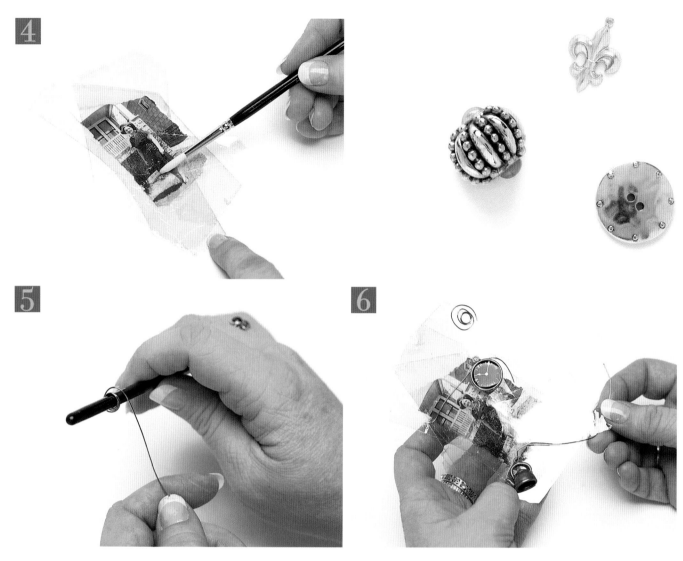

FOUR: Add several smaller tiles to the top of the copy.

FIVE: Twist copper wire around the handle of a paintbrush to create even swirls. Add buttons or beads on the wire.

SIX: Arrange the wire around the mica tile pieces, leaving swirled ends on the front of the piece.

((((TIP))))

Shank buttons can be difficult to use on some projects, but for this project they can be the perfect embellishment, especially if they are from the same era as the photo. Military shanks would be great on old army or navy photos!

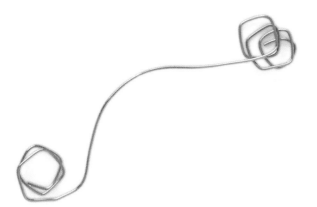

seven: Apply a thin layer of clear glue to a note card; add a torn piece of contrasting cardstock to the front.

eight: Using more clear glue, layer the tile piece to the front of the card.

nine: Stamp a word on a tiny flag of paper with a small metal alphabet. Attach it by curling it around a wire.

rusty
DRAGONFLY *card*

There are many interesting metal pieces available at craft, stamp and

paper arts stores. These particular pieces come in many shapes and sizes

and are rusted and ready to go!

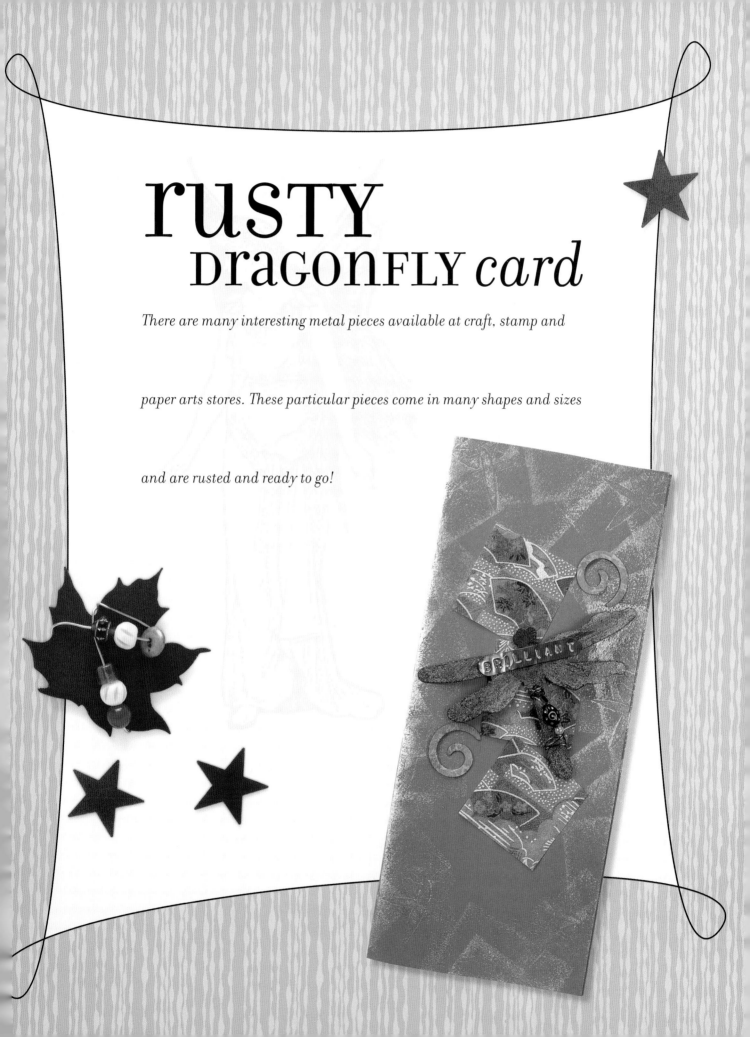

WHAT YOU'LL NEED

••••

metal dragonfly • white iridescent ink pad • beads

copper wire • small hammer • metal alphabet

clear glue • blue cardstock • 1" (3cm) square punch

swirl punch • decorative papers • Asian stamp

blue dye ink • thin copper sheet

••••

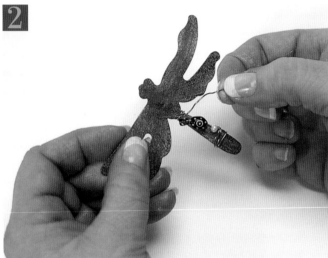

ONE: To soften the color of the metal, apply white iridescent ink directly on the dragonfly. Let dry.

TWO: Decorate the front of the dragonfly with copper wire strung with beads.

THREE: Using a metal alphabet and a small hammer, stamp a word into a thin copper sheet.

4

5

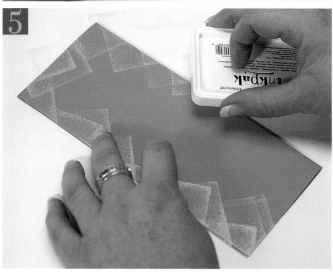

6

FOUR: Adhere the copper piece to the dragonfly with a drop or two of clear glue.

FIVE: Lightly dab the same iridescent white ink pad used on the dragonfly to the edge of a tall blue card.

SIX: Punch three 1" (3cm) squares and several swirls out of a decorative printed paper.

(((∞)) **TIP** (∞)))

If you like a softer appearance, use a sea sponge to apply the iridescent ink to the edge of the card.

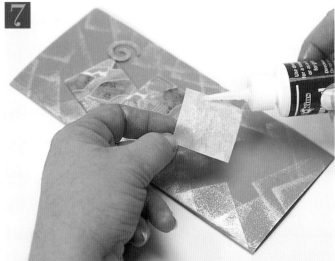

seven: Adhere the printed papers as shown directly to the tall card.

eight: Stamp an Asian image along the edge of the cardstock in a medium blue dye ink.

nine: Spread clear glue along the back of the dragonfly, then apply to the front of the card.

FRAMED
GAL *card*

By using foil tape from the local stained glass supplier or stamp store,

you can create a mini-framed photo on the front of your next card. These

little frames make a great decorative

element. Also, you can simply add a pin

to the back of such three-dimensional

items for a neat gift.

one: Create a piece of sculpture paper (see Chapter Two) by applying white gesso over a piece of tissue paper on aluminum foil. Allow the paper to dry thoroughly, then apply a layer of Diamond Glaze mixed with green PearlEx.

TWO: While the mixture is wet, use a rubber brush to create a pattern in the wet surface. Let dry.

THREE: Dip the rubber brush into pink iridescent ink.

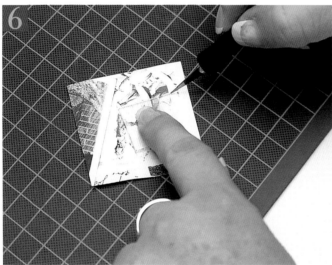

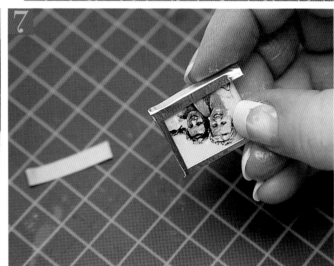

four: Paint pink iridescent ink into the pattern.

five: Place the piece of glass over the photocopy.

six: Crop the photocopy to the size of the glass.

seven: Foil tape is exceptionally sticky, so cut several 1" (3cm) pieces of foil tape before you begin. Apply the foil, leaving an even, straight edge along the photocopy. Press firmly. Trim the foil as each side is applied.

eIGHT: With a craft knife, cut holes in the card for the eyelets.

nIne: Insert the eyelets through the sculpture paper and cardstock.

Ten: Use a hammer and setting tool to set the eyelets on the back side of the card.

eLeven: Adhere the photo to the card with doublestick tape.

TRIPTYCH TEMPLATE

resources

❊ stamp, paper and ink companies

American Art Stamp
3870 Del Amo Blvd
Suite 501
Torrance, CA 90503
(310) 371-6593
www.americanartstamp.com
❊ stamps and supplies

Art Gone Wild!
3110 Payne Ave.
Cleveland, OH 44114
(800) 945-3980
www.agwstamps.com
❊ stamps and supplies

A Stamp in the Hand Co.
20507 S. Belshaw Ave.
Carson, CA 90746
(310) 884-9700
www.astampinthehand.com
❊ stamps

Claudia Rose
15 Baumgarten Road
Saugerties, NY 12477
(845) 679-9235
www.claudiarose.com
❊ stamps

Coffee Break Designs
P.O. Box 34281
Indianapolis, IN 46234
❊ eyelets, watch crystals, brads

ColorBox / Clearsnap / Ancient Page
Box 98
Anacortes, WA 98221
(888) 448-4862
www.clearsnap.com
❊ stamp pads

Great American Stamp Store, Inc.
1015 Post Road E.
Westport, CT 06880
(203) 221-1229
www.greatamericanstampstore.com
❊ stamp supplies, punches

Craft World (head office)
No. 8 North St., Guildford
Surrey GU1 4AF
England
Tel: 07000 757070
❊ retail craft stores

The Creative Block
25967 Detroit Rd.
West Lake, OH 44115
(440) 333-7941
❊ stamps and supplies

Draggin' Ink
P.O. Box 24135
Santa Barbara, CA 93121
(805) 966-5297
www.dragginink.com
❊ templates and supplies

February Paper
P.O. Box 17043
Salem, OR 97305
(360) 705-1519
www.febpaper.com
❊ fibers and paper

HobbyCraft
7 Enterprise Way
Aviation Park
Bournemouth Int'l Airport
Christchurch
Dorset BH23 6HG
United Kingdom
Tel: 0800 272387
www.hobbycraft.co.uk
❊ retail craft stores

Hot Potatoes
2805 Columbine Place
Nashville, TN 37204
(615) 269-8002
www.hotpotatoes.com
❊ stamps and fabric kits

Jacquard Products
Rupert, Gibbon and Spiders, Inc.
P.O. Box 425
Healdsburg, CA 95448
(800) 442-0455
www.jacquardproducts.com
❊ PearlEx, fabric paints, supplies

Judi-Kins
17803 S. Harvard Boulevard
Gardena, CA 90248
(800) 398-5834
www.judikins.com
❊ Diamond Glaze, stamps, supplies

Krylon Products
(800) 797-3332
www.krylon.com
❊ Krylon leafing pens

Lighthouse Memories
(909) 879-0218
www.lighthousememories.com
❊ circle cutters

Magenta
351 Blain
Mont-Saint Hilaire
Quebec, Canada J3H3B4
(514) 446-5253
www.magentarubberstamps.com
❊ stamps, supplies, paper

McGill, Inc.
131 E. Prairie St.
Marengo, IL 60152
(800) 982-9884
www.mcgillinc.com
❊ punches, scissors

Marvy Uchida
3535 Del Amo Blvd.
Torrance, CA 90503
(800) 541-5877
www.uchida.com
✳ dye inks and supplies

Meer Image
P.O. Box 12
Arcata, CA 95518
(707) 822-4338
www.meerimage.com
✳ stamps

Pam Bakke Paste Papers
1419 37th St.
Bellingham, WA 98226
(360) 738-4830
✳ handmade papers

Paper Parachute
P.O. Box 91385
Portland, OR 97291-0385
✳ stamps and supplies

paula best and co. Rubberstamps
507 Trail Dr.
Moss Landing, CA 95039
(831) 632-0587
www.paulabest.com
✳ stamps and silver charms

On the Surface
3423 Church
Skokie, IL 60076
(847) 675-2520
✳ fibers and beads

Postmodern Design
P.O. Box 720416
Norman, OK 73070
✳ stamps and supplies

Postscript Studio / Carmen's Veranda
P.O. Box 1539
Placentia, CA 92871
(888) 227-6367
www.postscriptstudio.com
✳ stamps and supplies

Rubber Monger
P.O. Box 1777
Snowflake, AZ 85937-1777
(928) 536-5128
www.rubbermonger.com
✳ stamps

Rubbermoon Stamp Company
P.O. Box 3258
Hayden Lake, ID 83835
www.rubbermoon.com
✳ stamps

Ruby Red Rubber
P.O. Box 2076
Yorba Linda, CA 92885
(714) 970-7584
✳ stamps

Scattered Pictures
13852 NE Sandy Blvd.
Portland, OR 97230
(503) 252-1888
✳ scrapbooks supplies and stickers

Skycraft Designs / Papers
26395 S. Morgan Road
Estacada, OR 97023
(503) 630-7173
✳ handmade papers, pastels, supplies

Speedball Art Products Company
2226 Speedball Rd.
Statesville, NC 28687
(800) 898-7224
www.speedballart.com
✳ C-thru ruler and supplies

Stamp Addicts
Park Lane Lodge, Park Lane
Gamlingay
Bedfordshire SG19 3PD
England
Phone/fax: 01767 650329
www.stampaddicts.com
✳ stamps and stamp supplies

Stamp Camp
P.O. Box 222091
Dallas, TX 75222
(214) 830-0020
www.stampcamp.com
✳ stamps

Stamp Your Art Out
9685 Kenwood Rd
Cincinnati, OH 45242
(513) 793-4558
www.stampawayusa.com
✳ templates, supplies, stamps

Stamp Your Heart Out
141-C Harvard Ave.
Claremont, CA 91711
(909) 621-4363
www.stampyourheart.com
✳ Japanese screw punch, stamps, supplies

Stampa Rosa Inc.
2322 Midway Dr.
Santa Rosa, CA 95405
(707) 527-8267
✳ stamps and supplies

Toybox Rubber Stamps
P.O. Box 1487
Healdsburg, CA 95448
(707) 431-1400
www.toyboxrubberstamps.com
✳ stamps and supplies

USArtquest
7800 Ann Arbor Road
Grass Lake, MI 49240
(517) 522-6225
www.usartquest.com
✳ mica tiles and supplies

Viva Las Vegastamps
1008 East Sahara Avenue
Las Vegas, NV 89104
(702) 836-9118
www.stampo.com
✳ stamps and supplies

Wilde-Ideas Craft Supplies
625 Pinellas St. Suite A
Clearwater, FL 33756
(800) 558-8680
www.wilde-ideas.com
❋ Xyron machines

Zettiology / The Studio Zine
(253) 638-6466
www.zettiology.com
❋ stamps and magazine

❋ PUBLICATIONS

The Rubberstamper
(800) 260-9028
www.rubberstamper.com

RubberStampMadness
P.O. Box 610
Corvallis, OR 97339-0610
877-STAMPMA
www.rsmadness.com

Stampers' Sampler & Somerset Studio
22992 Millcreek, Suite B
Laguna Hills, CA 92653
(877) STAMPER
www.somersetstudio.com

Vamp Stamp News
P. O. Box 386
Hanover, MD 21076-0386
www.vampstampnews.com

❋ MY FAVORITE PRODUCTS

Coffee Break Designs
❋ mini beads, eyelets, watch crystals, tiny brads
ColorBox
❋ pigment inks, Ancient Page inks
Draggin' Ink
❋ embossing powders, templates
February Papers
❋ decorative threads and yarns
Great American Stamp Store
❋ assorted punches
Judi-Kins
❋ acetate, laminating sheets, Diamond Glaze,

picture pebbles, ROXS
Jacquard Products
❋ PearlEx
Krylon
❋ gold, silver and copper leafing pens
Lighthouse Memories
❋ circle cutter
Lyra
❋ watercolor crayons, pastel chalks
Marvy Uchida
❋ dye inks
McGill, Inc.
❋ punches
On the Surface
❋ fibers
Pam Bakke Paste Papers
❋ specialty papers
Scattered Pictures
❋ assorted punches, scrapbooking stickers
Skycraft Designs
❋ specialty papers
Speedball
❋ C-thru ruler
Stamp Your Heart Out
❋ Japanese screw punch
USArtquest
❋ PearlEx, mica tiles
Wilde-Ideas Craft Supplies
❋ Xyron supplies

Stamps Used in this Book:
page 289, Paper Parachute. page 286, Judi-Kins.
page 287, Rubbermoon. page 296, Ruby Red
Rubber. page 302, Stamp Camp. page 305,
Judi-Kins. page 309, Rubbermoon. page 310,
Rubbermoon. page 312, Postscript Studio.
page 314, Postscript Studio. page 315, Judi-Kins.
page 318, Postscript Studio. page 323,
Rubbermoon. page 330, Twenty Two. page
333, River City. page 350, River City. page 360,
Zettiology. page 365, Zettiology. page 372,
Judi-Kins.

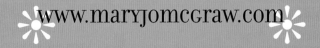

MaryJo is available to answer questions about all

her books through her website:

❋ www.maryjomcgraw.com ❋

simple
glass seed beading

simple
glass seed beading

Dorothy Wood

David & Charles

contents

introduction

There is no doubt about it; seed beading is a fun and potentially addictive craft. These tiny beads, which come in such a myriad of colours and finishes, can be used in lots of different ways to make some really wonderful things. If this is your first foray into the world of beads, there will be new techniques to learn - although you may find that you already have many of the skills required to become a successful beader. The book is designed to inspire as well as instruct and so that you don't feel too restricted, the beads are simply described by size and colour on the project pages. You can enjoy looking for similar beads in your local bead shop or even try a different colour scheme to create some truly unique pieces. But don't despair: for those lacking the confidence to branch out on their own straight away, the exact beads used are listed at the back of the book on page 492.

The bead projects are divided into five groups, each using a different set of skills: bead loom work, needle weaving, fringes and tassels, bead embroidery and wirework. You may like to start with something you're familiar with or take the plunge and learn a completely new technique.

Although the projects all have simple step-by-step instructions, it is worth reading through the techniques section beginning on page 396, where you will find lots of tips and helpful advice. There are also clear instructions for some of the more common bead techniques used in the book, such as how to set up and use a bead loom and the basic needle weaving stitches.

Whatever your level of expertise there are plenty of projects to inspire and delight. Those new to the craft should begin with something simple, like the friendship bracelet and then work through the book, making lovely things and learning new skills as they go. Experienced beaders on the other hand can use the book as a source of ideas, choosing wonderful colours and textures to tailor the projects to suit their own taste.

materials and equipment

Beading requires very little specialist equipment - in fact all you need to begin is a needle and thread. Although it is possible to use any fine needle and thread, proper beading needles and thread will start you off in the right way and prevent problems arising later. All materials and equipment used in the book are readily available from craft or jewellery suppliers. If you don't have a local shop, check the supplier's list at the back of the book to find companies who operate a mail-order system or have Web sites.

Needles

Beading needles are longer than normal sewing needles with a flat eye that can pass through the small holes in seed beads. The two most common sizes are 10 and 13. Size 10 is a good standard needle, but if you are going to pass the needle through a bead several times, you will need the finer size 13. Because they are so long and thin, beading needles can bend or break easily so make sure you have a good supply.

Thread

Polyester sewing thread is ideal for couching or embroidery techniques but a specialist beading thread is more suitable for all other beading techniques. Nymo thread is a strong, flat, nylon thread available in a range of sizes. The standard size for seed beads is D and the finer size B is ideal when passing the thread through a bead several times. Both thicknesses are available in a range of colours that can be matched to your beads. Cord threads are more suitable for making fringes and tassels as they allow the beads to swing attractively.

Thread conditioners

Thread conditioners strengthen and protect thread and make it less prone to tangling. It is not always necessary to condition threads when working with seed beads, but bugle and hex beads have sharp edges so condition your threads when using these. Run your thread through the conditioner, avoiding the needle area, and then pull the thread back through between your finger and thumb to remove any excess conditioner and smooth the thread.

Scissors

A sharp pair of embroidery scissors is useful for cutting thread to length and snipping off threads close to the beadwork. Use larger dressmaking scissors for cutting fabric.

Bead mats

Use a bead mat to spread the beads out while you work, so you can discard any misshapen ones and pick the beads up easily on the needle. To make one, cut a piece of chamois leather, or glue a square of velvet to card. The close pile on these materials prevents the beads from rolling away as you pick them up.

Jewellery findings

Choose the method of fastening your jewellery before you begin beading so that you leave enough thread to attach the findings or to make a bead fastening. Clasps and ear wires are readily available from bead suppliers. More unusual fastenings are available by mail order. Use wood beads to make small beaded toggles and tassle heads.

Embroidery hoop

An embroidery hoop or frame keeps the fabric taut while you embroider with beads and prevents puckering.

Fabric markers

Use a vanishing ink pen to mark out motifs on fabric. The ink marks will disappear after a few hours.

Wire

Wire is used in beadwork when the beads have to hold a particular shape or if the wire is part of the decorative effect. Jewellery wire and coloured enamel wire are available in a wide range of colours and thicknesses, from 0.2mm (36swg) to 1.2mm (18swg). 0.4mm (27swg) wire is ideal for stringing size 11 seed beads. Standard wire gauge (swg or SWG) is a UK scale of wire thickness.

Pliers and wire cutters

Bend wire with flat-nosed pliers or use them to pull the needle through a bead that is tightly packed with thread. Flat-nosed pliers are also useful if you have threaded too many beads on to your thread. To avoid taking off all the beads from the thread, simply grasp the unwanted bead in the tip of the pliers and squeeze until it breaks.

Cover your eyes, as the bead will shatter into tiny glass shards.

Round-nosed pliers are used to bend wire to make jump rings in a range of sizes. You can cut wire with most pliers, but it is much easier to cut close to the beadwork with wire cutters.

Bead looms

There are several different bead looms available, some are wooden and others have a stiff wire frame. Basic looms are suitable for making bead bands up to 6cm (2⅜in) wide, although the wire spring restricts the number of warp threads that can be strung on the loom. For weaving bands of beads wider than 30–35 beads, you will need to buy or make a wider loom with a longer spring or coil.

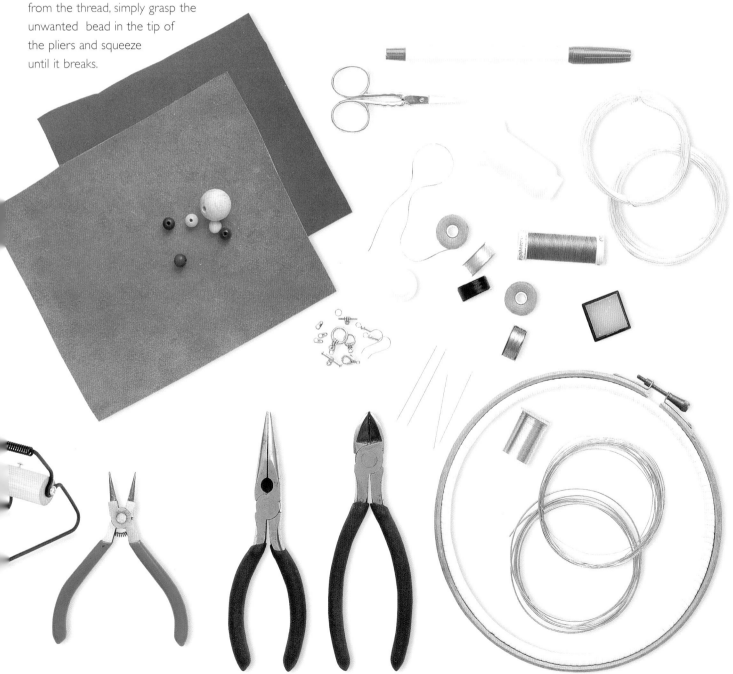

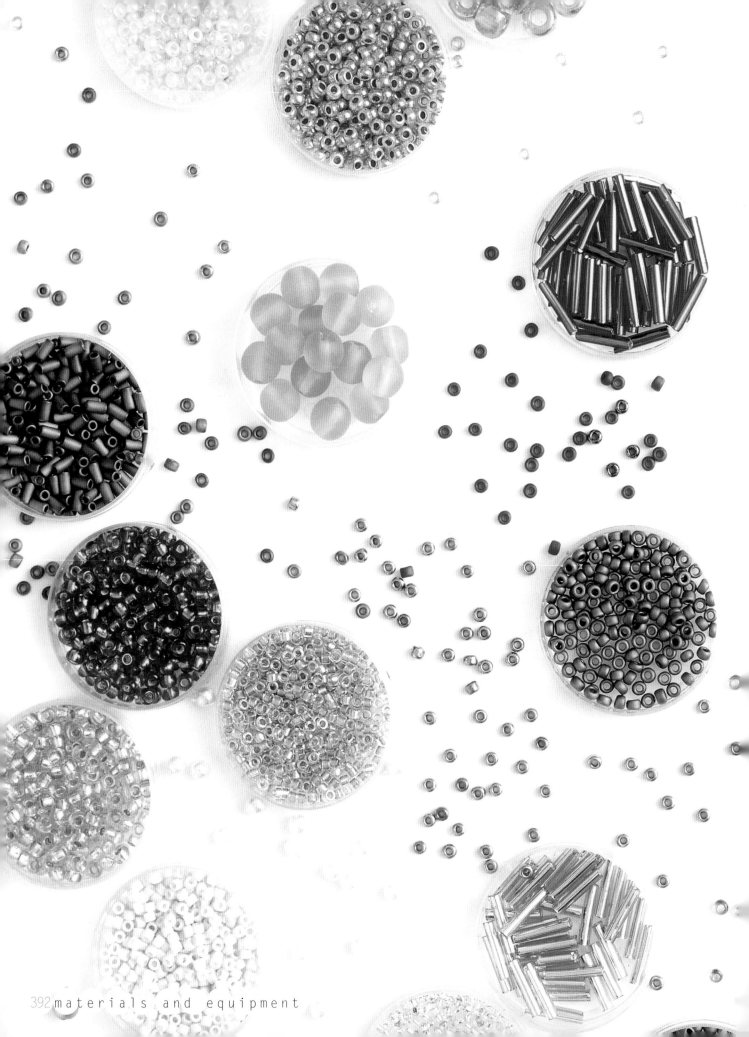

beads

At first sight all the beads in a bead shop look the same, but close inspection reveals a wide variety of shapes and sizes. When buying beads from a catalogue or on the web it helps to know the different types of beads and the names of the different finishes, as it is not always obvious what the beads actually look like from the photograph.

Seed beads are round, donut-shaped beads ranging in size from 5 to 15. Larger seed beads are known as **pony** beads and the smaller ones as **petites.** The most common sized seed beads are size 11 or 12.

Hex beads are cylindrical beads made from a six-sided glass cane. They are like a squat bugle bead and are useful for creating texture.

Cylinder beads, also known by their trade names **Delicas**, **Antiques** and **Magnificas**, are precision-milled tubular beads. They are ideal for needle and loom weaving as the beads sit next to one another and create an even bead fabric. They have a large hole enabling you to pass a needle and thread through each bead several times.

Bugle beads are made in a similar way to seed beads. The glass canes are cut to a variety of lengths from 2–30mm (1/16–1 1/4in). The most common sizes are 4mm (3/16in), 6mm (1/4in), 9mm (3/16in) and 15mm (5/8in). Twisted bugle beads are made from five- or six-sided tubes that have been twisted while the glass is still hot.

bead finishes

Beads often have two or more different descriptive words that explain exactly what the bead looks like. For example 'SL purple AB' is a silver-lined purple bead with an iridescent, rainbow effect on the surface (AB meaning aurora borealis). It is like a code system - once you know the code you can tell exactly what you are buying (see facing page, choosing and buying beads.) The combinations of these different finishes produce a huge variety of different beads.

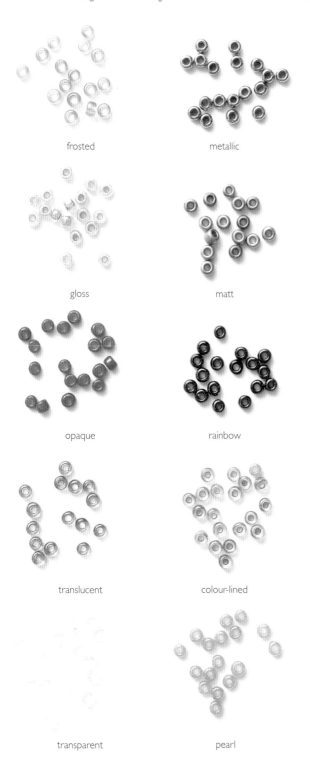

frosted

metallic

gloss

matt

opaque

rainbow

translucent

colour-lined

transparent

pearl

Transparent beads are clear or coloured glass that allow the light to pass through. Using a dark-coloured thread can alter the bead colour. **Opaque** beads are solid colour beads that don't allow any light to pass through. **Translucent** beads are in between transparent and opaque and are also known variously as greasy, opal and satin. **Greasy** beads are made from cloudy-looking glass while **opal** beads are slightly more transparent. **Satin** beads have tiny bubbles in the glass, which give the bead a directional sheen.

Gloss beads are very shiny, like glass. **Matt** beads are opaque beads that have been tumbled or dipped in acid to give them a dull, flat surface. **Frosted** beads are clear or translucent beads, which have been treated in a similar way.

Lustre beads have a transparent coating, either coloured or clear, that gives the beads a subtle shine. **Ceylon** beads have a milky, pearlized lustre.

Colour-lined (CL) beads have the hole in the bead lined with another colour. The beads can be clear or coloured. **Silver-lined** (SL) beads have the hole in the bead lined with silver and look very sparkly. These beads can be bleached to remove the silver lining leaving a more subtle finish.

Metallic beads include any bead that looks metallic. The finish can be painted on or in the case of galvanized beads the finish is electroplated to the surface of the bead. Beads with painted metallic finishes cannot be washed. **Iris** or **rainbow** beads have been treated with metal salts to create a coating that resembles an oil slick. They are often made from dark or black opaque beads and are also known as aurora borealis (AB) beads.

choosing and buying beads

It has never been easier to buy beads because even if you don't have a bead shop nearby there are lots of mail order and internet companies to choose from. The beads are usually clearly illustrated, with precise details of their size, colour and finish. Look at the suppliers listed on page 111 for some useful addresses to get you started stocking up on your own supply of beads.

The quality of seed beads available on the market varies, and you generally get what you pay for. The finest quality beads come from Japan, and this is often marked on the packet. When needle weaving or loom weaving it is essential to buy good quality beads that are of an even size, although it is fine to use less expensive beads for netting, fringing and coiling on wire.

Make use of your knowledge of the different types of beads when choosing them for your projects. Even if the beadwork appears to be all one colour, pick a selection of beads with different finishes to give the beadwork interest and vitality. You can use any size of seed bead for the projects although best results will be achieved using the correct size and type of bead specified in the text. For a unique finish, choose your own colours but if you would rather buy the exact beads used in the projects, full details are listed on page 492.

Seed beads, cylinder beads and bugles are sold in a variety of packets, bags and tubes with no standard bead packet sizes. The packets or containers usually have the weight of beads marked, making it easier to decide how many packets you require. Some beads are sold in round weights such as 5g or 100g; others are sold with a particular number of beads and so have an odd weight such as 4.54g. Unfortunately the number of beads is not marked. Do check the weight of each different bead – some companies keep the bead quantity the same in each packet and vary the price, whereas others keep the price the same and alter the quantity.

Depending on the size or type of bead there are an average number of beads per gram so that it is fairly easy to work out what quantity of beads you need for a certain project. Use the chart here to help you work out how many beads you require.

Type of bead	Size of bead	5g bag (approx.)
Pony bead	5	65
Seed bead	8	200
Seed bead	9	300
Seed bead	11	450
Seed bead	12	500
Petite bead	15	950
Cylinder bead	Delicas	800
Bugle bead	3mm	20
Bugle bead	7mm	150
Bugle bead	9mm	90
Bugle bead	15mm	55

techniques

If you are new to beadwork it is worth working through this section to learn the skills required for some of the projects. Although most of the projects have full instructions enabling you to work the project from the step-by-step instructions, this section has useful tips and diagrams as well as detailed instructions for using a bead loom, embroidering with beads and all the needle weaving stitches used in the book.

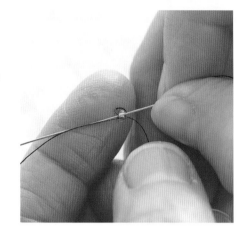

beginning a piece of beadwork

Work with as long a length of thread as you can comfortably sew with to reduce the number of joins – between 1–2m (1–2yd) is ideal. Nymo thread is easier to thread straight off the reel. If you are using a round thread such as quilting thread, flatten the end and trim at an angle before threading the needle. To prevent the thread from knotting, let the needle hang loose from time to time to unwind. If it does coil up and loop into a knot don't panic and pull the thread tight, simply put the needle into the loop and pull gently to one side to ease the knot out.

When needle weaving, a stop bead will stabilize the first row and prevent the beads from falling off. You can use the first bead in the row or use a bead in a different colour that can be removed at a later stage.

Pick up a bead and pass the needle back through it once or twice to anchor it. Leave a tail of at least 15cm (6in) for finishing off or adding a fastening.

joining on another thread

Don't work right to the end of a thread. Leave a tail of 15cm (6in) to make it easier to attach a new thread and weave the ends back into the work.

1 In closely packed beadwork, weave the new thread back and forward across the beadwork several times bringing the new thread out through the same bead as the old thread. At a later stage, weave the old thread through the new beadwork in the same way and trim off the ends.

2 When working nets or fringes, knot the two threads together using a reef knot (see facing page). Using a needle, manoeuvre the knot between two beads or to the edge of the work before tightening. Weave the ends into the work and trim close to the beads. A tiny drop of fray check liquid or clear nail varnish will secure the knot permanently.

knots used in beading

There are several simple knots used in beading to anchor threads or for tying off ends securely and it is worthwhile learning these knots so that your beadwork remains intact and fastenings firmly attached during use. For extra security use a cocktail stick to drop a tiny amount of fixative, such as clear nail polish or a fray check liquid, on the knots.

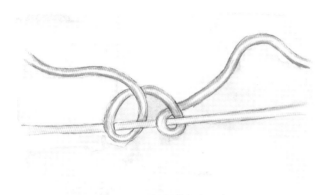

double half hitch

Use this knot to secure a thread in netting or fringes before feeding the end through several more beads and trimming the end.

reef (square) knot

This is the basic knot for joining two threads of equal thickness. Feed each end back through several beads before trimming the ends.

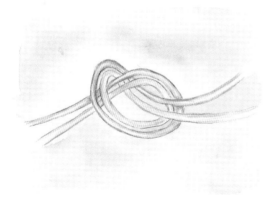

overhand knot

Use this knot to tie threads together before fitting on a bead loom or to join two threads together at the edge of a piece of work. The knot can be easily manoeuvred into position with a needle.

surgeon's knot

This knot is similar to a reef knot but each thread end is taken over and under twice. The knot is more secure than a reef knot and doesn't loosen while it is being tied.

bead loom weaving

Bead loom weaving is a quick method of producing flat bands of beading. The width of the band is only restricted by the width of the loom. Bead weaving on a loom produces a similar result to the square stitch in needle weaving. The beads are arranged in straight rows and so the design can be worked out on a square grid in the same way as cross stitch. There are two sets of threads on a bead loom. The warp threads run lengthways through the beadwork and are fitted to the loom. The weft threads are crossways threads, which carry the beads and are woven in with a beading needle.

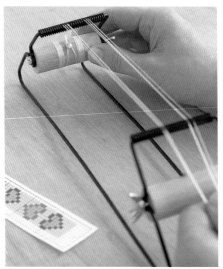

1 Count the number of beads across the design and add one to find the number of warp threads required. Add 60cm (24in) to the finished length of the project for attaching the threads to the loom and finishing off. Cut the warp threads and tie an overhand knot (see page 397) at one end.

2 Split the bundle in two and loop the knot over the tack on the top roller. Loosen the wing nut and, holding the threads taut, wind the warp threads on to the roller, stopping when there is just enough thread to tie on to the other roller.

3 Hold the threads firmly and arrange along the top spring. Use a 'T' pin to sort one thread into each coil. Line the threads up across the bottom spring in the same way, so that they run parallel to one another and don't cross at any point.

4 Tie an overhand knot and loop the knot over the tack on the bottom roller. Wind the rollers back until there is about 30cm (12in) on the bottom roller and tighten the wing nuts.

5 Thread a needle with a 2m (2¼yd) length of thread and tie to the left-hand side warp thread with an overhand knot leaving a 15cm (6in) tail. Beginning at the bottom, read the beadwork chart from right to left and pick up the required number of beads in the right order.

6 Hold the beads under the warp threads and push them up between the warp threads so that there is a thread either side of each bead.

7 Feed the needle back through the beads from left to right, making sure that the needle passes on top of the warp threads. If the needle goes below the warp thread the beads will not be secured.

8 Pick up the next row of beads according to the chart and repeat the process, passing the needle back through the beads above the warp threads. After the first few rows it will become much easier to work.

9 When you have about 13cm (5in) of thread left on the weft thread remove the needle and leave the thread hanging. Thread a new length of thread and feed through five or six beads, leaving a 13cm (5in) tail hanging below the beadwork. Both ends can be woven in later.

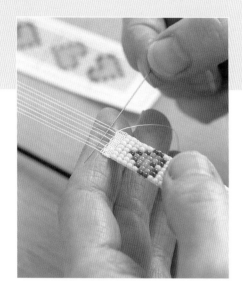

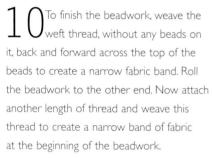

10 To finish the beadwork, weave the weft thread, without any beads on it, back and forward across the top of the beads to create a narrow fabric band. Roll the beadwork to the other end. Now attach another length of thread and weave this thread to create a narrow band of fabric at the beginning of the beadwork.

11 Lift the beadwork off the loom. Tie pairs of warp threads together using a surgeon's knot (see page 397). Take the thread ends left over right, twice, and then right over left, twice, and pull tight.

12 Weave the ends of the thread into the beadwork for at least five beads and then double back for at least five beads. Trim the ends close to the beadwork on the reverse side and then trim the warp threads at each end to 6mm (¼in).

needle weaving

Needle weaving is a way of stitching beads together to create a flat or tubular beaded fabric. There are lots of different stitches that can be used, each with distinct characteristics that determine the finished look and feel of the beadwork. The stitches may appear to be similar in samples but are not readily interchangeable, as their different characteristics become evident in larger pieces. Square stitch, ladder stitch, brick stitch, peyote stitch and chain stitch are described below.

ladder stitch

This simple stitch is often used to make the base for brick stitch. It is usually worked with bugle beads but seed beads can also be used.

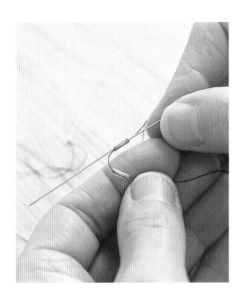 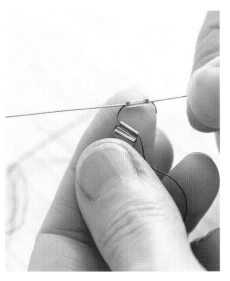 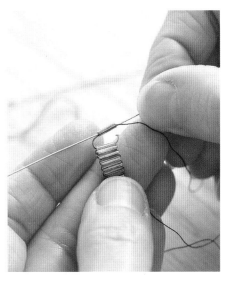

1 Cut a 2m (2¼yd) length of thread and thread a needle on to each end. Pick up two bugle beads and let them drop down to the middle of the thread. Now put the other needle through the second bead in the opposite direction.

2 Pull the threads tight. Pick up another bead with one needle and put the other needle through the bead in the opposite direction.

3 Continue adding beads in the same way until the band is the length you require. To make the band into a tube, pass each needle through the first bead again and pull tight.

square stitch

Beads worked in square stitch look similar to beads woven on a loom. The needle passes through each bead several times and so you may need to use a size 13 needle and a fine thread in a toning colour. Square stitch has a wonderful draping quality and is ideal for bracelets.

1 Pick up the required number of beads for the first row. For the second row, pick up a bead and pass the needle back through the last bead on the first row.

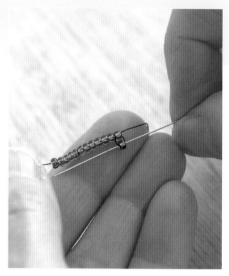

2 Pass the needle through the first bead on the second row again and back through the bead just added. The bead should be suspended below the first row.

3 Pick up a second bead and take the needle back through the second last bead on the previous row. Continue working along the row adding on one bead at a time.

4 To strengthen the fabric, at the end of the row go back through the previous row and the one just worked, ready to begin the next row.

brick stitch

Brick stitch is one of the easiest stitches to work and is so called because it looks like a brick wall. The stitch is flexible crossways but rather stiff lengthways and can be worked flat or in a tube. It is often used to make tiny bags, such as the amulet purse (see page 428).

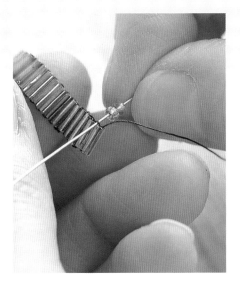

1 Make the foundation row the required length in ladder stitch (see page 401), using either seed beads or bugle beads. For the first row of brick stitch, pick up two beads and pass the needle under the first loop of thread joining the foundation row of beads.

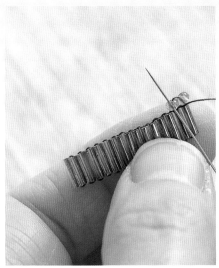

2 Pass the needle back through the second bead you picked up. Pick up another bead. Pass the needle under the next loop and back through the bead again. Continue adding one bead at a time in this way to the end of the row.

3 Turn the beading round and pick up two beads to begin the next row. Repeat steps 2 and 3 until the beadwork is the size that you require.

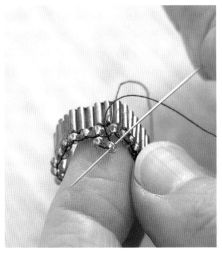

4 To work in a tube, make a foundation tube with ladder stitch. At the beginning of each row pick up two beads and at the end of the row join the beads together and bring the thread out ready to begin the next row.

peyote stitch

Peyote stitch is a versatile stitch that can be
worked flat or in a tube. It is easiest to work
with an even number of beads in each row. Peyote
stitch is ideal for bags with a flap, as the fabric
is very flexible along its length.

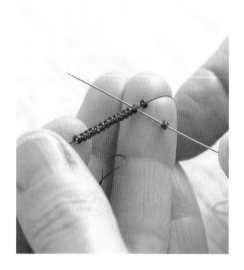

1 Pick up a bead and anchor it by taking
the needle back through it again leaving a
15cm (6in) tail. Pick up enough beads to give
the required width for the first row, ending up
with an even number. Pick up a bead and,
missing the last bead on the first row, pass the
needle through the next bead.

2 Pick up another bead, miss a bead on the
first row and pass the needle through the
next bead. Continue to the end of the row
missing every second bead.

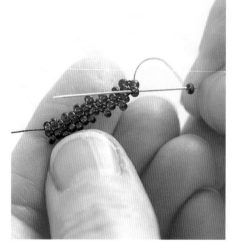

3 In subsequent rows the beads are in a
more obvious zigzag pattern. Work back
and forward in the same way, picking up one
bead at a time and passing the needle
through the next 'dropped down' bead.

chain stitch

Chain stitch is an ideal stitch for making straps and can be embellished to make more ornate bracelets and necklaces. The number of beads can be varied in each chain to create different effects.

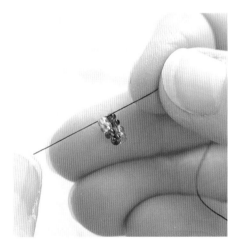

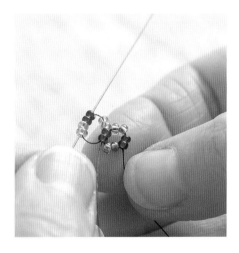

1 Pick up two light beads, two dark beads, two light beads and two dark beads. Tie the beads into a circle using a reef knot (see page 397), leaving a 15cm (6in) tail.

2 Pass the needle back through two dark, two light and two dark beads. Pick up two light, two dark and two light beads and put the needle back through the top two dark beads on the previous chain.

3 Pass the needle through the first two light and two dark beads just added, ready to add the next chain. Continue adding six beads at a time until the chain is the length required.

joining pieces of beadwork

From time to time it is necessary to make a seam and join two pieces of beadwork. In beadwork it is possible to make an invisible join. Square stitch and peyote stitch both have flat sides and can be butted together. Pass the needle and thread through one bead at a time alternating from side to side to join the seam.

To join pieces of brick stitch, it is necessary to slot the two pieces together using the beads jutting out in the alternate rows as shown.

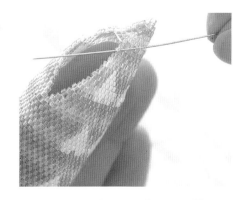

Put the needle through the jutting-out bead on one side. Take it through the jutting-out bead on the opposite side and pull tight. Continue working down the seam.

bead embroidery

Bead embroidery transforms everyday objects into luxury items. Beads can be attached individually, in groups or in rows to most fabrics, and two stitches, backstitch and couching, are described below.

preparing to embroider

If the fabric is flimsy it needs to be supported in a hoop or frame while working so that the beadwork does not scrunch up. If possible use a backing fabric to anchor any threads on the reverse side. Use a double length of sewing thread in the needle or one strand of a beading thread such as Nymo.

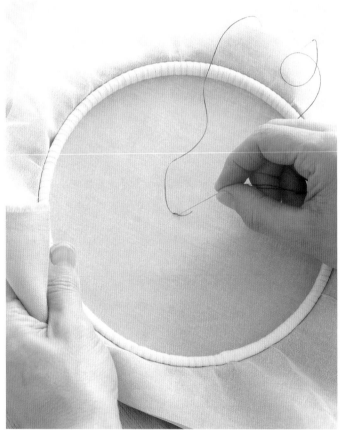

1 Cut the fabric and any backing fabric at least 5cm (2in) larger all round than the finished piece. Fit the fabric into an embroidery hoop or on to a rotary frame.

2 Take two tiny backstitches on the reverse side and bring the needle out on the right side where you want the beadwork to begin. You are now ready to start your bead embroidery.

backstitch

Backstitch is a useful stitch in bead embroidery as it can be used to add individual beads or several at a time. Only pick up one or two beads to follow a curved line but pick up more the straighter the line, taking the needle back through the last bead each time.

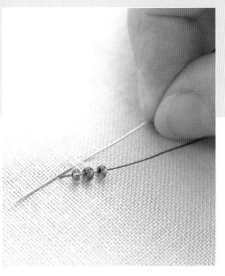

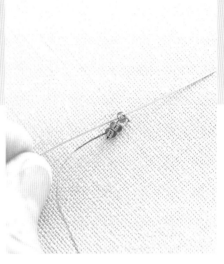

1 Pick up three beads and drop them down to where the thread emerges. Put the needle back into the fabric at the end of the three beads. Take a small backstitch and bring the needle out between the last two beads.

2 Put the needle back through the last bead and then pick up another three beads ready to begin again.

couching

Couching is used to apply a string of beads to fabric in a straight line or curve. You need to use two needles on separate lengths of thread – one beading needle and one sewing needle.

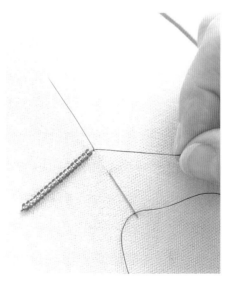

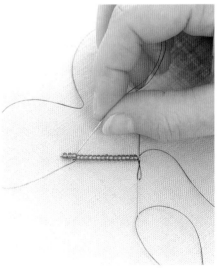

1 Bring the beading needle out where you want the beadwork to begin. Pick up sufficient beads to complete the line. If the beads are being couched in a straight line, put the beading needle in the fabric and wrap the thread around to hold the beads taut.

2 Bring the second thread out between the first and second beads. Take the thread over the bead string and back through the fabric. Work down the bead strand, stitching between every bead or in groups of three or four. At the end take both threads to the reverse side and secure them.

the projects

The beauty of seed beads is that they are so versatile - tiny pieces of glass that can be put together in so many different ways to create wonderful things. As with any craft there are techniques to be learnt but once these skills have been perfected the possibilities are endless.

In this book there are projects for the home, some beautiful pieces of jewellery and a few personal items that have been trimmed with beads to make them quite unique. Many of the projects are ideal for gifts; although they are all so beautiful I'm sure you'll be reluctant to give away anything you make! A bracelet only takes a few hours and can be made in any colour you choose or you could make a set of rose-scented sachets and decorate them with pretty beads. For a more substantial gift, add a net fringe to a beautiful devoré scarf or make a tiny amulet purse to give to your best friend. To finish off, why not make a beaded card to send with your gift or decorate a pretty gift bag with a few wire flowers.

Beads can be used to embellish all sorts of items in the home - add a sparkly fringe to a lampshade, wrap a beaded wire around plain glass candlesticks or trim a trinket box with iridescent beads. Some items around the home can be made almost entirely of beads, such as an exquisite bead tassel to hang from a wardrobe key, a delightful bead frame for your favourite photograph, or a set of coiled wire coasters for the dining room.

Finally, there are beautiful things to make just for you. Embroider a silk cover for a notebook or address book, make a natural linen rucksack embroidered with classic matt beads or step out in style in a pair of silk mules decorated with exquisite paisley motifs.

friendship bracelet

Loom weaving is a quick and easy way of creating flat bands of beading and this simple bracelet is the ideal first bead loom project. It is made using tiny tubular beads called Delicas, which are very even and lock together tightly to make a smooth bead fabric. It has been cleverly designed with fastenings made entirely of beads and so no clasps or hooks are required. As the name implies, these pretty bracelets are intended to be given as tokens of friendship. If you have an extra special friend, why not add a delicate picot edging down either side of the bracelet to finish it off?

friendship bracelet

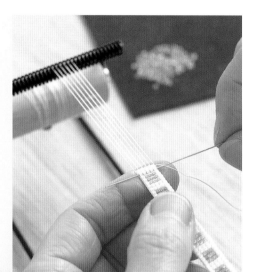

you will need

- bead loom
- beading needle
- white Nymo thread
- 2g white delicas
- 1g lime delicas
- 1g aqua delicas
- 1g bright blue delicas
- scissors

1 Set up the bead loom with six 76cm (30in) long white Nymo threads (see bead loom weaving, page 398). To calculate the length of the bracelet, measure the circumference of your wrist and take off 1cm (½in) for the fastening. Following the beadwork chart on page 490, work the bead design to this length ending with two white rows. Put the needle back through the second last row of beads.

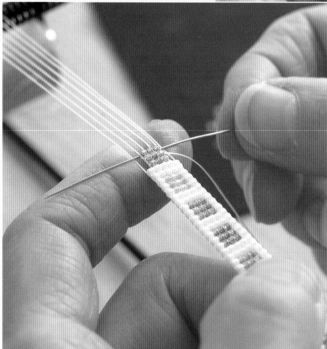

2 Bring the needle out between the first two beads on the last row. Pick up three aqua delicas and fit under the centre four threads. Take the needle back through the beads. Work another two rows avoiding the outside threads.

try this

If you prefer, you could leave the bracelet without the picot edging and make a short length of beadwork to create a pretty matching ring.

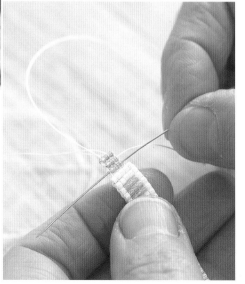

3 Wind the loom back to the other end of the bracelet and add a block of nine aqua delicas to that end as well. Take the beadwork off the loom. Sew the thread ends back into the bracelet leaving one thread next to the centre aqua bead at each end.

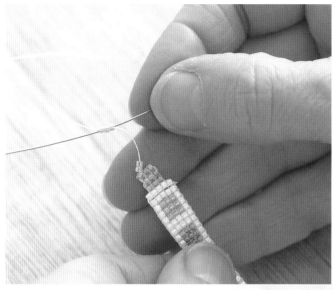

4 To make a toggle pick up five lime beads and put the needle back through the last three to make a circle. Pick up a bead and put the needle through the centre of the circle. Keep adding beads one at time, putting the needle through the cluster until you make a 6mm (¼in) toggle.

tip

Tie a double half hitch knot (see page 397) between two beads before sewing the thread ends of the loop into the bracelet to make it extra secure.

5 At the other end of the bracelet pick up enough lime delicas to make a loop that will pass over the toggle snugly. Put the needle back through the other side of the centre aqua bead and then back through the loop before securing the end in the bracelet.

6 To add a picot edge, attach a thread at one end of the bracelet and bring it out at the edge of the bracelet opposite the centre lime delica. Pick up three lime delicas and put the needle through the bracelet, bringing it out on the other side.

7 Pick up another three beads and put the needle back through the first two in the bracelet. Feed the needle down to the next coloured centre bead and then out to the edge. Make a picot on either side and continue down the bracelet adding matching picots either side of each square. Secure the end of the thread in the bracelet to finish.

bead frame

Inspired by the wonderful patterns on a zebra's coat and designed using neutral colours reminiscent of the Sahara Desert, this unusual frame is created using more than 8,000 beads. Using a wide bead loom, it is surprisingly quick to weave. The beadwork is woven in strips which are then sewn together invisibly before being made into a picture frame. The beads used to make the frame are cylinders, also known as Delicas, Magnificas or Antiques. Unlike seed beads, which are donut-shaped, cylinder beads are short tubes that slot together to make a more even, flat bead fabric.

bead frame

tip

If you find that you have missed one of the warp threads after lifting the beadwork off the loom, thread the beading needle and weave another length of thread in to correct the error.

1 Fit thirty-four 1.25m (49in) lengths of thread into the bead loom (see bead loom weaving, page 398). Following the beadwork chart on page 488, weave both side panels on these threads, leaving a 30cm (12in) gap between panels. Weave a thread panel at both ends of each panel before lifting off the loom. Now weave the top and bottom panels on fifty-one 1m (1yd) lengths of thread leaving a 30cm (12in) gap between the panels. Weave a thread panel at both ends of each panel before lifting off the loom. Sew in any side threads. Secure the bead panels to the work surface with masking tape and tie the thread ends together in pairs using a surgeon's knot (see page 397).

2 Stick a piece of double-sided tape along the top and bottom edges of each bead panel on the reverse side. Fold the threads back on to the double-sided tape and trim the threads to 6mm (¼in).

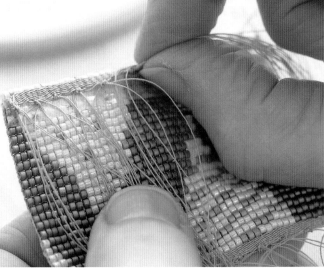

3 Lay the bead panels out on a flat surface. Weave a thread into one of the side panels bringing it out in the inside corner. Feed the needle through the first three beads in the adjacent panel.

4 Take the needle back through the three beads in the next row and then through the first three beads in the adjacent panel. Work along the seam, sewing back and forward through the beads to join the seam.

5 Join all four seams in the same way. Measure the height and width of the bead panel leaving one row of beads all round. Cut two pieces of mount board that size.

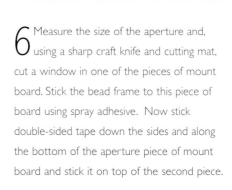

6 Measure the size of the aperture and, using a sharp craft knife and cutting mat, cut a window in one of the pieces of mount board. Stick the bead frame to this piece of board using spray adhesive. Now stick double-sided tape down the sides and along the bottom of the aperture piece of mount board and stick it on top of the second piece.

try this

For a more substantial frame, cover each piece of mount board in fabric and stitch the bead panel in position rather than using glue.

7 To make a stand, cut a 5 x 15cm (2 x 6in) piece of mount board and score a line 5cm (2in) from one end. Apply double-sided tape above the score line and stick the stand on the back of the frame. Place your photo in the frame through the top opening.

trinket box

Three different bead
techniques are combined
to make this beautiful
trinket box. The rim is
covered with a stunning
piece of bead loom
weaving, the padded lid
is decorated with hand
embroidered beads and
the box is finished off
with an exquisite,
three-dimensional beaded
blackberry. Use a soft
fabric such as georgette
that drapes well to
cover the outside of the
box. The inside of the
box can be as luxurious
or plain as you like.
Cover the inside raw
edge with a strip of
co-ordinating ribbon or
cut a strip of card to
fit inside and cover
this with plain or
padded fabric.

trinket box

you will need

- bead loom
- petrol blue Nymo thread
- beading needle
- 6g iridescent pale aqua seed beads
- 5g iridescent blue rainbow seed beads
- 6g iridescent green/blue iris seed beads
- 3g deep blue seed beads
- 3g blue/green seed beads
- 3g dark olive green seed beads
- 3g pink seed beads
- scissors
- circular papier mâché box 12cm (4¾in) diameter
- 1.25cm (½in) wide double-sided tape
- 30cm (12in) lilac georgette
- 50g (2oz) wadding (batting)
- 15cm (6in) diameter circle of organdie
- 7mm (⁵⁄₁₆in) wooden bead
- dressmaker's pin
- spray adhesive
- thin card

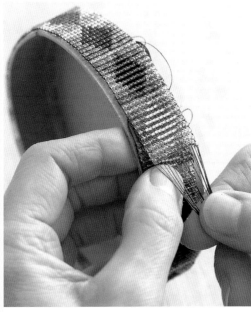

1 Fit fourteen 1m (39in) lengths of petrol blue Nymo thread into the loom, (see bead loom weaving, page 398). Work the bead design following the chart on page 490. You will need four repeats plus one extra diamond to fit this size of box. Take the beading off the loom and check the length against the box rim. Allow 6mm (¼in) for the fabric covering and remove a row or two of beads if required. Put the beadwork back on the loom and weave the fabric ends.

2 Stick double-sided tape around the inside and outside of the lid rim. Cut a 5 x 40cm (2 x 15¾in) strip of georgette and stick it halfway down the rim on the outside. Fold over the raw edge of the overlap and use double-sided tape to secure. Smooth the strip of fabric over to the inside of the lid.

3 Cut six circles of wadding (batting) the same size as the lid. Cut another slightly larger and two smaller circles. Stick another piece of double-sided tape around the rim of the lid. Pile the wadding (batting) on top of the lid beginning with the smallest circle and finishing with the largest one.

4 Position the organandie over the wadding (batting) and stretch it gently on to the double-sided tape. Adjust the organdie until the top is a smooth dome and trim any excess fabric.

tip

Don't be tempted to skip step 4. Organdie is a fine, closely woven fabric that gives a superior finish to the padding on the box lid. Softer dress fabric does not give a smooth result.

5 Stick more double-sided tape around the rim of the lid. Stretch a 15cm (6in) diameter circle of georgette on to the double-sided tape and trim off the excess fabric. Tie off the threads on the bead strip and fold the woven fabric under. Stick the bead strip around the rim, butting the ends together.

6 Using the point of a pair of embroidery scissors, make a hole in the centre of the lid from the inside. Tie a knot in the end of a length of Nymo thread and feed it through the hole. Leaving a 1cm (½in) circle in the centre clear of beads, begin to stitch green/blue iris beads in the middle of the lid. Work out from the centre, spacing the beads out further and using progressively lighter iridescent beads.

7 To make the blackberry, thread the beading needle and pick up the wooden bead, tying the thread to it, leaving a 10cm (4in) tail. Cover the bead with rows of 8 dark olive green seed beads. Begin to fill the gaps with some of the other colour beads, threading the needle under the dark olive green rows.

8 Keep adding beads used in the design until the wooden bead resembles a blackberry. Feed the thread ends through the centre of the lid and out of the hole on the reverse side.

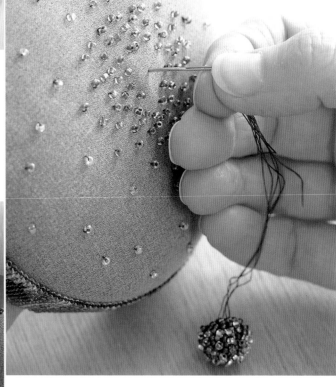

9 From inside, lay an ordinary dressmaker's pin across the hole. Push down on the blackberry to sink it into the wadding (batting) and tie the threads across the pin using a surgeon's knot (see page 397). The pin stays in place.

10 Cut a strip of georgette fabric 3cm (1¼in) deeper than the box base and long enough to wrap around it. Stick double-sided tape on the inside of the rim and around the base. Stick the fabric around the box and then tuck the excess inside. Stretch the fabric gently on to the base of the box.

11 Cut two circles of thin card the same size as the base of the box and trim one slightly smaller. Spray adhesive on one side of each circle and stick to a piece of georgette. Trim the fabric to 1cm (½in) and snip into the card all round. Spray with adhesive and stretch the fabric on to the reverse side.

try this

Create an attractive card to match the trinket box by weaving a small square, using the chart on page 490. Weave the fabric border at each end and use double-sided tape to stick the beadwork inside the aperture.

12 Stick the larger covered circle inside the lid and the smaller circle on to the base of the box. To finish the inside of the box simply cover the raw fabric edge with a piece of co-ordinating ribbon.

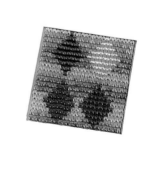

spiral bracelets

Needle weaving, described fully on page 401, is perfect for creating jewellery so why not add a finishing touch to your favourite outfit with this set of matching bracelets? Although they look very delicate, these spiral bracelets are made with a strong beading stitch that is unlikely to break. You can use any beads you like to make the bracelets but it is better to choose contrasting colours or textures for the inside and outside beads so that the spiral is quite obvious. To make a chunkier bracelet, use larger beads on the outside of the spiral and finish off with a heavier toggle fastening.

spiral bracelets

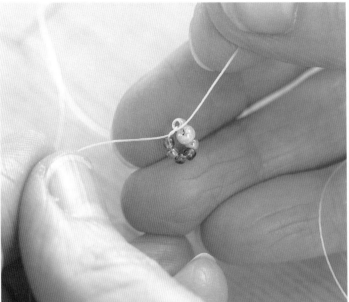

you will need

- white Nymo thread
- beading needle
- 2g grass green seed beads
- 3g mint green seed beads
- 3g aqua size 8 seed beads
- scissors
- toggle fastening

1 Thread the beading needle with a 2m (2¼yd) length of white Nymo thread. Pick up 4 grass green beads, then 1 mint green bead, 1 aqua bead and another mint green bead. Tie the beads into a circle, leaving a 15cm (6in) tail.

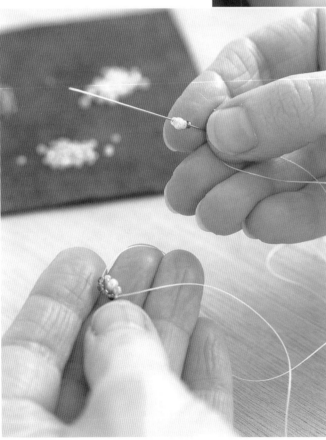

2 Pass the needle through the 4 grass green beads. Pick up 1 grass green bead, 1 mint green, 1 aqua and another mint green. Let the beads drop down to the work.

tip

Use a fine size 13 beading needle and size 'b' thread to make the bracelet so that you are able to take the needle and thread through some of the beads several times.

try this

Make a matching bracelet using the more unusual hex beads to create a distinct pattern that looks like a helter-skelter. Create a different effect by using dark beads on the outside and pale beads on the inside.

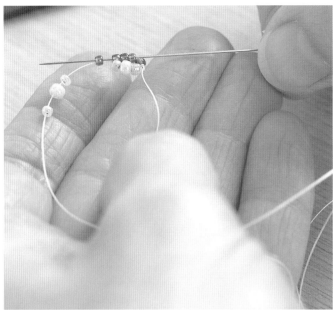

3 Pass the needle back through the last three grass green beads and the one just added. Pull the thread tight and position the beads next to the previous group of mint green/aqua beads.

4 Pick up 1 grass green bead, 1 mint green, 1 aqua and 1 mint green. Let the beads drop down to the work. Repeat steps 3 and 4. The spiral will only become obvious when you have made about eight repetitions.

5 Continue adding beads until the spiral is the length required, approximately 17cm (6¾in). Oversew the two halves of the toggle fastening to the ends of the bracelet. Feed the needle back down through 3 or 4 beads, tie a double half hitch knot and feed the needle through another 3 or 4 beads. Trim the thread close to the beads.

amulet purse

An amulet is a charm, something worn as protection from misfortune or evil spirits. Traditionally, these delightful purses were hung around the neck with the charm tucked safely inside. Nowadays an amulet purse has a more decorative purpose and is worn as a rather unusual necklace. It is worked in brick stitch from a chart, with the design repeated twice so that the back and front are identical. The purse is rather tiny and doesn't hold very much, but it could still protect you from misfortune: keep a little money folded up inside and you should get home safely!

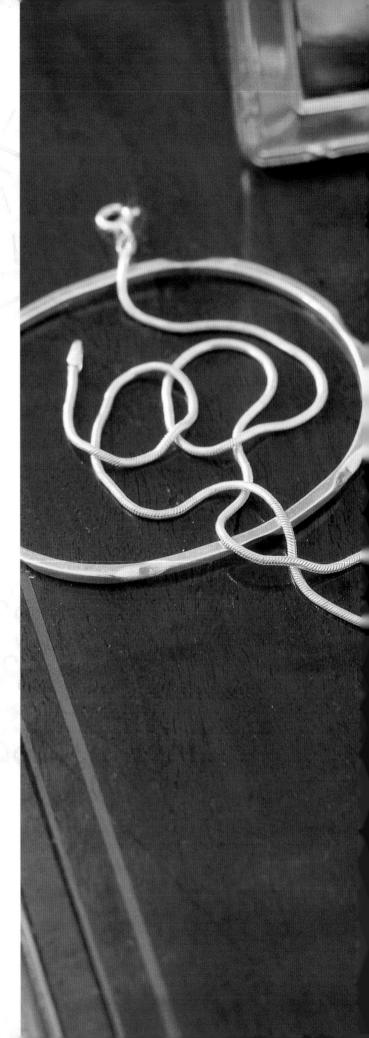

amulet purse

you will need

- two beading needles
- white Nymo thread
- 4g silver-lined clear crystal 3mm bugle beads
- 2g white delicas
- 10g light pink delicas
- 8g pink delicas
- scissors
- cord thread

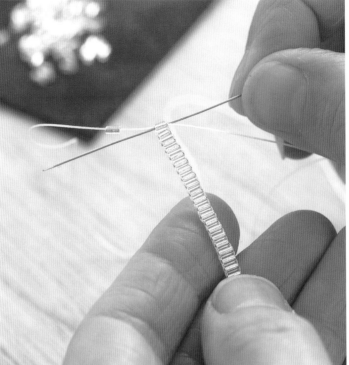

1 Thread a long length of white Nymo thread with a beading needle at each end. Work ladder stitch (see page 401) using the bugle beads until there are 50 beads and then join the strip into a circle.

2 Working in brick stitch (see page 403) follow the chart on page 489, starting on Row 1. Pick up two light pink delicas and put the needle through the first loop and back through the second bead threaded. Continue working brick stitch, repeating the chart twice until you reach the first bead again.

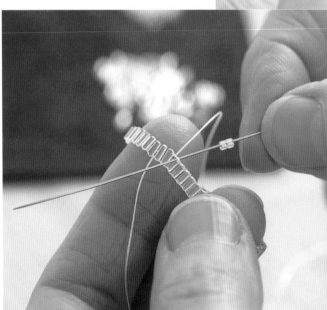

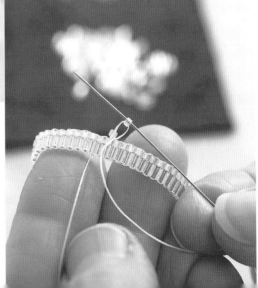

3 Stitch these two beads together and then begin the next row as in step 2. Keep following the chart, working tubular brick stitch until you complete Row 30. Now fold the purse in half so that the hearts are in the centre.

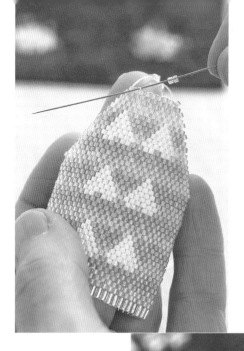

4 From now on you will not be stitching a tube but should continue working brick stitch one side at a time, decreasing the beads at each edge, as shown on the chart. To decrease, pick up two beads as usual but put the needle through the second loop from the edge and work across the row as normal. Now join on a thread on the other side of the amulet and complete the back of the purse in the same way. Once both sides are complete, stitch the side seams together invisibly (see page 405).

(see page 405)

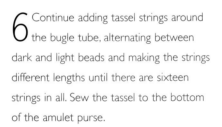

5 Make an eight-bugle strip in ladder stitch and join into a tube. Add a second row of bugles using brick stitch. To make a tassel string, cut a 2m (2¼yd) length of cord thread and pick up 20 light pink beads and 2 bugles. Take the needle back through the delicas and through next loop below the bugle tube.

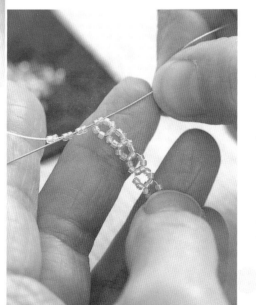

6 Continue adding tassel strings around the bugle tube, alternating between dark and light beads and making the strings different lengths until there are sixteen strings in all. Sew the tassel to the bottom of the amulet purse.

7 The strap is made using chain stitch (see page 405). Start by picking up 2 pink, 2 light pink, 2 pink and 2 light pink delicas and tie the beads into a circle. On the next and subsequent chains, pick up 2 light pink, 2 pink and 2 light pink delicas. Put the needle through the two pink beads at the top of the previous chain and through the first two light pink and pink beads just added. Work chain stitch until the strap is 60cm (23½in) long. Attach the strap securely on either side of the amulet purse.

beaded mules

Transform a pair of plain silk mules with these delightful paisley-pattern motifs. The motifs are worked in brick stitch using petite beads, which are the smallest seed beads, and have a pretty picot edging around the outside. These tiny beads make dainty motifs that can be stitched or glued on to the front of each shoe. The motifs are quite intricate and you will find it best to gain a little experience of stitching brick stitch (see page 403) before beginning as you will need to shape the design by introducing extra beads on the curves and adding beads to create the point.

beaded mules

- pale pink Nymo thread
- size 13 beading needle
- 2g crystal petite beads
- 2g green rainbow petite beads
- 2g dark rainbow petite beads
- 4g crystal aqua petite beads
- 2g crystal pink petite beads
- 2g pale mauve petite beads
- scissors
- silk mules
- flat-nosed pliers

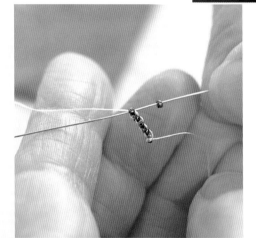

1 Thread the needle with a 1m (1yd) length of Nymo thread. Pick up a dark rainbow bead and put the needle back through the bead again. Pick up a second dark rainbow bead and put the needle back through the previous bead and then back through the one just added.

2 Add a further 4 dark rainbow beads and 3 aqua crystal beads. Take the needle through the last crystal bead again and then pick up 2 aqua crystal beads. Put the needle through the first loop and back through the second bead. Work brick stitch (see page 403) down the first side. Work 3 aqua crystal beads in the loop on the first rainbow bead and then work back up the second side in brick stitch.

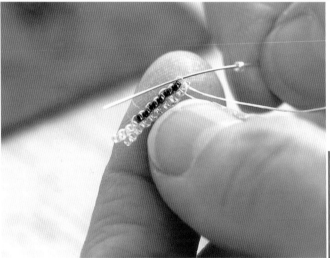

tip

It is much easier to make the paisley motifs using a magnifying lamp. The petite beads are very small and you will be able to pass the needle under loops more easily when they are magnified.

3 Bring the needle out at the top crystal bead and pick up two green rainbow beads. Work one row of brick stitch. To keep the motif flat, increase the number of beads around the bottom curve by working a second bead into a loop twice.

4 Work a second row of brick stitch. At the point end pick up a green rainbow bead and take the needle back through the bead on the opposite side to make a point. Add a row of dark rainbow beads.

try this Make a matching brooch by stitching a beaded paisley motif and sticking it to fabric-covered card. Attach a brooch fastening to the back.

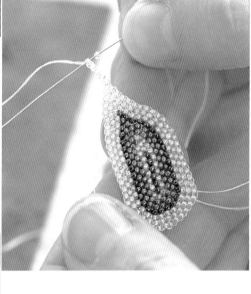

5 Beginning at the top bead on the motif work three rows of crystal aqua beads, tapering the beads to shape the motif. Add 6 crystal aqua beads to the point in the same method as step 1. Work a row of brick stitch back down to the motif and then feed the needle back through the beads to add a row of 5 more beads at the top and then another row of 3.

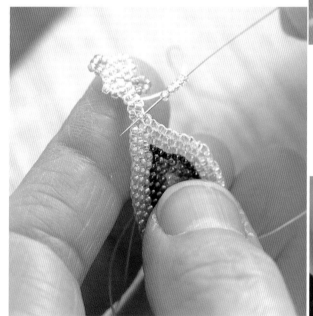

6 To make the picot edging, pick up 5 pale mauve beads. Miss a bead on the motif and take the needle down through the next. Bring it out at the next bead and pick up 5 crystal pink beads. Work round the motif alternating the colours.

7 Make three motifs for each mule, checking the arrangement of the motifs on the front of each mule. Secure a thread with a double backstitch under the first motif and stab stitch through the motif and the mule front to secure. Use a pair of flat-nosed pliers to pull the needle through. Finish off the thread under the motif and trim. Add the other two motifs to the mule in the same way. Repeat for the other mule.

zigzag necklace

Although it looks quite unassuming, this pretty necklace will hang beautifully around your neck, and because it is such a simple design you can easily change the colour of the beads to suit the colour of your outfit. The fringe has been designed to fit inside a 'V' neck but can be altered in length and shape to suit the neckline of any dress or top. The necklace is worked in square stitch, an ideal stitch for this design as it has a wonderful draping quality which allows the necklace to fall into the contours of your neck.For a more formal occasion, you could make a set of earrings to complement the necklace.

zigzag necklace

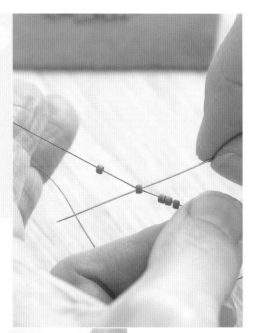

1 Thread your needle with a long length of red Nymo thread. To make the first block of 8 beads in square stitch (see page 402), string on 5 red seed beads. Take the needle back through the fourth bead and pull the thread tight so that the fifth bead is suspended below the fourth bead.

tip
To make the necklace as strong as possible, stabilize the blocks by taking the thread back though the last two rows of beads at every opportunity.

2 Put the needle back through the fifth bead and pick up another bead, the sixth. Put the needle back through the third bead and through the sixth bead again so that it is also suspended below the first row. Add the seventh and eighth beads in the same way.

3 Take the needle back through the first four beads and down the second row to stabilize the block. Add another row of 4 beads and stabilize again.

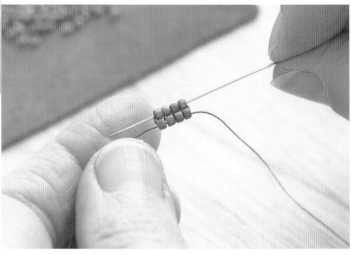

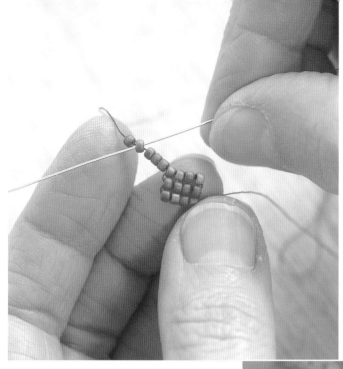

4 Pick up 5 beads. Put the needle back through the second last bead and through the last bead again. Work down the row of eight beads in square stitch.

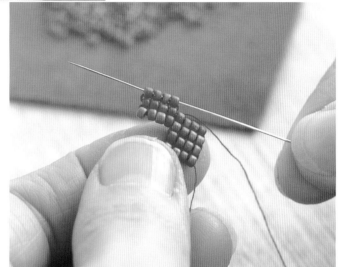

5 Take the needle back through the last two rows twice bringing it out in the middle of the last row. Add 4 beads with square stitch and take the needle down through the first 4 beads on the previous row and back up the last row. Repeat steps 4 and 5 until there are 44 blocks of 16 beads.

6 To add the fringe, thread the needle with another long length of thread. With the ends of the zigzag facing up, take the needle through the first block of beads and out at the first 'V' of the zigzag.

7 Pick up a red bead, then a gold and another red. Take the needle back through the large bead and the first red bead. Feed the needle through the beads in the zigzag chain to the next V. Add a fringe strand of 3 beads at the next ten Vs.

8 On the next and subsequent Vs add on another red and gold bead each time until there are 12 gold beads in the centre of the necklace. Decrease the fringe strands two beads at a time to complete the other side of the necklace.

9 Attach a toggle fastening at each end. Secure the ends by threading back and forwards three times through the necklace and snip off the excess thread.

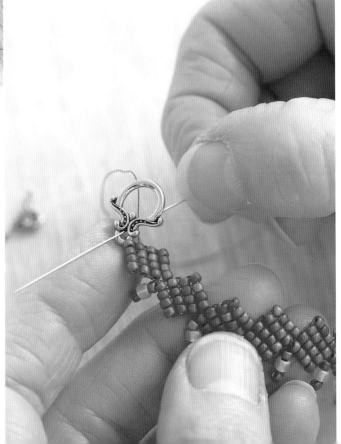

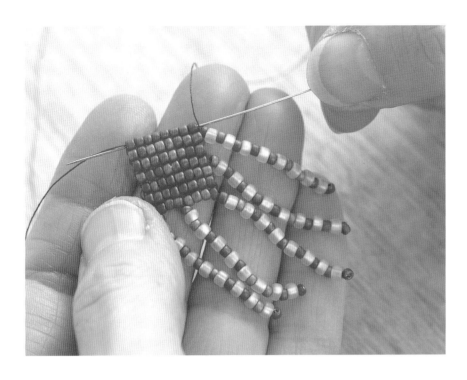

try this

Make a set of
matching earrings by
working seven rows of 8 beads
in square stitch. Attach five fringe
strands of 9 red beads and 8 gold
beads to the block. Finish by
stitching an earring hook
to the top corner of
the block.

bead-fringed cushion

This section features beaded fringes and tassels and shows how ordinary items can be transformed into something quite special. Cushions are one of the most creative pieces of soft furnishing and can be used in almost any room. Tucked in the corner of a chair, scattered on a sofa or arranged at the head of a bed, they add a splash of colour that can complement or lift a decorative scheme. Adding a beaded fringe will transform the plainest cushion and introduce texture and sparkle into a room. Choose fabrics with a slight sheen to complement the beads and add the fringe to a piece of grosgrain ribbon that matches the fabric.

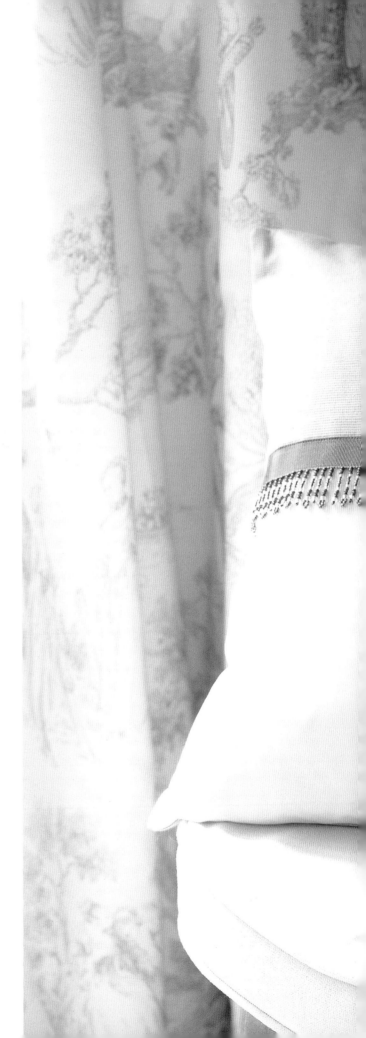

bead-fringed cushion

you will need

- beading needle
- dark blue cord thread
- 41cm (16in) of 2cm (¾in) wide blue grosgrain ribbon
- 2g Caspian blue seed beads
- 2g frosted gunmetal seed beads
- 2g slate blue seed beads
- 2g frosted ice seed beads
- 6g blue iris seed beads
- 2g green iris seed beads
- 6g silver-lined clear size 8 seed beads
- scissors
- 0.5m (½yd) blue fabric
- 26 x 41cm (10 x 16in) cream fabric
- cream and blue sewing threads
- pins
- sewing machine
- 40cm (16in) square cushion pad

1 To make the beaded fringe, thread the beading needle with a length of dark blue cord thread and tie a knot in the end. Insert the needle through some threads on the reverse side of the ribbon 2cm (¾in) from the end and bring it out through one of the tiny loops on the edge.

2 Pick up one each of the following beads: Caspian blue, gunmetal, slate blue, frosted ice and green iris. Then pick up a blue iris and work back down the list in the opposite direction, picking up 11 beads in all. Pick up a clear size 8 bead and a blue iris. Ignoring the last bead threaded, take the needle back up through the beads and into the loop at the edge of the ribbon.

3 Oversew through the next three loops and then pick up the same order of beads as above. Pick up a further 4 blue iris beads and then take the needle through the clear crystal bead and back up the other beads.

tip

If you can't find a grosgrain ribbon in a suitable colour, cover it with a satin or velvet ribbon that complements the fabrics.

4 These two strands are repeated along the ribbon to make the fringe. Stop on a longer strand about 2cm (¾in) from the end of the ribbon. Slip the thread through a few threads on the reverse side and take two small backstitches before trimming the excess thread.

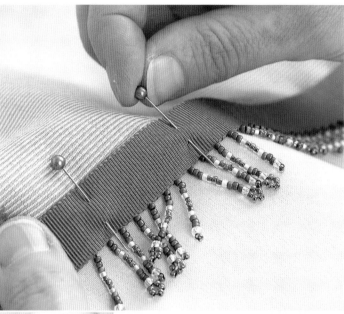

5 To make the cushion, cut the following pieces from blue fabric: front panel 18 × 41cm (7 × 16in); back panels 24 × 41cm (9½ × 16in) and 34 × 41cm (13½ × 16in). Pin the cream fabric piece and the blue front panel right sides together along one long edge and machine stitch. Trim the seam and press towards the blue fabric. Pin the beaded ribbon along the edge of the blue fabric and, using a zipper foot, machine stitch along the edge of the ribbon next to the blue fabric.

try this
Make a rectangular cushion to match using a similar type of envelope opening in the back panel. Insert the beaded ribbon in the seam at each end of the cushion cover before stitching and turning through.

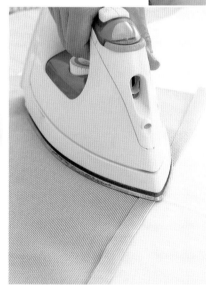

6 Press under a 6mm (¼in) turning and then a further 1cm (⅜in) hem along one long edge of each blue back panel and then machine stitch.

7 With right sides facing pin the small back panel along the top edge of the cushion. Lay the other panel on top with the hems overlapping and pin. Machine stitch all the way round the outside, double stitching where the hems overlap. Trim across the corners and turn the cover through. Press before inserting the cushion pad.

fringed lampshade

Although inspired by the ornate beaded lampshades found in Victorian boudoirs and lounges, this wonderful lampshade has a thoroughly modern look. Choose a bright contemporary colour for the lampshade and pick beads that complement the base of the lampshade too. This fringe uses shades of lilac and silver beads with a darker purple bauble at the end of each strand to add depth of colour and weight. The length of the fringe you make will depend on the height and width of your lampshade, and remember it doesn't have to be straight along the bottom - why not try a zigzag or curved fringe instead?

fringed lampshade

- 1.25cm (½in) wide seam tape, long enough to fit the shade
- beading needle
- cord beading thread
- 12g silver-lined crystal clear 3mm bugles
- 7g silver-lined crystal clear seed beads
- 7g lavender seed beads
- 7g violet/turquoise seed beads
- 7g silver-lined blueberry seed beads
- 7g violet rainbow seed beads
- 7g cobalt blue seed beads
- 20g deep blue rainbow seed beads
- scissors
- fabric glue
- glue brush
- 1.5cm (⅝in) satin ribbon, long enough to fit shade

1 Cut a piece of seam tape long enough to fit around the bottom edge of the lampshade, adding 4cm (1½in) seam allowance. Using cord thread, work a couple of backstitches into the tape at one end and bring the needle out at the edge of the tape 2cm (¾in) in.

2 To make the fringe, start by picking up a bugle then the beads in this order – lavender, violet/turquoise, silver-lined blueberry, violet rainbow, cobalt blue and deep blue rainbow. Miss the deep blue and work back down the list picking up 13 beads in all.

3 Repeat the sequence three times in all and then pick up 2 bugles. To make the bauble on the end, pick up 3 deep blue beads and put the needle back through the last bugle. Repeat five times in all.

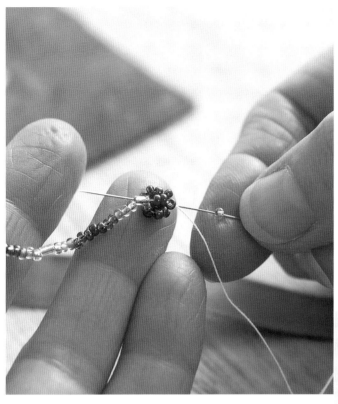

4 Pick up a crystal clear seed bead and take the needle back through the bauble and the other beads in the strand. Secure the thread in the tape and then work running stitch along 6mm (¼in), ready to make the next strand. Repeat until the fringe is long enough to fit around the lampshade.

tip

You will need to use a size 13 beading needle and fine beading thread so that you can stitch through the bugle several times when making the bauble at the end of the fringe.

5 Lay the finished fringe on a flat surface. Brush a thin layer of fabric glue along the reverse side of the tape. Lift the tape carefully and stick along the bottom edge of the lampshade. You may need a friend to help at this stage. Trim the ends and slipstitch together.

6 To finish, cut a piece of satin ribbon to fit around the lampshade. Pin the ribbon in place, fold under the raw edges at one corner and slipstitch the edges together. Sew a few tiny stitches on both edges of the ribbon at each corner to secure.

try this

If you can't find a lampshade in the colour you require you can cover a lampshade with silk/viscose velvet backed with Lamitex. This is a matt sheet that can be cut to size and ironed on to the reverse side of the fabric. Fold the top and bottom edges of the fabric over the lampshade rings and stick on the inside.

devoré scarf

An elegant scarf is
ideal for keeping the
chill off your shoulders
when wearing an evening
gown. A net fringe adds
colour and sparkle to a
plain scarf and the
weight of the beads
helps to hold the scarf
in place. Different
effects can be achieved
depending on how you
shade the seed beads
from dark to light
between the pearls.
I have given the order
and colours of the beads
I used but choosing your
own colour scheme is
half the fun. Devoré
velvet is made from silk
georgette with a viscose
pile. The pattern on the
scarf is created with
etching fluid, which
removes the unwanted
viscose pile, leaving
the plain silk georgette
in some areas.

devoré scarf

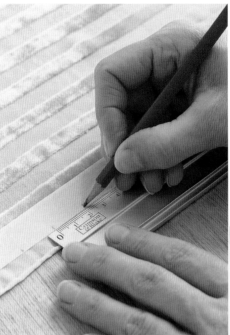

1 Stick a length of masking tape across the width of the scarf and stick the ends to the work surface. Measure the width of the scarf and mark approximately every 2cm (¾in) along the tape.

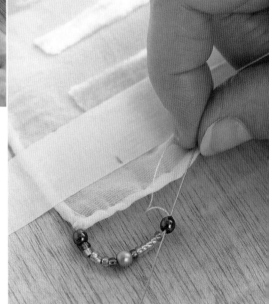

2 Beginning at one corner, attach a length of cord thread and pick up 1 dark brown pearl, 6 seed beads (1 burnt orange, 1 orange, 2 apricot, 1 orange and 1 burnt orange were used here), 1 gold pearl, 6 seed beads (as before) and 1 dark brown pearl. Take a tiny stitch into the scarf below the second mark then put the needle back through the dark brown pearl. Work across the scarf adding the same loop of beads between the marks. Sew in the end.

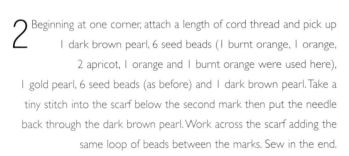

3 Secure a second thread with a couple of tiny stitches on the reverse side and bring it out through the first dark brown pearl. Pick up 8 seed beads (1 burnt orange, 2 orange, 2 apricot, 2 orange and 1 burnt orange were used here), then 1 brown pearl. Repeat three times. Add another string of beads down the other side.

4 Take a new length of thread up through the second dark brown bead at one side. Pick up 6 seed beads (order as in step 2) and take the needle through the gold pearl. Pick up another 6 seed beads (as before) and 1 dark brown pearl. Continue like this across the width.

try this

If you can't find a scarf in the right colour, simply buy a white silk/viscose scarf and dye it to match the beads. See suppliers list on page 493 for scarf stockists.

tip

When you need a new thread, join the ends together with a reef knot (see page 397) and sew the ends back through several beads before trimming close to the netting.

5 At the other end take the needle down through the dark brown pearl at the end. Work back across, feeding the needle through the dark brown beads. Continue adding rows of bead netting until you reach the last dark brown bead at each side.

6 Pick up 21 seed beads (order as in step 3 until there are 21 beads), 1 dark brown pearl and 1 burnt orange seed bead. Take the needle back through the dark brown pearl, the seed beads and the next dark brown pearl. Pick up 6 seed beads (as in step 2), feed the needle through the gold pearl at the bottom of the netting and pick up another 6 seed beads (as before) and 1 brown pearl. Repeat until the fringe and last row of netting is complete. Sew in thread ends securely.

tasselled key-rings

It will be difficult to misplace your keys when they are attached to wonderful tasselled key-rings that are not only practical but decorative too. The tassels can be made in a single colour to match your décor or in a combination of mixed colours for a different effect. Attach a beaded tassel to your key with some beautiful sheer ribbon for an elegant, artistic touch. Beaded tassels can also be attached to the corners of large square cushions and used to finish the flat end of bolsters.

tasselled key-rings

you will need

- quilting thread to match beads
- beading needle
- 22mm (⅞in) wooden bead
- 10g lime seed beads (or fuchsia)
- 12g lime 6mm (¼in) bugles (or fuchsia)
- scissors

1 Thread a length of quilting thread on to the beading needle and feed it through the centre of the wooden bead and tie with a surgeon's knot (see page 397). Pick up approximately 17 seed beads and put the needle back through the centre of the wooden bead. Hold your finger and thumb over the holes to stop the beads going in and then pull the thread tight.

tip

The tassel is much more tactile if you use quilting thread or another strong corded thread to make the strings. Nymo thread is rather stiff and will give a firmer finish to the tassel.

2 Continue adding 17 beads at a time until the bead strands touch near the holes with gaps in the middle – about 12 altogether. Now pick up 13 beads each time and fill every second gap around the wooden bead. Fill the remaining gaps with groups of 9 beads. Tie the thread ends together with a surgeon's knot and trim the ends.

3 To make the tassel loop, pick up 25 beads on a length of quilting thread. Feed the needle back through the beads to form a circle and then take it back through again for extra strength. Put both ends into the needle and take them through the wooden bead.

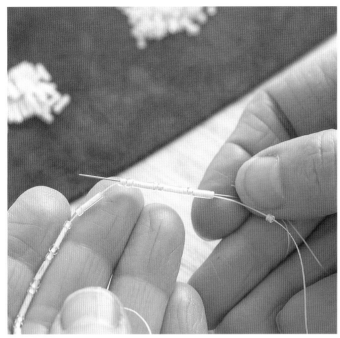

4 Thread a 2m (2¼yd) length of quilting thread on to the needle. Pick up 2 seed beads and a bugle bead. Repeat until there are 8 bugle beads on the thread. Pick up another seed bead. Leaving the last seed bead take the needle back through the other beads. Ease the bead string down the thread until there is a 10cm (4in) tail.

5 Keep adding further strings of beads and bugles until there are ten strings altogether. Tie the thread ends together and split the tassel string bundle in two. Loop the threads sticking out from the bottom of the wooden bead around the tassel strings and tie off using a surgeon's knot. Trim the thread ends.

try this

Make a spiral staircase loop (see spiral bracelet, page 424) long enough to fit around a napkin and attach the tassel to make a stunning napkin ring.

6 Thread another 2m (2¼yd) length of thread and secure the end to the base of the wooden bead close to the tassel strings. Thread on the seed beads and bugles to make a tassel string as in steps 4 and 5. Take the needle under one of the adjacent threads on the wooden bead and make another tassel string. Keep working around the wooden bead adding tassel strings until there are forty in all. Sew in the end and trim neatly to finish.

beaded notebook

Exquisite beadwork embroidery transforms a simple notebook or address book into something really special. By choosing beads that tone in with the fabric, the overall effect is subtle with a mix of couched bugles and seed beads creating a simple, textured surface. This beaded cover is not only beautiful but is practical too, as it is designed to be slipped off and fitted on to another notebook when required. Choose a luxury fabric such as silk dupion that will show the beads off at their best, and back the silk fabric with thin quilting wadding (batting) to give it an opulent feel.

beaded notebook

you will need

- two pieces 40 x 26cm (16 x 10in) of silk dupion
- 40 x 26cm (16 x 10in) thin wadding (batting)
- A6 notebook
- vanishing embroidery marker
- ruler
- tapestry needle
- rotary frame
- beading needle
- 10g pale coral seed beads
- 10g dark coral seed beads
- 10g pink pearl seed beads
- 18g small coral bugle beads
- scissors
- coral sewing thread
- sewing needle
- tacking (basting) thread
- sewing machine

1 Lay one piece of silk dupion on top of the wadding (batting) and fold in half crossways to mark the centre line. Position the notebook just right of the centre line. Mark the corners with a vanishing embroidery marker.

tip

Allow for the thickness of the notebook cover when marking and stitching. It is better that the cover is slightly too big than too tight a fit, so check your measurements carefully before stitching by machine.

2 Score between the first two dots with a tapestry needle and ruler and tack (baste) along the line. Repeat on all sides. Fit the silk and wadding (batting) into a rotary frame.

3 Thread the beading needle with coral thread and secure on the back with two small backstitches. Bring it out on the right side in the top corner of the tacked (basted) outline. Pick up a pale coral seed bead and then a bugle. Continue adding beads until there are 13 bugles and 12 seed beads. Insert the beading needle into the fabric below the tacked (basted) line at top left and wrap the thread around the beading needle several times to tension it.

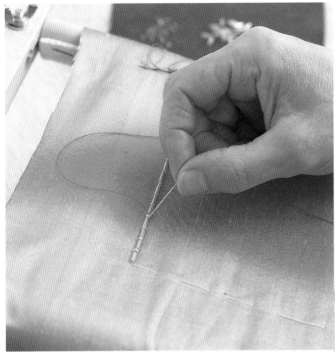

4 Thread a sewing needle with another length of coral thread. Secure it to the wadding (batting) and bring it out below the first seed bead. Couch between each bead, working along the line of beads (see couching, page 407). Couch the same order of beads along the bottom tacked (basted) line. Now couch a row of 17 bugles and 18 seed beads between the two beaded lines along the left-hand side tacking (basting) thread. Repeat the same order for a line of couched beads on the right side.

5 Now bead the area inside the bead border from the bottom up, as follows. For the first row, pick up a pale coral, a pink pearl, a pale coral and a pink pearl bead, repeating this order until there are approximately 80 beads strung. Couch the beads as before. For the second row repeat the order but on every alternate bugle row use dark coral beads instead of pale coral beads. Fill the area inside the bead border alternating these two rows. Once all the beading is complete, take the fabric and wadding (batting) off the frame and press the fabric lightly.

6 To make up the notebook cover, lay the fabric face down on the plain piece of silk and mark the outline of the open notebook on the wadding (batting) using a fabric marker. Trim along the lines. Extend the lines out 5cm (2in) on each side of the book for the flaps. Score the fabric to mark the stitching lines at each end and tack (baste) the two pieces of silk together along the top and bottom of the wadding and around the flaps.

7 Fit a sewing machine with a zipper foot so that you can stitch close to the beads. Stitch just outside the tacked (basted) line all round, leaving a gap for turning at one end. Trim across the corners. Trim the seam allowances to 6mm (¼in).

8 Turn the beaded cover through. Slipstitch the gap and press the cover if necessary. Fold the front flap back 5cm (2in) and slipstitch it to the front cover with tiny stitches.

9 Tuck the book into the first flap and fold the back flap inside. Check that it closes before slipstitching the back flap in position.

try this

Do you love the idea of a beaded notebook cover but are rather short of time? Try stitching a grid of machine stitching inside the tacked (basted) outline of the notebook and then fill every other square with a little circle of beads.

sequined decoraions

These delightful padded
shapes prove that
decorations are not just
for Christmas but for
any special occasion.
The sequins and beads
are sewn on in loops to
create an interesting
three-dimensional
surface which catches
the light, so hang them
in the corner of a room
or from a pergola in a
summer garden where they
will sparkle as they
turn. Choose beads and
sequins that match the
colour of the fabric or
dye the fabric to match
the beads - diluting the
dye to create delicate
pastel shades.

sequined decorations

you will need

- paper
- pencil
- scissors
- small amounts of velvet
- pins
- sewing thread to match fabric/beads
- sewing machine
- polyester stuffing
- sewing needle
- beading needle
- 15g crystal seed beads
- 5g crystal 8mm flat sequins
- 15g aqua seed beads
- 5g aqua 8mm flat sequins
- 15g blue seed beads
- 5g blue 8mm flat sequins

tip

When making the star decoration, trim across the points of the star and then trim close to the stitching down both sides of each point before turning through. Carefully ease the points out with a knitting needle or bodkin.

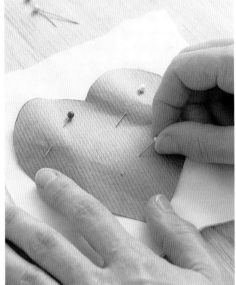

1 The instructions are for the heart decoration – use the picture on page 465 as a guide for making the other shapes. Begin by enlarging the heart template on page 491 by 200%, and cut out the shape. Place two pieces of velvet right sides together and pin a template to one side. Machine stitch around the edge of the template leaving a gap on one side for turning.

2 Trim the seam allowance to 6mm (¼in) and trim across the corners to reduce the bulk. Snip into the point at the top of the heart. Notch the outer curves for ease of turning. Turn the shape through to the right side, easing out the corners, and stuff with polyester stuffing. Slipstitch the gap.

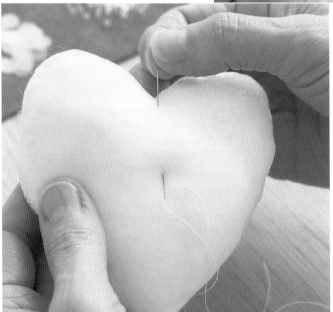

3 Thread the beading needle with sewing thread and tie an overhand knot (see page 397) at the end. Take a stitch into the centre of the decoration and tug to bury the knot in the stuffing.

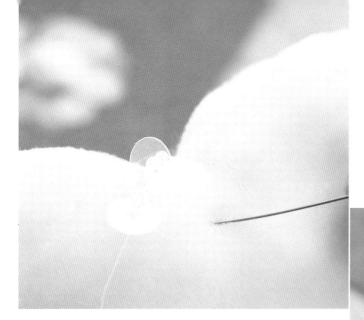

4 Using the colours of your choice, pick up 1 sequin, 4 seed beads, 1 sequin, 4 seed beads and then a final sequin. Put the needle into the decoration so that the last sequin will sit next to the first.

5 Bring the needle back out between the two sequins and slightly in front. Repeat step 4 so that this group of beads lies perpendicular to the first group. Continue adding groups of beads and sequins in a grid-like pattern until the front of the decoration is covered.

6 To hang, attach a double sewing thread at the top of the decoration. Pick up enough seed beads to make a cord about 30cm (12in) long. Carefully tie a small loop at the top and feed the end of the thread back through the beads.

try this

If you want to hang the decorations on a Christmas tree, make a loop by picking up 45 seed beads. Take the needle back into the top of the decoration, take two tiny backstitches and then a large stitch through the decoration and trim off the end of the thread.

7 On the heart and diamond decorations, attach a thread to the bottom of the decoration. Pick up 4 seed beads and 1 sequin. Repeat until there are 7 sequins. Pick up a further 4 seed beads. Miss the last seed bead and take the needle back through the other beads and sequins. Secure the thread to finish.

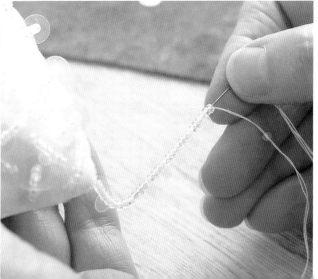

pot-pourri sachets

These little beaded cushions will fill your bedroom with the wonderful scent of roses all year round. The scent can be refreshed from time to time with a few drops of rose oil. Use the sachets individually to tuck in a drawer or tie the three together with a pretty ribbon to decorate the dressing table. Choose delicate pastel shades of silk organza to make the cushions to allow the rose pot-pourri to show through the sheer fabric. An added layer of tulle over the silk organza gives a slightly antique appearance.

pot-pourri sachets

you will need

- pencil and fine black marker
- pale green silk organza
- pale cream silk organza
- pale pink silk organza
- pale pink tulle
- scissors
- vanishing embroidery marker
- tacking (basting) thread
- sewing needle
- beading needle
- 18cm (7in) embroidery hoop
- 5g mid green seed beads
- 5g light green seed beads
- 5g crystal green seed beads
- 5g pink seed beads
- 5g pale pink seed beads
- sewing thread
- sewing machine
- rose pot-pourri
- 1m (1yd) of 15mm (⅝in) pale green sheer organza ribbon

tip

Stitch all the outline beads at one sitting as the marked design will vanish in a few hours.

1 Trace the design on page 491 and outline with a black marker. Cut a 25cm (10in) square in pale green silk organza and one in pale pink tulle. Position the template under the organza with the tulle on top and trace the design with a vanishing embroidery marker.

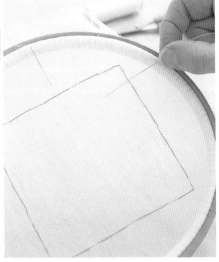

2 Tack (baste) around the square border and then fit the two fabrics into an embroidery hoop. Thread both needles with lengths of sewing thread and secure each length inside one of the petal shapes with two tiny backstitches.

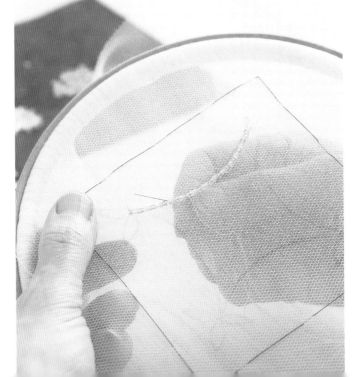

3 With the beading needle, pick up one each of the green beads and repeat until there are sufficient to fit along the first curved line of the motif. Couch the beads down with the other needle and thread (see couching, page 407). Work all four sides in the same way.

4 Pick up 11 pink beads and couch down one side of the middle petal. Couch 10 pink beads down the other side of the petal. On the side petals put the needle through the first two beads of the middle petal and then pick up only 9 beads. Couch 10 beads down the remaining sides.

try this

Using the same bead design, you could make a large cushion with the design embroidered in the centre. Tuck a rose pot-pourri sachet in the middle of the stuffing before closing the gap.

5 Fill the petals with pale pink seed beads stitched on individually from the reverse side. Now take the embroidery out of the hoop and press the fabric carefully.

6 Cut three 15cm (6in) squares of pale green organza and steam press together. Place these squares on top of the bead embroidery right sides together and pin. Machine stitch just inside the tacked (basted) line leaving a gap on one side.

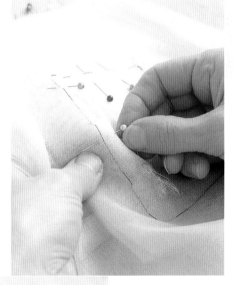

7 Trim the seam allowance to 6mm (¼in) and trim across corners. Turn through and ease out corners.

8 Fill the sachet with rose pot-pourri and slipstitch the gap. Make a pale pink and cream sachet in the same way but without any bead embroidery. Pile the sachets together and tie in a bundle with some sheer organza ribbon.

bead-embellished bag

Whether you're off to the shops or going out for the day, this stylish rucksack-type bag is ideal for all your bits and bobs. It is the perfect style of bag for a day in town as your hands are free to pick things up and to open doors. It is very easy to make, as it is really just a simple drawstring bag so why not make another for a day at the beach or to suit your usual colour scheme? For a beach bag, choose a bright, sunny fabric with colourful beads or use fabric and beads that complement your favourite outfit.

bead-embellished bag

you will need

- 3 x 38cm (5 x 15in) antique white linen
- 3 x 38cm (5 x 15in) iron-on interfacing
- tacking (basting) thread
- sewing needle
- vanishing embroidery marker
- beading needle
- white quilting thread
- 12g purple/olive matt seed beads
- 12g brown satin matt seed beads
- 12g stone matt seed beads
- 12g medium grey matt seed beads
- 12g of 3mm (⅛in) purple/olive bugle beads
- two pieces 56 x 38cm (22 x 15in) raw linen
- sewing thread
- scissors
- pins
- sewing machine
- two 2m (2¼yd) lengths of white cord
- two large eyelets and eyelet tool

1 Iron the interfacing on to the reverse side of the antique white linen. Tack (baste) two lines 5cm (2in) apart down the centre of the linen strip. Now tack (baste) lines across, to make five 5cm (2in) squares, 1.5cm (⅝in) apart along the strip (see diagram on page 109).

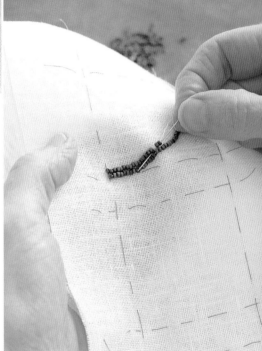

2 Using the vanishing marker, draw a curve on the right-hand square. Using quilting thread stitch a row of purple/olive beads with backstitch along the line. Continue filling in the area below the curve with beads and then fill in the last corner. Mark the next square into nine equal squares. Stitch brown satin beads in each little square, alternating the rows from horizontal to vertical.

3 On the middle square, divide the square into four equal vertical strips and work zigzag rows of stone matt beads to cover the area. In the next square begin stitching bugles around the outside edge and then work into the centre, completing a triangle each time. On the left-hand square use medium grey matt beads, beginning in the centre and spiralling out to make a circle. Fill in the corners to complete the square.

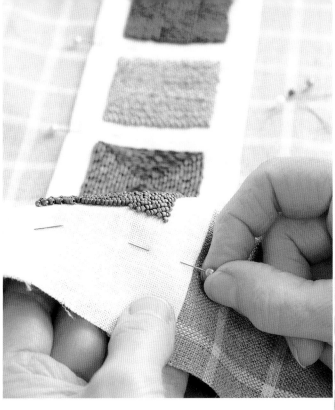

4 To make up the bag, remove the tacking (basting) thread. Turn under 2cm (¾in) down the long edges of the strip and pin it across one piece of the raw linen 10cm (4in) from the bottom. Machine stitch in place close to the edge.

5 Pin the two pieces of linen right sides together and machine stitch the side seams and along the bottom. Leaving 8cm (3in) clear at the top of each side seam, zigzag the seams and trim. Turn the bag through to the right side and press. Stitch diagonally across both bottom corners 4cm (1½in) from the point (the eyelets will be positioned here later).

try this

If you are short of time, stitch the beads in a pattern so that they are less solidly packed and make the bag up as shown in the steps.

6 To make a channel around the top edge, turn down 2cm (¾in) and then a further 3cm (1¼in) and pin. Machine stitch close to the hem edge and again along the top edge. Snip into the side seams between the casing lines. Thread the lengths of white cord through the casing, one from each side.

tip

Dip the white cotton cord in a very weak tea solution. This will darken it slightly so that it is not so stark and matches the antique linen.

7 Following the manufacturer's instructions fit an eyelet into each bottom corner of the bag. Feed the pairs of white cords through the eyelets and tie the ends in an overhand knot (see page 397) to complete.

coiled coasters

Using beads with wire is the theme for this section, so start by giving your dining table extra style with these eye-catching beaded coasters. These bright pink beads have a fresh summery feel to them but you could use any colour to co-ordinate with your existing tableware. As the beads are very small and packed closely together, they form a smooth surface on which to place your glass. Presented in a pretty, shimmering mesh bag, a set of six of these bead coasters would form a lovely gift. Or why not make a larger version of the coaster design as a pretty addition to any dressing table.

coiled coasters

1 Cut a 2.5m (2¾yd) length of wire and pick up a seed bead. Fold the first 1cm (½in) of the wire over the bead and twist to secure. Pour a small quantity of beads into your left hand (right hand if you are left-handed). Holding the other end of the wire, pick up about 10 beads at a time and let them drop down the wire.

tip

You can buy beads already strung – just loop the wire over the thread at one end and feed the beads on to the wire.

2 Keep picking up beads and letting them drop down the wire until the handful is finished. Continue pouring beads into the palm of your hand and feeding them on to the wire until there is a 2m (2¼yd) length.

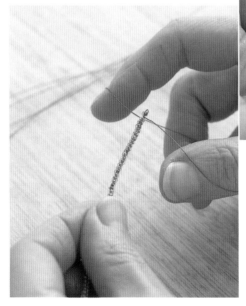

3 Make a loop on the end of the wire to prevent the beads falling off. Now cut five 30cm (12in) lengths of wire and fold each in half. Tuck one of the pieces of wire over the first bead and cross over the ends to secure it.

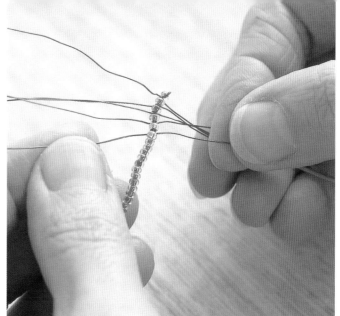

4 Add the other four pieces of wire in the same way, leaving a bead between each wire. These are the spoke wires. Now begin to coil the beaded wire. At each spoke wire cross the wires over between two beads.

5 Keep coiling the beaded wire and crossing over the spoke wires. The spokes should be evenly spaced at an angle of about 72 degrees. Continue until the coaster is about 7.5cm (3in) in diameter.

try this

Make an organza bag in which to keep the coasters. Pin two 30 x 12cm (12 x 4¾in) pieces of organza together and machine stitch around the edge leaving a gap. Trim the seams and cut across corners then turn through and press. Fold into three and oversew the side seams. Draw a swirl on the front flap and sew beads along the line.

6 Fold the ends of the spokes back over the outside row of beads and trim the wire close to the beads. Remove any beads that remain on the wire beyond the last spoke. Fold the wire back and weave it into the coaster for a row or two. Snip the end close to the coaster to finish.

sparkling candlesticks

These days meal times are becoming increasingly casual, with ready-made meals and TV dinners the norm, but there are still some meals that merit a little extra effort. These two elegant candlesticks decorated with spirals of beaded wire will add a touch of glamour to the simplest table setting to make it fit for any special occasion. Choose a fresh colour scheme such as lilac and white to match your décor, or one that reflects the occasion. White and gold would look stunning for a christening or wedding breakfast whereas deep red and green are ideal at Christmas time.

sparkling candlesticks

you will need

- 1.25m (48in) of 1mm (19swg) silver-plated wire
- 10m (5½yd) of 0.4mm (27swg) silver-plated wire
- round-nosed pliers
- wire cutters
- safety glasses
- 5g frosted pale lilac seed beads
- 5g matt lilac seed beads
- 5g heather seed beads
- 5g lilac iris seed beads
- 10 white opal hearts
- 10 amethyst hearts
- 10 white opal flowers
- 10 amethyst flowers
- 20 amethyst pony beads
- two 18cm (7in) tall glass pillar candlesticks

try this

Why not create a set of matching napkin rings by making 25cm (10in) lengths of beaded wire to coil around a napkin?

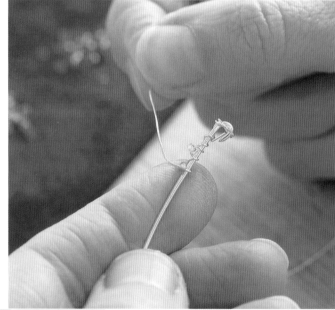

1 Cut a 60cm (24in) length of 1mm wire and bend over one end using round-nosed pliers. Cut a 1.5m (1¾yd) length of 0.4mm wire and attach one end to the bent end of the wire. Wrap the thin wire down the core wire a couple of times.

2 Pick up a pale lilac and a matt lilac seed bead and let them drop down to the work. Wrap the thin wire around the core wire several times, trapping both seed beads as you go. Wrap 2 seed beads on to the core wire between each of the following.

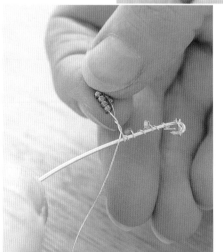

3 Pick up 7 heather seed beads and let them drop down to the work. Make a loop with the thin wire. Hold the seed beads at the top of the loop and twist to form a 6mm (¼in) stem.

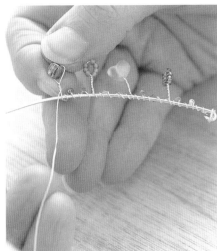

4 Pick up a white opal heart. Make a loop as before and twist the heart to form a stem. Make a cluster with 7 lilac iris seed beads. Add a pony bead in the same way as the heart followed by a cluster of 7 heather beads.

5 Pick up a pale lilac seed bead, a flower and another pale lilac seed bead. Fold the wire back over the first seed bead leaving a 1cm (⅓in) stem. Twist the stem halfway down. Hold the flower bead 7mm (⅜in) away and twist to form a short stem.

6 Twist the stem for the seed bead on the other side and then twist all the beads together to complete the stem down to the core wire. Repeat this sequence five times in all, alternating the colours of the hearts and flowers.

7 To finish, bend the end of the core wire over and wrap the thin wire around to secure, trimming the excess wire. Wrap the beaded wire around the stem of the candlestick and secure by hooking each end of the wire over where it meets the beaded wire.

tip

Wear safety glasses while cutting and wrapping the wire to protect your eyes and prevent an accident.

483

flower gift bags

Pretty gift bags are the ideal way to wrap an awkwardly shaped present and can make even the smallest gift seem quite special and substantial. One or two lipsticks or bottles of nail polish make a wonderful gift for a teenager if presented in one of these delightful little bags and you can easily make a simple card to match. Enlarge the diagram on page 108 and make your own bag using crisp handmade paper, or decorate a ready-made bag. Change the colour to suit the occasion – off-white paper and gold beads would be ideal for a wedding gift.

flower gift bags

you will need

- 5.5m (6yd) of 0.4mm (27swg) silver-plated wire
- wire cutters
- safety glasses
- 12g baby pink seed beads
- 15g deep pink seed beads
- 12g baby blue seed beads
- 15g mid blue seed beads
- masking tape
- silk paper
- tapestry needle
- double-sided tape
- sticky-backed labels

tip

Choose a crisp paper that will hold a crease well and which is thick enough to support the weight of the bead flowers and handles.

1 To make the wire flowers, start by cutting a 45cm (18in) length of wire and bend one end over 5cm (2in). Pick up 15 pale blue seed beads on the long end and let them drop down to the bend.

2 Bend the wire over at the other end of the beads. Pick up another 15 pale blue beads. Hold the beads between your finger and thumb and twist round once or twice. Make 5 petals in all, leaving the long end protruding from the centre.

3 Pick up 30 deep blue beads and let them drop down to the centre of the flower. Coil the wire round and feed the end through the first bead again. Pull the wire through to the reverse side and twist the ends together.

4 Cut six 20cm (8in) lengths of wire. Fill 18cm (7in) of each wire with beads, making 2 deep pink strands, 2 mid blue and 2 baby blue. Now plait one of each colour together to make the handles using masking tape to hold one end.

try this

Why not make a simple greetings card to match the gift bags? Fold a piece of white card in two. Tear a square of handmade paper and punch a hole in the centre and feed the wire ends of the flower through. Secure the wires with tape and stick to the front of the card.

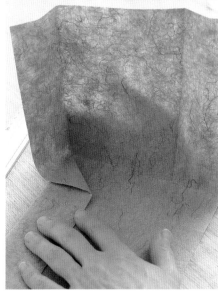

5 To make the paper bag, use the diagram on page 490, transferring the lines of the design on to the silk paper. Pre-crease the paper along the lines as indicated – dotted lines are 'mountain' folds and other dashed lines are 'valley' folds. Fold the side sections in one at a time. Fold the edge along the centre diagonal and then fold the other edge up. Secure at the top with a small piece of double-sided tape.

6 Turn under the top edge. Snip two notches on each side of the bag and tuck the handles in. Open out the bag flap, spread out the wire ends of the handles and stick a piece of double-sided tape across the wire ends. Fold the flap back down to secure.

7 Using a tapestry needle, punch a hole for each of the flowers in the front of the bag. Trim the flower wires and feed the ends through a hole. Open out the wire on the inside and use a sticky-backed label on the inside to secure each flower.

charts and diagrams

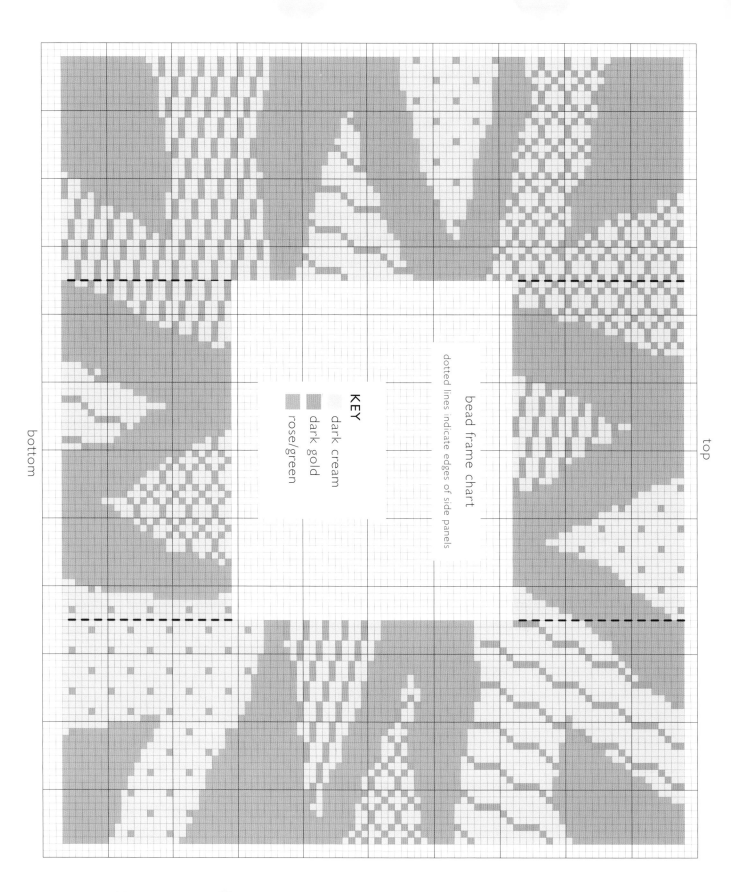

KEY

dark cream
dark gold
rose/green

bead frame chart

dotted lines indicate edges of side panels

bottom

top

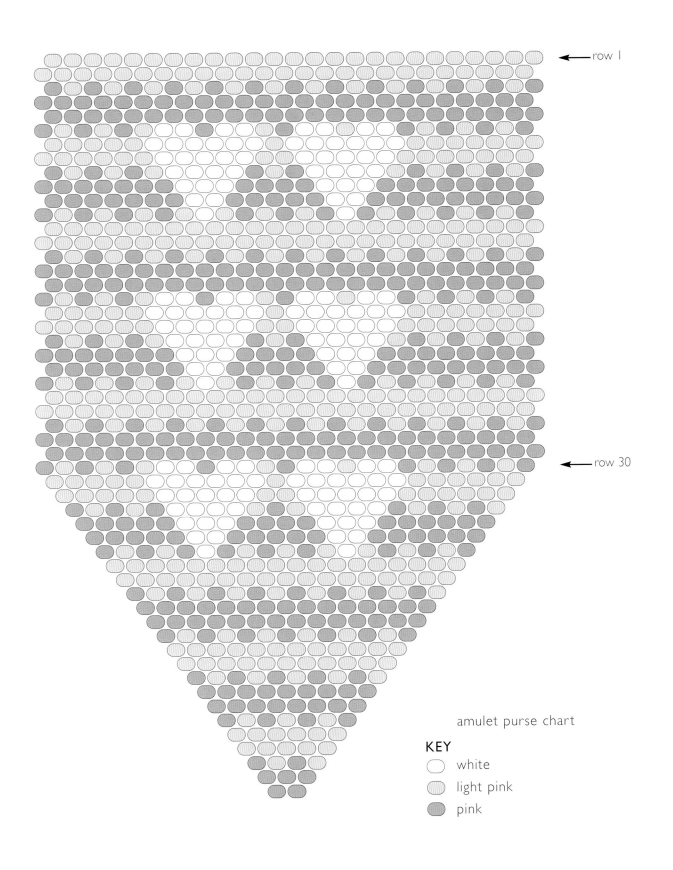

row 1

row 30

amulet purse chart

KEY

⬭ white

⬭ light pink

⬭ pink

trinket box chart

card chart

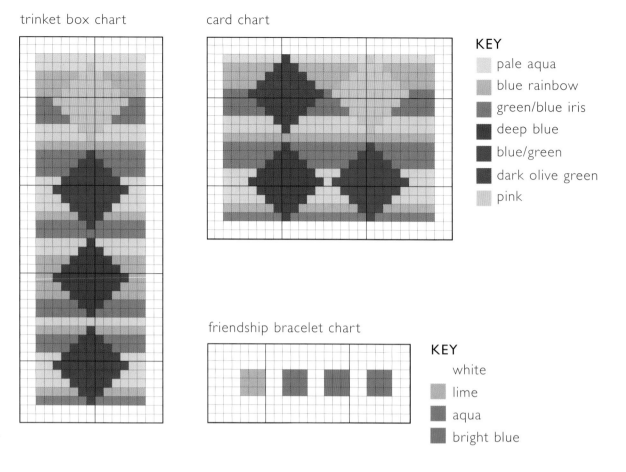

KEY

- pale aqua
- blue rainbow
- green/blue iris
- deep blue
- blue/green
- dark olive green
- pink

friendship bracelet chart

KEY

- white
- lime
- aqua
- bright blue

flower gift bag diagram

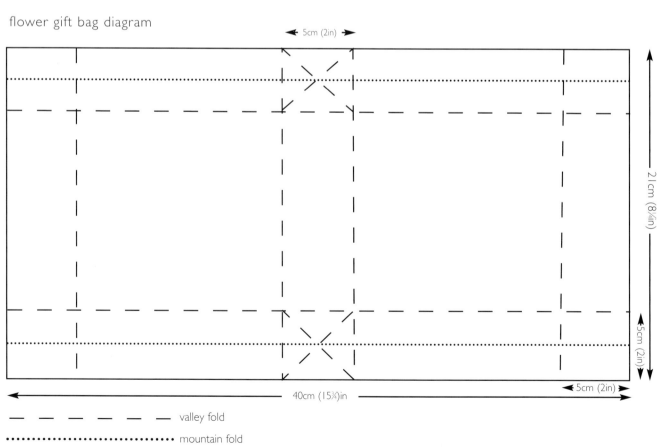

5cm (2in)

21cm (8¼in)

5cm (2in)

5cm (2in)

40cm (15¾in)

– – – – – – – valley fold

•••••••••••••••• mountain fold

sequined
decorations templates

enlarge by **200%**

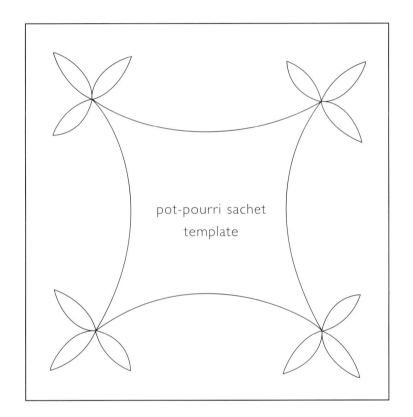

pot-pourri sachet
template

bead-embellished
bag diagram

enlarge by **200%**

1.5cm
⅝in

5cm (2in)

5cm (2in)

bead project details

This list contains details of the various beads used in the projects, giving their specific colours and codes. However, the list is not exhaustive, and the availability of beads can change. The list of suppliers on the facing page will assist you in sourcing a vast variety of beads and accessories for your projects.

friendship bracelet
Beadbox – delicas:
White lustre D201, limeaid D237, aqua D79, medium blue iris D76.

bead frame
Beadbox – delicas:
Matt dark gold metallic D334, OP medium flesh lustre D204, matt rose/green metallic D380.

trinket box
Beadesign – size 11 seed beads:
Pale aqua T0170D, rainbow multi M0283, blue M0279, pink T0038, blue/blue M0386, peacock green M0147, forest green/deep blue T0384.

spiral bracelets
London Bead Company – hex and size 11 and 8 seed beads:
Size 8 aqua green 335, hex bright green 259, hex green 452; Size 11 mint green 336, grass green 547.

amulet purse
Beadesign – delicas and 3mm bugles:
Bugles – SL crystal clear TB10021, lined light pink DBV 0082, pink DBV0106.
Beadbox – delicas white lustre D201.

beaded mules
Mill Hill Beads – petite beads:
Crystal 40161, tapestry teal 42029, rainbow 40374, crystal aqua 42017, crystal pink 42018, heather mauve 42024.

zigzag necklace
Beadbox – size 11 and 8 seed beads:
SL ruby multi matt 21202, SL gold matt 28352.

bead-fringed cushion
Mill Hill Beads – size 11 seed beads:
Caspian blue 03027, frosted gunmetal 62021, slate blue 03010, frosted ice 62010, blue iris 03047, shimmering sea 02087, mercury 00283.
London Bead Company – size 8 seed beads:
SL clear size 8 seed beads 034.

fringed lampshade
Beadesign – size 11 seed beads and 3mm bugles:
Seed beads – SL crystal clear T0021, CL lavender M0269, CL violet/turquoise T0937, SL blueberry M0029, rainbow violet T0327, cobalt blue T0116, rainbow deep blue T0408; Bugles – SL crystal clear TB10021.

devoré scarf
Gütermann – 4mm glass pearls and 9mm seed beads:
Pearls – dark brown 3350, gold 2885;
Seed beads – apricot 1345, orange 1850, burnt orange 1970.

tasselled key-rings
London Bead Company – size 11 seed beads and 6mm bugles:
Lime 239, fuchsia 255.

beaded notebook
Mill Hill Beads – size 11 seed beads and 6mm bugles:
Seed beads – frosted pink coral 62036, cherry sorbet 03057, tea rose 02004;
Bugles – peach crème 72003.

sequined decorations
Gütermann – 9mm seed beads and 8mm flat sequins:
Seed beads – crystal 1030, aqua 7500, blue 6510;
Sequins – crystal 1030, aqua 7165, blue 6510.

pot-pourri sachets
Beadesign – size 11 seed beads:
Adventurine green T0156, light French green M0143A, crystal green M0268A, pink M0168, pale pink T0011.

bead-embellished bag
Beadesign – size 11 seed beads and 3mm bugles:
Seed beads – purple olive T0614, brown satin T0702, stone T0566, medium grey T0613;
Bugles – purple olive TB10614.

coiled coasters
London Bead Company – size 11 seed beads:
Deep bright pink rainbow 309.

sparkling candlesticks
Mill Hill Beads – size 11 seed beads, pebble beads and glass treasures:
Seed beads – frosted heather mauve 62024, matt lilac 02081, heather 02025, shimmering lilac 02084;
Pebble beads – amethyst 05202;
Glass treasures – hearts: opal 12090, amethyst 12091, flowers: opal 12297, amethyst 12295.

flower gift bags
Beadesign – size 11 seed beads:
Baby pink T0145, blossom pink T0906, baby blue T0143, mid blue T0917.

suppliers

UK Suppliers

ARTY'S
For nearest stockist of silk/viscose velvet,
devoré scarves, dyes, lamitex (for backing
lampshades)
Sinotex UK Ltd
The Courtyard Business Centre
Lonesome Lane, Reigate
Surrey RH2 7QT
tel: +44 (0) 1 737 24 5450
www.artys.com

Beadbox, Inc.
tel: (800) BEADBOX
www.beadbox.com

Homecrafts direct
For bead looms
tel: +44 (0) 116 269 7733
www.homecrafts.co.uk

Gütermann Beads
tel: +49 7681-21 0
www.gutermann.com

London Bead Company/Delicate Stitches
339 Kentish Town Road
Kentish Town
London NW5 2TJ
tel: 0870 203 2323
www.londonbeadco.co.uk

Mill Hill Beads
tel: (608) 754-9466
www.millhillbeads.com

The Scientific Wire Company
18 Raven Road
London E18 1HW
tel: 020 8505 0002
www.wires.co.uk

The Spellbound Bead Company
45 Tamworth Street
Lichfield
Staffordshire WS13 6JW
tel: 01543 417650
www.spellboundbead.co.uk

US Suppliers

ARTY'S
For nearest stockist of silk/viscose velvet,
devoré scarves, dyes
Janlynn
tel: (800) 445-5565
www.artys.com

Beadbox, Inc.
3006 S. Priest Dr.
Tempe, Arizona 85282
tel: (800) BEADBOX
www.beadbox.com

Gütermann of America Inc
8227 Arrowridge Blvd
Charlotte, NC 28273
tel: (704) 525-7068
www.gutermann.com

Mill Hill Beads
For nearest stockist:
Gay Bowles Sales Inc
PO Box 1060, Janesville
WI 53547-1060
tel: (608) 754-9466
www.millhill.com

Get creative with North Light Books!

How to Be Creative if You Never Thought You Could

Let Tera Leigh act as your personal craft guide and motivator. She'll help you discover just how creative you really are. You'll explore eight exciting crafts through 16 fun, fabulous projects, including rubber stamping, bookmaking, papermaking, collage, decorative painting and more. Tera prefaces each new activity with insightful essays and encouraging advice.

ISBN 1-58180-293-5, paperback, 128 pages, #32170-K

The Essential Guide to Handmade Books

Gabrielle Fox teaches you how to create your own handmade books—one-of-a-kind art pieces that go beyond the standard definition of what a "book" can be. You'll find 11 projects inside. Each one builds upon the next, just as your skills increase. This beginner-friendly progression ensures that you're well prepared to experiment, play and design your own unique handmade books.

ISBN 1-58180-019-3, paperback, 128 pages, #31652-K

Stenciling & Embossing Greeting Cards

Judy Barker introduces you to the basics of stenciling and embossing attractive greeting cards. You'll also learn how to embellish them with foil, polymer clay, shrink plastic and more. It's everything you need to make one-of-a-kind cards for family and friends alike.

0-89134-997-9, paperback, 128 pages, #31613-K

The Big Book of Greeting Cards

This book presents a variety of fun, festive and stylish ideas for making cards perfect for any occasion. Discover more than 40 step-by-step projects using a wide range of techniques including rubber stamping, stenciling, quilling and embroidery.

ISBN 1-58180-323-0, paperback, 144 pages, #32287-K

Handcrafted Soap

Create your own luxurious bars of soap today—the kind that lather, clean and smell better than store-bought—and start babying your skin tonight. Simply combine ingredients, cook as directed, add fragrances, place in molds and voila! Using equipment as easy as your oven or crock pot, you've made soap that'll be ready to use in an hour!

ISBN 1-58180-268-4, paperback
128 pages, #32138-K

Home & Garden Metalcrafts

You can create gorgeous home decor and garden art using today's new, craft-friendly metals, meshes and wire. You'll find 15 projects inside, ranging from lamps to picture frames. Most can be completed in an afternoon! You'll learn how to texture, antique and emboss your work, then embellish it with glass beads, scented candles, colorful ribbons and more.

ISBN 1-58180-330-3, paperback
96 pages, #32296-K

Create Your Own Tabletop Fountains

You can make your own tabletop fountains and add beautiful accents to your living room, bedroom, kitchen and garden. These 15 gorgeous step-by-step projects make it easy, using everything from lava rock and bamboo to shells and clay pots. You'll learn to incorporate flowers, driftwood, fire, figurines, crystals, plants and more.

ISBN 1-58180-103-3, paperback
128 pages, #31791-K

Wreaths for Every Season

These 20 beautiful wreath projects are perfect for celebrating those special times of year. You'll find a range of sizes and styles, utilizing a variety of creative materials, including dried herbs, cinnamon sticks, silk flowers, Autumn leaves, Christmas candy and more. Clear, step-by-step instructions ensure beautiful, long lasting results every time!

ISBN 1-58180-239-0, paperback
144 pages, #32015-K

The material in this compilation appeared in the following books previously published by North Light and David & Charles and appears here by permission of the authors. (The initial page numbers given refer to pages in the original work; page numbers in parentheses refer to pages in this book.)

Janes, Susan Niner	Bright Ideas in Papercrafts © 2003.	Pages 1-3, 6-125 (5-127)
Janes, Susan Niner	New Ideas in Ribboncraft © 2003.	Pages 1-3, 6-141 (128-267)
McGraw, Mary Jo	Making Greeting Cards with Creative Materials © 2001.	Pages 1-3, 6-110, 112, 123-127 (268-381)
Wood, Dorothy	Simple Glass Seed Beading © 2003.	Pages 1-3, 5-111 (382-493)

Other fine North Light Books are available from your local bookstore or direct from the publisher.

08 07 06 05 04   5 4 3 2 1

A catalog record for this book is available from the Library of Congress at http://catalog.loc.gov.
All works of art reproduced in this book have been previously copyrighted by the individual artists.

Creative Crafts You Can Do In a Day/ edited by editors of North Light Books-1st ed.
    p.cm.
ISBN 1-58180-664-7 (hc: alk. paper)

Cover Designer: Clare Finney
Production Coordinator: Kristen Heller